Women in the New Testament

Women
in the
New Testament

Mary Ann Getty-Sullivan

THE LITURGICAL PRESS
Collegeville, Minnesota

www.litpress.org

Nihil Obstat: Robert C. Harren, *Censor deputatus.*
Imprimatur: ✢ John F. Kinney, Bishop of St. Cloud, Minnesota, July 21, 2001.

Cover design by Ann Blattner. Illustration: *The Visitation,* Jacopo da Pontormo, 1514–1516, fresco. S. Michele, Carmignano.

6   7   8

Library of Congress Cataloging-in-Publication Data

Getty-Sullivan, Mary Ann, 1943–
    Women in the New Testament / Mary Ann Getty-Sullivan.
        p.   cm.
    Includes bibliographical references and index.
    ISBN 0-8146-2546-0 (alk. paper)
    1. Women in the Bible.   2. Bible. N.T.—Biography.   I. Title.

    BS2445.G48   2001
    225.9'22'082—dc21   2001029592

To Florine Getty Sands,
my aunt and inspiration, wise woman,
and to the Sisters of Mercy,
partners in grace;
biblical women if ever there were.

Contents

Prologue

The stories of creation and of salvation begin with woman and a promise. In Genesis humans are made "male and female," in the likeness of God. The story of creation and of the Fall cannot be told without the participation of both men and women. Before the "curse" came the promise of salvation through the "seed of the woman" (Gen 3:15), a promise addressed to woman, although the struggle between humankind and evil will also bring pain and death. In both the Old and New Testament, what is most striking about the way the story of salvation is told is that in a society where patriarchy is the most prominent accepted value, the story of woman, embodied in the stories of so many women, is told.

It is expected that the story told by men to men and about men would reflect the views of a patriarchal society. That this story is suffused also with the stories of women is a loud voice insisting that it could not, and still cannot, be told without women's active participation. Women's stories in the Bible often function as a kind of anticulture, an underground swell that could not be suppressed. In other words, it is most "natural" that these accounts that came together to make up the whole of the Church's story of creation and salvation be told from a male viewpoint. That perspective naturally overlooked the roles and the voices of women; the feminine perspective would understandably have been neglected. The surprise is that it was not erased. It is there because it is essential and could not be left out. Our challenge is to try to make sense of its inclusion and to take the story from here.

1. Women of Expectant Faith

Elizabeth, Mary of the Infancy Narratives, Anna

Suggested Readings: Luke 1:5-56; 2:1-52; also Matthew 1–2

The Gospel According to Mark, the first Gospel to be written, begins with the preaching of John who baptizes by the Jordan River. As if out of nowhere, Jesus of Nazareth suddenly appears and is baptized. He announces the coming of the kingdom of God (Mark 1:14-15) and calls disciples (1:16-20) to witness his ministry, which is characterized both by mighty works and by controversy, before Jesus meets his death in Jerusalem. Matthew and Luke use Mark extensively, adding two important elements to Mark's story of Jesus: both Matthew and Luke supplement Mark's account with a "Sayings" source called *Quelle* (or "Q"), which is German for the word "source." Additionally, Matthew and Luke each add a two-chapter introduction to the story Mark had begun with John's baptism. This introduction is commonly called the "infancy narratives." These narratives, especially Luke's, will serve as the context for examining the first three women of the New Testament.

Matthew and Luke were writing around the same time (A.D. 85),[1] but for different communities. Matthew addressed a

---

[1] We use the currently accepted abbreviations for dates: B.C.E. ("before the Common Era") and C.E. ("Common Era") in this volume.

largely Jewish-Christian audience, while Luke, a Gentile, was writing for Gentile Christians. Matthew and Luke have varying emphases and themes that correspond to the needs and interests of the faith communities they addressed. Apparently these evangelists both had access to basic elements of traditions about Jesus' origins. And perhaps they each had other sources that they used to develop their respective narratives about where and when Jesus was born. Their common traditions include the general timing (during the reign of Herod), Jesus' parentage, his roots in Nazareth, and his birth in Bethlehem. Both claim that Jesus was born of a virgin and that some welcomed him while others rejected him.

MATTHEW'S INFANCY NARRATIVE (MATTHEW 1–2)

Matthew, writing for a community rooted in Judaism, portrays Jesus as the fulfillment of the longings and hopes articulated in the Old Testament Scriptures. As he will do throughout his Gospel, Matthew will consistently follow a prophecy-fulfillment pattern as he shows in his infancy narrative who Jesus is, where he came from, and what his coming means. For Matthew, Jesus is a new Israel, a new Exodus, a new Moses, a new David. It is as if, for each element of Jesus' story, Matthew finds an appropriate Scripture text that serves as "prophecy." Even when he sometimes has to force the text to fit the situation, Matthew will scan the Scriptures and show Jesus as their fulfillment. For example, Jesus is from Nazareth. But no great prophet or messianic figure was expected to come from there.[2] Yet Matthew finds a quotation in Judges 13 in reference to Samson's being a nazirite, and that is close enough for Matthew. In explaining Jesus' upbringing in Nazareth, Matthew says, "He shall be called a Nazorean" (Matt 2:23).[3]

Matthew tells the story of Jesus' birth through the experience of Joseph. Like his Old Testament namesake, Joseph of Nazareth had to interpret God's will through the medium of

---

[2] So, in John, Nathaniel says, "Can anything good come from Nazareth?" (John 1:46). And later some say Jesus is a prophet, but others object that "no prophet arises from Galilee" (7:40-41, 52).

[3] For the meaning of "nazirite," see below, pp. 13–14.

dreams. In his infancy narrative, Matthew reports three dreams of Joseph. The first deals with his marriage to Mary despite the shadow of suspicion about her pregnancy (Matt 1:20-24). Secondly, Joseph dreams that he should take the child and his mother into Egypt to escape Herod's massacre of male infants under two years old (2:13-18). Finally, Joseph is instructed in a dream to return and raise his child in Nazareth (2:19-23).

Joseph is portrayed in Matthew's Gospel as the quintessential Old Testament "just man" (1:19). Joseph searched to do God's will by fulfilling the Torah. His dilemma is to accept how God is working in his life and in history to fulfill the Old Testament promises. Joseph is the main figure of Matthew's infancy narrative. Mary, like other women preparing for and expecting the birth of the Messiah, is a peripheral character in the infancy narrative as well as in the rest of Matthew's Gospel. This is not very surprising when we consider that Matthew's singular objective is to show how Jesus fulfills the Scriptures.

Yet there is a remarkable qualification to the observation that Matthew's infancy narrative focuses on Joseph and other male characters. Matthew begins the whole narrative with a genealogy that will contextualize the birth of Jesus (Matt 1:1-17). Matthew will demonstrate that Jesus is "the son of David, the son of Abraham" (1:1). In so doing, Matthew mentions five women ancestors of Jesus: Tamar (1:3); Rahab (1:5); Ruth (1:5); the mother of Solomon, wife of Uriah (1:6); and Mary, the mother of Jesus (1:16).

Tamar's story in Genesis 38 tells how she seduced her father-in-law Judah in order to force him to obey the Law and honor her right to a levirate marriage.[4] Rahab was a prostitute who helped the Israelite scouts enter the Promised Land (see Josh 2). Ruth tricked Boaz into marrying her (see Ruth 2–4). Bethsheba is unnamed by Matthew, but his Jewish-Christian audience would immediately identify her. Her beauty was renowned, and David committed adultery and murder to have her (2 Sam 11). Matthew hints at the possibility of impropriety on Mary's

---

[4] A levirate marriage could take place when the eldest son of a family died before producing an heir. His widow (Tamar in this case) could then be married to her late husband's brother, and any son would be the heir of the deceased brother.

part and claims that Joseph, somewhat reluctantly, covers up for her at the direction of the angel (Matt 1:18-20).

These are the female ancestors Matthew found worthy to include in Jesus' genealogy. Even though for him women are beside the point (which is to trace Jesus' ancestry back to Abraham through David), Matthew seems to be unable to tell the story of Jesus' birth without including women. The Abrahamic-Davidic line could not have survived without such courageous women, who, at great personal risk and despite all odds, kept the line going. In spite of the fact that women are not portrayed as furthering Matthew's primary goal, they are included from the outset of his account, as if to say that the story cannot be told without them. It is as if their contribution, while expected, cannot be taken for granted. These women have to be remembered; they deserve to be mentioned. And while these women do not warrant further description in Matthew's account, he still will include in his Gospel other examples of women who are outstanding for their courage and strength in the pursuit of justice (for instance, Matthew's presentation of the mother of the sons of Zebedee at the cross in 27:56 or the prophetic but unheeded intervention of Pilate's wife in 27:19).

LUKE'S INFANCY NARRATIVE (LUKE 1–2)

It is Luke who will develop the account of Jesus' birth, infancy, and youth in a way that will intrigue us most in this initial chapter on women in the New Testament. Luke fills in the gaps of the scanty information provided by the traditions he knew about Jesus' origins by developing for us a triptych of three great women saints: Elizabeth, Mary, and Anna. Luke, who shows a certain interest in women's stories,[5] begins his

---

[5] Not only does Luke have more stories featuring women than the other Gospels do, but the language of the stories he includes illustrates female concerns. For instance, in the infancy narrative, the term "womb" occurs seven times (1:15, 31, 41, 42, 44; 2:21, 23), as Bonnie Thurston observes. See *Women in the New Testament: Questions and Commentary* (New York: Crossroad, 1998) 15. It certainly seems plausible that such stories as these would have enjoyed wider circulation among female believers; such groups could have been Luke's source for these stories.

Gospel account with the tales of three women whose faith held potent expectation. Faith means hope and expectation. Indeed, the only definition we have of faith in the New Testament includes this idea. The author of the Letter to the Hebrews tells us that "faith is the realization of what is hoped for and evidence of things not seen. Because of it the ancients were well attested" (Heb 11:1-2).

We would not know the stories of Elizabeth, Mary, Anna, and other women were it not for Luke, whose Gospel is sometimes called the "Gospel of women."[6] Scholars debate whether Luke is promoting women by giving them special mention and attention or denigrating them by portraying them only as models of submissive service. The least we can say is that when it comes to the subject of women, Luke appears to promise more than he delivers. Regarding women, Luke's text has even been called "dangerous,"[7] in the sense that it could seduce us into an uncritical reading beyond the happy observation that more women appear in Luke than in the other Gospels. Yet, although our final judgment may be that Luke does seem to diminish or erase the contribution of women as he presents the rest of his Gospel and Acts, his beginnings are promising. We are indebted to him for the story of these women of Jesus' birth. Some background on the narrative itself will set the stage to learn about these women.

Luke's infancy narrative is structured around several scenes, each laid out in pairs of stories featuring both men and women. These scenes include annunciations to Zechariah (1:5-25) and to Mary (1:26-38); Zechariah's and Elizabeth's reactions at the birth of John (1:57-79); and the joyous testimony of Simeon

---

[6] It is a hopeful portent for the Gospel that three women are named there: Elizabeth, Mary, and Anna. But only six more will find their names worked into the fabric of the rest of Luke's Gospel: Mary Magdalene (8:2; 24:10), Joanna (8:3; 24:10), Susanna (8:3), Mary and Martha (10:38-42), and Mary, the mother of James (24:10). This contrasts with the thirty-nine men named men in Luke's Gospel, excluding the seventy-six found in Luke's genealogy. There are also ten unnamed women in Luke's Gospel.

[7] See Jane Schaberg, "Luke," in *The Women's Bible Commentary,* ed. Carol A. Newsom and Sharon H. Ringe (Louisville: Westminster/John Knox, 1992) 275–292, at 275.

and Anna at Jesus' presentation in the Temple (2:25-32). The angel's annunciations are connected by a visit of the two mothers-to-be (1:39-56), which functions as a transition to the births of the two babies (John in 1:57-80 and Jesus in 2:1-21). These events are celebrated in canticles by Zechariah, Mary, and Simeon, who all recite hymns of praise and thanksgiving based on various Old Testament passages.

Luke's infancy narrative is also structured using the technique of comparison-contrast between a number of elements, including men and women, and between the predecessors of John the Baptist and of Jesus. For example, at the announcements, John's father Zechariah doubts the angel, but Jesus' mother Mary believes from the beginning. Luke masterfully sets up a parallelism between the events surrounding the births of John the Baptist and Jesus, including:

- annunciations by the angel Gabriel (1:11-20 and 1:26-38);
- the unexpected nature of the pregnancy of the mothers (1:18-25 and 1:29-34);
- canticles, derived from the Old Testament, expressing gratitude and praise of God (1:46-55 and 1:68-79);
- the reaction of joy and praise on the part of witnesses to these events (1:58; 2:8-14, 18-20, 28-32, 38);
- the shadow of suffering and rejection that is present from the beginning (1:65-66, 80; 2:34-35, 50-51).

In fact, Luke's entire infancy narrative presents a comparison and contrast between the two main figures, John and Jesus. The greatest parallel is in the announcement stories. John and Jesus are born as a result of God's will and grace. All the people anxiously await the births of these babies. John will be great before the Lord (1:15); Jesus will be the Son of the Most High. The origin of both is in God.

This parallelism between John and Jesus has further been described as "step parallelism, that is, a parallelism of one-upmanship. The Jesus side always comes off better."[8] Luke

---

[8] See J. A. Fitzmyer, *The Gospel According to Luke*, Anchor Bible 28 (New York: Doubleday, 1981) 315. Luke does something similar in Acts by

means to insist that although John is a great figure in the history of salvation, Jesus is the fulfillment of every salvation hope. Jesus is the long awaited Messiah. John came to announce Jesus and then to recede into the background until he is arrested and killed. John baptized with water, but Jesus, who is "mightier" than John, will baptize with the Holy Spirit (3:16).

Luke's infancy narrative serves as a kind of introduction to the themes of the entire Gospel. Those themes include a fascination with women and their roles in the early Christian community, God's predilection for people who are poor, those who are weak, those whom society disregards. Other Lukan themes show hospitality as a way of proclaiming the Gospel, the joy of those who receive the Gospel with faith, as well as the suffering necessarily involved with this acceptance.

Writing in the eighth decade of the first century, Luke was concerned with offering a defense for the Christian way of life to the dominant Greco-Roman society, which regarded this new sect with suspicion and often animosity. Luke is at pains to show that one could be a Christian and a good and pious member of Roman society. For example, the fact that Luke shows Joseph and Mary traveling to Bethlehem for the census could be one indication that Luke is trying to depict them as conscientious Roman citizens. They had no quarrel with Rome (2:1-5). They complied with the government. They also observed their own religious traditions. They are portrayed as pious and upright.

At the same time, Luke will be encouraging believers to persevere in faith despite inevitable hostility or suffering. He will also insist that a kinship of faith transcends blood ties. Believers form a new society, a new family based on their common faith. The infancy narrative of Luke thus serves as a kind of descriptive family tree, showing the Church's roots in the Old Testament and therefore continuity, while also looking forward to the full coming of the new age of the Spirit. Luke presents the story of salvation as a kind of progressive sequence

---

comparing Peter (see Acts 1–8) and Paul (16–28) with Acts 9–15, providing the transition from a church anchored in Judaism to one with a universal mission exemplified by the Pauline ministry to the Gentiles.

from the age of the prophets, to the dawning of the messianic age with the coming of Jesus, to the age of the Church characterized by the empowerment of the Spirit. John the Baptist is the last of the prophets. The death of Jesus is not the end, but its meaning is clarified by the resurrection. Finally, we are living in the age of faith and of the outpouring on the Church of the Spirit of God. These progressive stages in the unfolding of salvation will feature the examples of women as well as men believing and bearing witness to their faith.

Although they contain themes found in the rest of the Gospel of Luke, chapters 1–2 stand alone for several reasons. Characters who appear here are not found in any other Gospel, and except for Mary and John the Baptist, are not found in the rest of the Gospel of Luke.[9] These chapters are also unique in their introduction of hymns into the Gospel narrative. In general, these initial chapters read very differently than the rest of Gospel. One can skip from 1:4 to 3:1 and find the transition smooth. Luke seems to have used the Greek translation of the Old Testament known as the Septuagint.[10] The pattern of the material found in the infancy narrative of Luke seems to be based on the story of Hannah in 1 Samuel 1:1–2:11.[11]

The infancy narrative focuses especially on three women: Elizabeth, Mary, and Anna. By thus beginning with a focus on female characters, with women in leading roles, the narrative implicitly calls for a reversal of the world's values if readers are to understand. As Barbara Reid so elegantly puts it, Luke opens what is for him the most important chapter of salvation history with the least important people in society: a barren

---

[9] In fact, Mary does not appear in Luke's Gospel outside the infancy narrative; she is present with the rest of the disciples at the beginning of Acts, awaiting the coming of the Holy Spirit (Acts 1:14). Luke will include two other references to Jesus' mother: one in Luke 8:19-21, where Jesus' family is described as those who hear the word of God and act on it, and the other in 11:27-28, when the woman praises her as the "womb that carried [Jesus] and the breasts at which [he] nursed," and Jesus countered that she is blessed because she heard the word of God and observed it.

[10] An abbreviated way of referring to this translation is the LXX.

[11] See a summary of the story of Hannah at the end of this chapter, pp. 40–41.

wife, a young peasant girl, and an elderly widow.[12] These are ideal Lukan believers, totally reliant upon, trusting in, and submissive to the will of God.

ELIZABETH

Suggested Reading: Luke 1:5-25, 57-66; see 1:36, 40, 41; also 1 Samuel 1:1–2:11

Elizabeth is the first woman we meet in Luke's Gospel. Yet in both Luke's telling and in subsequent interpretation of her story, Elizabeth appears to get short shrift. She is identified primarily in terms of the relationships in her life: to her husband and her son and then to Mary, mother of Jesus. In a sense, Elizabeth represents the thread that binds the story of these others together. Initially more attention is given to her husband Zechariah, until the visitation from Mary. After that the focus shifts to Elizabeth's son John, who in turn is overshadowed by Jesus.

Yet it is significant that what Luke does say about Elizabeth suggests the depth of her faith and her cooperation with God's call to play a remarkable role in salvation history. Elizabeth will be described as demonstrating the virtues Luke most consistently recommends as characteristic of believers: readiness and expectation of the coming of God's Messiah, perseverance, faith, obedience, joy, and openness to receive the word despite difficulties.

Significantly, Elizabeth has her own name rather than being referred to only as Zechariah's wife or John's mother or Mary's kinswoman. As part of the husband-wife team, Elizabeth's credentials are on a par with those of her husband, who holds a place of honor in the Old Testament priesthood. Moreover, in contrast with her husband, Elizabeth shows no sign of reluctance, hesitation, or doubt when she learns of her divinely appointed role. As part of the John-side of the parallelism,

---

[12] Barbara Reid, *Choosing the Better Part? Women in the Gospel of Luke* (Collegeville: The Liturgical Press, 1996) 94–95.

Elizabeth's role is subordinate to that of Jesus' mother, for example. But within the family of John, Elizabeth is a more remarkable figure than her husband Zechariah. Thus we need to read between the lines to glean the importance of this remarkable woman, even though Luke's word count about her lags behind the attention he gives the other characters in her story.

Luke introduces the story of salvation with a married couple, Zechariah and Elizabeth. They are righteous. They are childless too. They are old, beyond childbearing age. Then God heard their prayers and sent a messenger to them with good news. In an amazing way, God rewards their faithfulness in Elizabeth's conception. The gift of the Holy Spirit, a particular concern for Luke, comes first to Elizabeth and Mary, who prefigure the women in the rest of Luke's Gospel. Luke tells the story this way.

ANNOUNCEMENT OF THE BIRTH OF JOHN (LUKE 1:5-25)

[5]In the days of Herod, King of Judea, there was a priest named Zechariah of the priestly division of Abijah; his wife was from the daughters of Aaron, and her name was Elizabeth. [6]Both were righteous in the eyes of God, observing all the commandments and ordinances of the Lord blamelessly. [7]But they had no child, because Elizabeth was barren and both were advanced in years. [8]Once when he was serving as priest in his division's turn before God, [9]according to the practice of the priestly service, he was chosen by lot to enter the sanctuary of the Lord to burn incense. [10]Then, when the whole assembly of the people was praying outside at the hour of the incense offering, [11]the angel of the Lord appeared to him, standing at the right of the altar of incense. [12]Zechariah was troubled by what he saw, and fear came upon him. [13]But the angel said to him, "Do not be afraid, Zechariah, because your prayer has been heard. Your wife Elizabeth will bear you a son, and you shall name him John. [14]And you will have joy and gladness, and many will rejoice at his birth, [15]for he will be great in the sight of [the] Lord. He will drink neither wine nor strong drink. He will be filled with the holy Spirit even from his mother's womb, [16]and he will turn many of the children of Israel to the Lord their God. [17]He will go before him in the spirit and power of Elijah to turn the hearts of fathers toward children and the disobedient to the under-

standing of the righteous, to prepare a people fit for the Lord." [18]Then Zechariah said to the angel, "How shall I know this? For I am an old man, and my wife is advanced in years." [19]And the angel said to him in reply, "I am Gabriel, who stand before God. I was sent to speak to you and to announce to you this good news. [20]But now you will be speechless and unable to talk until the day these things take place, because you did not believe my words, which will be fulfilled at their proper time."

[21]Meanwhile the people were waiting for Zechariah and were amazed that he stayed so long in the sanctuary. [22]But when he came out, he was unable to speak to them, and they realized that he had seen a vision in the sanctuary. He was gesturing to them but remained mute. [23]Then, when his days of ministry were completed, he went home. [24]After this time his wife Elizabeth conceived, and she went into seclusion for five months, saying, [25]"So has the Lord done for me at a time when he has seen fit to take away my disgrace before others."

Zechariah and Elizabeth both are described as having impressive religious credentials. "Both were righteous in the eyes of God, observing all the commandments and ordinances of the Lord blamelessly" (Luke 1:6). Zechariah held a position of honor in Judaism. He was "of the priestly division of Abijah" (the note in the New American Bible tells us that this is a reference to the eighth of twenty-four divisions of priests who, for a week at a time, twice a year, served in the Jerusalem Temple). Elizabeth was also from priestly progeny. She is further described as a "daughter of Aaron," who was the brother of Moses. The priests were called the "sons of Aaron," claiming to trace their ancestry back to Aaron. Elizabeth had the same name as Aaron's wife (Exod 6:28). The name Elizabeth incorporates a Hebrew word for God *(el);* her name means "God is my treasure" or possibly "God is the one by whom I swear."

Elizabeth, like her husband, observed all the commandments blamelessly. She is the only woman called "righteous" (or "just") in the New Testament. It is interesting that Tamar, one of the women Matthew names in Jesus' genealogy, is the only woman referred to as "righteous" in the Old Testament. This special attribute summarizes the religious aspirations of a dedicated Old Testament person. It is ascribed to Tamar in recognition of her persistence, risking all, to gain justice from her father-in-law Judah. Indeed the attribute of righteousness is reserved for only a few people in either Testament.[13]

According to the Old Testament, justice properly belongs to God; it is the goal of the Torah people. To be righteous meant to be focused on God and on the will of God as revealed in the Law. Israel's hope was to follow the Law and thus learn the way of God's justice. Righteous living meant not only moral integrity but observing all the Law and ordinances of God.[14] Luke depicts Elizabeth as doing this unquestioningly. While such righteousness was expected of men, there was less emphasis on women's keeping all of the mandates of the Law, which was male-oriented. Women were exempt from many of the Law's requirements because their duties to their husbands and families took precedence in their lives. But Elizabeth is described as "just," as "righteous," no less than her husband; she is presented as every bit as zealous and every bit as longing for the redemption of Israel, as Simeon and Anna both are.

Like Sarah, Elizabeth was barren and well on in years. Zechariah's protest to the angel includes Elizabeth's advanced age, as well as his own. The elderly are special wards of God. Long life is a blessing. It is also a covenant. Those who live long not only show God's graciousness but testify to their own dedication, faith, and trust. They are living evidence that God is faithful. But to have reached old age without having children who carry on one's life and represent the future demands real courage and trust. Elizabeth's advanced age means that she had lived righteously for many long years. Luke describes perseverance as a particularly desirable Christian virtue (see Luke 8:15; 18:1-8), and Elizabeth's advanced age suggests that she is

---

[13] Righteousness or justice is the attribute of God invoked under this title in the Old Testament. In Luke's Gospel, Jesus is recognized by the centurion as "righteous" at his death (Luke 23:47, NAB note).

[14] This is one of many examples, especially in Luke, that shows that there is no polemic against the Law or against Judaism. Although Jesus sometimes quarrels with various interpretations of the Law, Luke insists that the Law can and should be obeyed. It was fulfilled by Jesus, who was an observant Jew; and many of the people who are praised for their faith are also searching for the way of justice symbolized by the Law.

a model of perseverance. This is so despite the fragility of her future in human terms since she was barren. Her faith, her perseverance, her trust and obedience never wavered, even into old age, when it would seem that she could easily have become disillusioned and angry that her fidelity had gone unnoticed and unrewarded by God. She, like Anna after her, represents the truly poor, since her worth and her hope would have been measured by her children; she has none. Their stories anticipate the restoration of the son of the widow of Nain, the bereaved Jairus and his wife, who lost their daughter, the ostracized but brave woman with a hemorrhage, and the widow who gave her whole life as offering at the temple.

Thus a collage of Old Testament themes forms the background of John and his family. His parents are firmly rooted in Judaism and in the priestly traditions. The "angel of the Lord" is associated with the coming of the "Day of the Lord," a day of judgment against God's enemies and a time of vindication for God's faithful ones. The angel also symbolized the coming of the Lord to his temple, an experience of holiness and of deliverance (Dan 9:20-26; 10:7, 12, 16-17).

In announcing John's birth, the angel echoes lines from the story of the birth of Samson, which likewise was a result of God's favor to a childless couple. Judges 13:3 says that an angel of the Lord came to Manoah's wife, who was barren and childless. The angel instructed her to

> take no wine or strong drink and to eat nothing unclean. As for the son you will conceive and bear, no razor shall touch his head, for this baby is to be consecrated to God from the womb. It is he who will begin the deliverance of Israel from the power of the Philistines (Judg 13:4-5).

The Hebrew word *nazir* means "to set apart as sacred, to consecrate or vow." To take a nazirite vow meant to dedicate oneself for a certain mission. This dedication would be signified by abstinence from strong drink and by letting the hair grow (see Num 6:2-8), without cutting it. The Law says, "As long as he is a nazirite he is sacred to the Lord" (Num 6:8). This vow could be for a limited amount of time, for example until the mission was accomplished. In this case, a man would shave his head at the time of taking a vow of dedication and then let his hair grow for as long as it took to fulfill the vow. The length of his hair thus symbolized the time he had been dedicated under his vow.[15] Or, in the case of some nazirites, the consecration could be a lifelong commitment, as was supposed to be the case for Samson. But at the instigation of the Philistines, Delilah discovered the source of Samson's strength and betrayed him. As the story is told in the book of Judges, Delilah, after nagging him relentlessly, finally wrenched from Samson the secret and source of his strength:

> No razor has touched my head, for I have been consecrated to God from my mother's womb. If I am shaved, my strength will leave me, and I shall be as weak as any other man (Judg 16:17).

Samson allowed himself to be seduced and distracted before his mission to conquer the Philistines had been accomplished. Later, after he had rededicated himself and his hair grew long again, his strength returned (16:22).

Like Samson, John is also portrayed as a nazirite for life, consecrated, even before his birth, in the tradition of the prophets. The image of Elijah also comes to mind in reading about the birth of John:

> He will be great in the sight of [the] Lord. He will drink neither wine nor strong drink. He will be filled with the holy Spirit even from his mother's womb. . . . He will go before (the Lord) in the spirit and power of Elijah to turn the hearts of fathers toward children and the disobedient to the understanding of the righteous, to prepare a people fit for the Lord (Luke 1:15, 17).

John is the messenger sent before God to prepare the people for the coming of God. Luke must have been inspired by the beginning of Mark's Gospel, which portrayed John's mission as such:

> Behold, I am sending my messenger ahead of you;
>   he will prepare your way.

[15] The practice may have been continued among some Christians, according to Luke (see Acts 21:23-26).

A voice of one crying out in the desert:
    "Prepare the way of the Lord,
    make straight his paths" (Mark 1:2-3).

Although Mark attributes this saying to Isaiah, it is a combination quotation. Isaiah 40:3-5 says:

A voice cries out:
In the desert prepare the way of the LORD!
    Make straight in the wasteland a highway for our God!
Every valley shall be filled in,
    every mountain and hill shall be made low;
The rugged land shall be made a plain,
    the rough country, a broad valley.
Then the glory of the LORD shall be revealed,
    and all mankind shall see it together;
    for the mouth of the LORD has spoken (Isa 40:3-5).

To Isaiah's quote, Mark adds an excerpt from Malachi, who said:

Lo, I am sending my messenger
    to prepare the way before me;
And suddenly there will come to the temple
    the LORD whom you seek,
And the messenger of the covenant whom you desire.
    Yes, he is coming, says the LORD of hosts.
But who will endure the day of his coming?
    And who can stand when he appears?
For he is like the refiner's fire,
    or like the fuller's lye (Mal 3:1-2).

A little further on, Malachi adds, speaking on God's behalf:

Lo, I will send you
    Elijah, the prophet,
Before the day of the LORD comes,
    the great and terrible day" (Mal 3:23).

Elijah was described as taken to heaven in a fiery chariot (2 Kgs 2:1). Therefore he shall return to earth, his coming portending the "Day of the Lord." Although this will be a day of judgment against the unjust, it will also mean vindication for the just who welcome Elijah. John is described in language reminiscent of Elijah, whom he resembles in lifestyle and even in dress and appearance (see 2 Kgs 1:8; Mark 1:6). Jesus will identify John the Baptist with Elijah (see Mark 9:11-13; Matt 17:10-13).

Returning to Luke's story, after Gabriel announced John's birth, Zechariah's disbelief is implied in his question to the angel. Zechariah asks, "How shall I know this?" (Luke 1:18). The prophets often asked for a sign, but Zechariah appears to be incredulous. He represents an attitude many will show toward John and toward Jesus: "What sign do you give?" The reply of the angel shows impatience with such a test of God, "I was sent with good news, but you ask for proof." Nevertheless, a sign is given: "you will be speechless and unable to talk until the days these things take place . . . ." (Luke 1:20). Abruptly, the apparition is concluded. The rest is up to God. Zechariah goes home after the days of his ministry and Elizabeth conceives.

Meanwhile, Luke says, although Zechariah had been troubled, the people were amazed. They had been "waiting" outside as Zechariah went in to offer sacrifice. Luke could be anticipating those to whom Anna will prophesy about Jesus, those, Luke says, who awaited the redemption of Jerusalem (Luke 2:38). The people are still there waiting, while Zechariah remains inside a long time. The people will gather again, at the home of Elizabeth and Zechariah, when this promise is fulfilled and John is born. And again they will be described as amazed (Luke 1:21, 58, 63, 66).

Luke involves the "people" (the Greek word Luke uses often is *laos*, from which the term "laity" is derived) as a kind of chorus, a kind of collective person in the drama. The people's longing and waiting becomes amazement. And the amazement of the people often turns to praise, joy, and thanks. They frequently express these reactions by giving testimony about what they have seen and heard and believe. So, for example, the people ask regarding John, "'What, then, will this child be?' For surely the hand of the Lord was with him" (Luke 1:66). And the people are described later by Luke as "filled with expectation," wondering whether John could be the Messiah they so much longed for (Luke 3:15).

The story, to this point at least, seems to be more about Zechariah and John than about Elizabeth. Yet, whereas Zechariah was disbelieving, Elizabeth has no such reaction. She conceives and gives thanks, saying, "So has the Lord done for me at a time when he has seen fit to take away my disgrace before others" (Luke 1:25). Luke tends to attribute dialogue to persons, developing the drama as it unfolds, as if on stage. Elizabeth speaks the sentiments of many Old Testament women who were tested with barrenness, one of the greatest trials for women in a patriarchal society that so valued sons. Elizabeth voices the thoughts of Sarah and of Rachel, of Leah and of Hannah, when at last they conceived a child. Elizabeth praises God for the blessing of her pregnancy.

For Elizabeth, this is a new beginning, but only the beginning. She shows no signs of the skepticism of her husband. He remains dumb and apparently also deaf, since she and the people have to make signs for him to understand (1:22, 62-63). Elizabeth withdraws into seclusion for five months. Luke presents this less as a sign of her modesty than as accordance with God's own time to draw her out with a visit from Mary.

Luke has a way of interjecting into the sequence of things even more momentous tidings. So he does with the announcement of the birth of Jesus. After that announcement Mary will come to Elizabeth, and the two will celebrate the blessings God has given them.

THE BIRTH OF JOHN (LUKE 1:57-66)

After describing the annunciation of Jesus' birth to Mary, Luke returns to the story of Elizabeth, telling how she gave birth to John. Luke tells us:

> [57]When the time arrived for Elizabeth to have her child she gave birth to a son. [58]Her neighbors and relatives heard that the Lord had shown his great mercy toward her, and they rejoiced with her. [59]When they came on the eighth day to circumcise the child, they were going to call him Zechariah after his father, [60]but his mother said in reply, "No. He will be called John." [61]But they answered her, "There is no one among your relatives who has this name." [62]So they made signs, asking his father what he wished him to be called.

⁶³He asked for a tablet and wrote, "John is his name," and all were amazed. ⁶⁴Immediately his mouth was opened, his tongue freed, and he spoke blessing God. ⁶⁵Then fear came upon all their neighbors, and all these matters were discussed throughout the hill country of Judea. ⁶⁶All who heard these things took them to heart, saying, "What, then, will this child be?" For surely the hand of the Lord was with him.

Luke simply says that Elizabeth gave birth "when the time arrived." Her neighbors and relatives rejoiced at God's mercy to her. As pious Jews, Elizabeth and Zechariah fulfilled the Law, having John circumcised on the eighth day as prescribed. The expectation was that he would be named according to family tradition. As with the rest of the angel's announcement, Elizabeth must have learned from Zechariah that God had chosen the name of this child, John, a name that means "favored." This time the people protest (rather than praise) in chorus, complaining that he had no relatives by this name. But Elizabeth is adamant. Yet even though she is the mother, her word is not enough; they inquire by gestures to Zechariah, who, at last believing, writes, "His name is John." Then the people believe and are once again amazed.

In commentaries, Zechariah's disbelief is often contrasted with Mary's belief; it should also be contrasted with Elizabeth's. Although Zechariah had the word of an angel, he doubted. Elizabeth had only the second-hand account of a doubter and she believed. Although he was a priest of the temple, Zechariah did not recognize the visit of God's messenger. Elizabeth was an old and barren woman but was alert to the ways God's presence could be felt. Zechariah asked for a sign and was made deaf and mute. Elizabeth recognized the blessing of God and testified in a "loud voice" (1:42) before her relatives and neighbors, starting with Mary. Elizabeth is the first person to make a Christological statement, when, upon greeting Mary, she said, "How does this happen to me that the mother of my Lord should come to me?" (Luke 1:43). We are not finished with Elizabeth yet. Her story continues. The significance of her role in the story is all the more enhanced by her encounter with Mary in the visitation. This is also the scene in which Elizabeth yields to Mary, who then takes center stage, while Elizabeth exits, her preparatory role accomplished.

MARY

Suggested Reading: Luke 1:26-56; 2:1-52

Mary is first and foremost a disciple of Jesus, a model believer. That is how she comes across in the annunciation scene. That is how Mary is greeted by Elizabeth at the visitation. And that is how she appears in the rest of the infancy narrative and in Luke's Gospel. She is a believer all along, waiting for the fulfillment of the Last Times, which finally come with the outpouring of the Spirit and the birth of the Church (Acts 1:14).

THE ANNUNCIATION TO MARY (LUKE 1:26-38)

The angel Gabriel links the experience of Mary to that of Elizabeth. To show that the angel rather than rumor told her of Elizabeth's pregnancy, Luke notes that Elizabeth was in seclusion for five months (Luke 1:24). In the sixth month the angel Gabriel, the same messenger who had told Zechariah of the birth of John the Baptist, appears to Mary with a comparable but greater announcement. The basic pattern of a call narrative appears again, as it did in the appearance to Zechariah:

- the angel Gabriel appears unexpectedly (1:28; see 1:11);
- Mary is troubled (1:29; see 1:12);
- address and commission (1:30-33; see 1:13-17);
- objection of Mary (1:34; see 1:18);
- sign and reassurance (1:35-37; see 1:19-20).

Luke concludes the announcement with Mary's acceptance (1:38) and the angel's leaving her. Here's how Luke records the announcement of Jesus' birth to Mary in 1:26-38:

> [26]In the sixth month, the angel Gabriel was sent from God to a town of Galilee called Nazareth, [27]to a virgin betrothed to a

man named Joseph, of the house of David, and the virgin's name was Mary. [28]And coming to her, he said, "Hail, favored one! The Lord is with you." [29]But she was greatly troubled at what was said and pondered what sort of greeting this might be. [30]Then the angel said to her, "Do not be afraid, Mary, for you have found favor with God. [31]Behold, you will conceive in your womb and bear a son, and you shall name him Jesus. [32]He will be great and will be called Son of the Most High, and the Lord God will give him the throne of David his father, [33]and he will rule over the house of Jacob forever, and of his kingdom there will be no end." [34]But Mary said to the angel, "How can this be, since I have no relations with a man?" [35]And the angel said to her in reply, "The holy Spirit will come upon you, and the power of the Most High will overshadow you. Therefore the child to be born will be called holy, the Son of God. [36]And behold, Elizabeth, your relative, has also conceived a son in her old age, and this is the sixth month for her who was called barren; [37]for nothing will be impossible for God." [38]Mary said, "Behold, I am the handmaid of the Lord. May it be done to me according to your word." Then the angel departed from her.

The angel Gabriel appears to Mary in God's time, when the moment is right, when Elizabeth is in her sixth month. This angel was already introduced in the appearance to Zechariah, the father of John. Belief in angels grew in popularity in Israel, especially after the exile in Babylon (587–539 B.C.E.), when Judaism came into contact with surrounding cultures and their beliefs in lesser gods and superhuman, semidivine heroes. This was a belief disputed by the Sadducees but accepted by Pharisees in the first century (see Acts 23:8).[16]

In some of the older books of the Hebrew Scriptures, "angels" were hardly distinguishable from God. Partly as a way of preserving the transcendence of Yahweh while also asserting God's immanence and care for human beings, belief developed in spiritual forces that were messengers (the meaning of the Greek word *angelos*, "angel") of the divine. By about the third

---

[16] A resurrection from the dead is a similarly disputed idea between these groups. Such divergent beliefs are an indication that Judaism is not a monolithic religion, adhering to a single set of teachings.

century before Christ, these spirits were sometimes personified.[17] There are three such angelic spirits named in the Old
Testament: Gabriel (Dan 8:16; 9:21), Michael (Dan 10:13; 12:1),
and Raphael (Tob 3:17). Their names all end in *"-el,"* a Hebrew
name for God. This is an indication that angels are to be understood as God's messengers, sent by God and speaking for God.

An "angel of the Lord" appeared to only two women in the
Old Testament, each time bringing a message that she would
bear a son. In Genesis 16, an "angel of the Lord" came to
Hagar and confirmed her pregnancy with Ishmael, her son by
Abraham:

> You are now pregnant and shall bear a son;
>   you shall name him Ishmael,
> For the LORD has heard you,
>   God has answered you" (Gen 16:11; see vv. 7-11).

It is with a similar message that an angel comes to the wife of
Manoah, telling her that she would become the mother of
Samson, saying, "Though you are barren and have had no
children, yet you will conceive and bear a son" (Judg 13:3).

The angel named Gabriel first appears in the Book of Daniel,
explaining to him disturbing visions of the end of time. The
book of Daniel is an example of apocalyptic literature. Apocalyptic developed out of the extreme suffering of the Babylonian
Exile, when Judah was struggling with unbearable persecution
and confusion. Apocalyptic is a coded way of encouraging
God's people that their faith would be vindicated and that the
victory of God over evil would come soon. Meanwhile, outsiders are prevented from comprehending the symbolic language that forecasts their own punishment and destruction.

Daniel is a seer who has an unearthly vision full of all sorts
of strange images. He borrows on the older prophetic image of
the "Day of the Lord," which is a time of wrath, vengeance,
judgment, punishment, and unspeakable suffering (see Amos
5:18-20). Yet it will also be a day of hope, consolation, and vindication for the "remnant" of Israel, those who remain faithful

---

[17] It is a later belief that evil is also personified and named as Satan
(see Job) or Beelzebul (see Gospels).

despite persecution and all sorts of threats and temptations against faith (see Amos 5:15). The Day of the Lord in apocalyptic literature represents the "end" of this world and a new time that will witness the reversal of the present. Oppressors will be punished and the oppressed will be rewarded.

The apocalyptic perspective is universal. The struggle is between good and evil, including not only human life but all levels of creation. Good and evil spirits, conceived as angels and demons, are involved in this same struggle. Thus in Daniel 12 and also in the New Testament book of Revelation 12, the angel Michael leads the struggle against Satan and is victorious in the end. Apocalyptic figures to some extent in the New Testament books as they grapple with explaining the meaning and implications of Jesus' proclamation that the kingdom of God has come. Apocalyptic views are part of the stock images used at times by New Testament writers.

Such views help us to understand not only the role of Gabriel but the "disturbed" reaction of Mary. In apocalyptic literature the angel Gabriel is associated with the last days. But Luke will link Gabriel with the beginning of the new age of salvation promised to all of God's faithful people, including the poor, the little ones, the outcasts. They represent the universalism of the Gospel.

Gabriel addresses Mary by name. Gabriel speaks to her in a jubilant tone, saying, "Hail, Mary!" This is a common greeting in Greek; but Gabriel goes further, calling Mary "favored one." Gabriel's greeting could be an abbreviated reflection on Zechariah 2:14, which says, "Sing and rejoice, O daughter Zion! See, I am coming to dwell among you, says the LORD." In Luke the angel continues, "The Lord is with you!" This is a phrase frequently found in the Old Testament, but it only occurs as a greeting in two places: in Ruth 2:4, where it expresses a wish as "May the Lord be with you!" and in Judges 6:12, when an angel comes to Gideon and declares, as Gabriel says to Mary in Luke 1:28, "The Lord is with you!" "The Lord" *(Kyrios)* is one of the ways the Septuagint refers to Yahweh, the God of Israel. That is the reference in this statement to Mary, of course. But later in the New Testament, especially in Luke, the title "Lord" will be used of Jesus himself (for example, Luke 5:8, 12; 6:46; 7:6, 13, 19; 9:54, 59, 61).

After greeting Mary, the angel begins the message from God, saying, "Do not be afraid." The attitude of awe or reverence, expressed as "fear," is typical for those who experience an epiphany. Gabriel continues, "You have found favor (*charis* meaning 'grace') with God." The choice of Mary has nothing to do with merit or worthiness. God is gracious, abundant in generosity. God's choice is based on who God is rather than who Mary is. Mary could easily be "troubled" by the immediacy of the grace she experiences. Her next question indicates wonderment, not doubt, "How can this be?"

Mary is troubled at hearing the greeting of the angel. Her confusion is based on both the appearance of the angel and on what the angel has said. Mary "pondered" *(dielogizeto)* what these could mean. Luke goes further, later noting that Mary "treasured" *(syneterei)* the words of Simeon (Luke 2:19) and concluding the infancy story with the comment that Mary "treasured" *(dieterei)* "all these things in her heart" (2:51). Mary's perplexity at the angel's visit and words may be associated with the great demands made on those who are favored by God, as many Old Testament examples show. Moses, for example, hoped he could decline the favor of being chosen to go to the pharaoh, protesting that he was "slow of speech and tongue" (Exod 4:10), maybe meaning that he stuttered or had stage fright. Moses begs, "If you please, Lord, send someone else!" (Exod 4:13). Besides, he implies as he pleads his case, he was wanted in Egypt for killing an Egyptian (see Exod 2:11-15). He was needed by his father-in-law in Midian to help tend the flocks (Exod 2:21). Moses does not appear to be a good candidate to go to the pharaoh or to lead the people.

Similarly, Jeremiah protests when chosen by God: "I know not how to speak; I am too young" (Jer 1:6). Even Isaiah complains that he has "unclean lips" (Isa 6:5), thereby implying that God should send someone else! Yet we ought not think that Mary's wonderment meant that she was reluctant, as Luke will make clear in the rest of the angel's announcement. Luke probably included Mary's "protest" as part of the call-story pattern. The reaction and assurance of the angel are much more positive than in the case of the incredulous Zechariah.

The angel continues with the divine message, which involves a *commission* to Mary. The angel said to her:

> Do not be afraid, Mary, for you have found favor with God.
> Behold, you will conceive in your womb and bear a son, and
> you shall name him Jesus. He will be great and will be called
> Son of the Most High, and the Lord God will give him the
> throne of David his father, and he will rule over the house of
> Jacob forever, and of his kingdom there will be no end (Luke
> 1:30-33).

Mary's commission transforms her from a frightened, defenseless girl, too young even to have been given in marriage to her
husband and transferred to his care, to the chosen one of God,
in God's favor. Her mission has to do with the child she will
bear, a clear indication that Luke's purpose is Christological
rather than Mariological.[18] Jesus, the name of Mary's child,
means "God saves" (as Matthew explains in 1:21). "Salvation"
is a term Luke uses to describe the work that Jesus does. Salvation is linked with peace as a messianic blessing. The salvation
Jesus brings is celebrated in the Canticle of Zechariah:

> He has raised up a horn for our salvation . . .
>   salvation from our enemies . . . .
> to give his people knowledge of salvation
>   through the forgiveness of their sins . . . .
>   (Luke 1:69, 71, 77).

In her Magnificat, Mary likewise praises God for salvation:
"My spirit rejoices in God my savior" (Luke 1:47). Similarly,
Simeon prays, "Now, Master, you may let your servant go in
peace . . . for my eyes have seen your salvation . . . . (Luke
2:30). In Luke, salvation is linked with faith and peace, as Jesus
says to the woman who anointed him: "Your faith has saved
you; go in peace" (Luke 7:50). And salvation is universal, extended to all people in Jesus, as Acts says: "I will pour out a
portion of my spirit upon all flesh" (Acts 2:17), and "everyone
shall be saved who calls on the name of the Lord" (2:21).

Divinely appointed names carry with them a mission.
Mary's child will be great. He shall be called the "Son of the
Most High." This absolute title for God, "Most High," is related
to a Hebrew name for Yahweh. "Most High" conveys the awe-

---

[18] See Fitzmyer, *The Gospel According to Luke,* 1:337–338.

some transcendence or otherness of God. "Most High" occurs only once in Mark (5:7) but is used several times as a reference to God in Luke (see Luke 1:35, 76; 6:35; 8:28; Acts 7:48; 16:17).

The relation between the greatness of Jesus, the Most High, and the identification of Jesus as God's Son may be linked with the image of David and may have been inspired by 2 Samuel 7, where the prophet Nathan conveys to David God's promise of an everlasting covenant. Nathan blesses David, promising on God's behalf that David will have a "great name" (2 Sam 7:9), and of his son, Solomon, God says, "I will make his royal throne firm forever. I will be a father to him, and he shall be a son to me. . . . Your house and your kingdom shall endure forever before me" (2 Sam 7:13-14, 16). For Luke, Jesus is the Savior, the descendant of David, the Messiah who fulfills God's promise to David.

But Jesus is even more than that—he is also God's Son. It is no mere human testimony but God who reveals Jesus' sonship at his baptism with the words, "You are my beloved Son; with you I am well pleased" (Luke 3:22). God testifies again to Jesus' sonship at the transfiguration, when a voice from a cloud said, "This is my chosen Son; listen to him" (Luke 9:35).

Mary's virginity is used by Luke in function of Jesus' identity as God's Son.[19] Mary objects to the words of the angel out of her perplexity: "How can this be, since I have no relations with a man?" (Luke 1:34). It is typical for Luke to supply dialogue to his characters, as he does here, for example, and in the story of Zechariah. Mary's question is a kind of plea for help, a query about what she should do, how she might prepare for this momentous event in her life. She is portrayed as willing, if not ready. This is grace unexpected, not unappreciated. Like the prophets in the Old Testament, she is portrayed as surprised by this call. Mary does not create obstacles. She asks for direction, relying on God for help.

Mary answers, "Behold, I am the handmaid of the Lord! May it be done to me according to your word" (Luke 1:38). The handmaid theme will appear again in Mary's canticle (Luke 1:48). It is inspired by the prophet Samuel's mother, Hannah

---

[19] For a good discussion of this, see Fitzmyer, *The Gospel According to Luke*, 1:340–341.

(1 Sam 1:11). Luke is also anticipating the final age of history when, with the gift of the Spirit, God's servants and handmaids alike will prophesy (Acts 2:18; a fulfillment of Joel 3:1-5).

Here is Mary's unqualified acceptance, and in the witness of her Magnificat, Luke foreshadows the way he will portray Mary later in the Gospel. Mary is both disciple and prophet. Indeed she will be described from here on, not in the usual terms of women of her times, that is, in relation to her husband and family; rather she takes on the identity of a model of the disciples, as Luke portrays them in his rendition of the parable of the sower: "they are the ones who, when they have heard the word, embrace it with a generous and good heart, and bear fruit through perseverance" (Luke 8:15).

Whenever Mary is described, similar terms are used in reference to her. She ponders Jesus' words in her heart. Jesus corrects the emphasis of the woman from the crowd who praises Mary for her physical relationship with him, implying that she is blessed "rather" for hearing the word of God and observing it (see Luke 11:27-28). In Luke 8:19-21, Mary and Jesus' brothers are described as hearing the word of God and keeping it, so unlike Luke's source, Mark, who describes Jesus' mother and brothers as thinking him "out of his mind" and wanting to silence him by taking him away (see Mark 3:20-22, 31-35). The angel referred to Mary as having found God's favor; Elizabeth will speak for generations who will recognize Mary as "blessed" because she believed the word that was spoken to her (Luke 1:45). Mary is a witness to Jesus and a model disciple. She is commissioned to bear testimony about Jesus and to bring forth fruit of the word in perseverance.

The parallelism with the story of the birth of John continues. The usual story of a call concludes with a *sign and reassurance*. The "sign" given to Mary is Elizabeth's pregnancy, which is already advanced into the sixth month. No ordinary word of mouth from other relatives reveals this to Mary, but the angel. Mary believes and will act on that belief in the visit that brings the women together. Mary is reassured that this shall come to pass because the "holy Spirit will come upon you, and the power of the Most High will overshadow you." Luke usually associates the Holy Spirit with power. So, for example, in Acts the disciples are instructed to wait in Jerusalem until the Holy

Spirit comes in power (see Acts 1:7-8). Then the timid, frightened disciples are empowered to be witnesses to the ends of the earth. The Holy Spirit and the power of the Most High are parallel. The Spirit is God's creative and active spirit.

The final reassurance to Mary is the reminder that nothing is impossible for God. And then, Luke says, "The angel departed from her" (1:38). So simply does Luke proceed from one scene to the other in this infancy narrative. God and God's will provide the transition and continuity. But the pace is quickened by the final line of each scene. For example, Zechariah "went home" (1:23). The angel departed from Mary (1:38). After the visitation to Elizabeth, Mary "returned to her home" (1:56). "The angels went away from them" (2:15). "They returned to Galilee, to their own town of Nazareth" (2:39). Things are happening according to God's plan and in God's time, which makes it all the more remarkable that part of this grand plan involves the meeting of ordinary people, two pregnant women, to celebrate the wondrous things God is doing for them. We turn now to the visitation of Mary to Elizabeth.

MARY'S VISIT TO ELIZABETH (LUKE 1:39-45)

As a result of learning of Elizabeth's pregnancy through the message of the angel, Mary sets out to see her kinswoman Elizabeth, an encounter that becomes part of Luke's Gospel. The story is told this way:

> [39]During those days Mary set out and traveled to the hill country in haste to a town of Judah, [40]where she entered the house of Zechariah and greeted Elizabeth. [41]When Elizabeth heard Mary's greeting, the infant leaped in her womb, and Elizabeth, filled with the holy Spirit, [42]cried out in a loud voice and said, "Most blessed are you among women, and blessed is the fruit of your womb. [43]And how does this happen to me, that the mother of my Lord should come to me? [44]For at the moment the sound of your greeting reached my ears, the infant in my womb leaped for joy. [45]Blessed are you who believed that what was spoken to you by the Lord would be fulfilled."

Mary's visit to Elizabeth is Luke's way of getting these two prophetic women together. A prophet is one who speaks and acts on God's behalf and intercedes with God on behalf of the people. That is how both Elizabeth and Mary are depicted, as well as Anna, who is designated with the title "prophet" in Luke 2:36. So far Luke has hinted at the relationship of Elizabeth and Mary through the parallelism of the announcement stories. Luke also tucked within the angel's announcement to Mary the "sign" of her kinswoman's pregnancy, already in its "sixth month" (1:36). Luke values faith ties over bloodlines, implying that we are kin to those with whom we share faith. A disciple may be required to "leave" house, wife, brothers and sisters, parents, or children for the sake of the kingdom of God (see Luke 14:26; 18:29). Only Luke includes spouses and children among those whom it might be necessary to leave behind for the sake of the Gospel. Physical family ties must not prohibit disciples from following Jesus. Jesus associates with sinners and outcasts, very often in the familial setting of a "house" and even a "meal." Luke consistently has Jesus move from synagogue to "house"; he is often rejected at the former but accepted and given hospitality at the latter, symbol of the Church (for example, compare Luke 4:16-30 with 4:38-39 and 5:27-32).

Table fellowship with sinners and outcasts is a critical point of his enemies' attack on Jesus according to Luke (see for example, Luke 7:39; 15:1-2). Luke pictures Jesus creating a fictive family of those willing to accept the cost of discipleship. His disciples become Jesus' sisters and brothers, a family based on common faith. Thus, in Acts, Luke refers to the community of believers as the "brothers and sisters." It is in their shared faith and related mission that Elizabeth is linked to Mary. That is not to say that there is no blood relationship between Mary and Elizabeth, an element of the story we would not otherwise be able to evaluate for lack of historical evidence. It is only to give priority to Luke's theological agenda.

Since God's time has already put things into motion, Mary acted right away on God's word made known to her by the angel. Mary hurried off "to the hill country in haste to a town of Judah, where she entered the house of Zechariah and greeted Elizabeth" (1:39-40). We ought to see here more than Mary's considerate kindness toward an elderly relative. Almost every word of Luke's narrative is potent with meaning. Mary's haste is an expression of her joy, faith, and gratitude, themes that dominate the two chapters of the infancy narrative up until the end, when the prophecy of Simeon warns that sorrow will also be part of discipleship.

Elizabeth and Mary will demonstrate what close relatives they are in the community of their belief and in the joy and humble praise with which they celebrate being part of God's plan for the salvation of the whole world. One of the major themes of Luke's Gospel is universal salvation. The theme is expressed in the infancy narrative, with its inclusion of women as representatives of the little ones, and also with the participation of angels and shepherds, even the fields and the flocks, the people who are awaiting the redemption of Jerusalem. This is the universe Jesus came to save.

Upon seeing Mary, Elizabeth greets her as the "mother of my Lord" (*Kyrios* in Greek). Thus Elizabeth, filled with the Holy Spirit, makes a prophetic statement. The women immediately express the overflowing sentiments of their hearts. Elizabeth first speaks a dual beatitude.[20] "In a loud voice," Elizabeth pronounces Mary blessed because she bears the Lord ("Most blessed are you among women, and blessed is the fruit of your womb") and because of her faith ("Blessed are you who believed that what was spoken to you by the Lord would be fulfilled"). The first part of Elizabeth's blessing is echoed later by another woman who "called out loud" and said to the adult Jesus, "Blessed is the womb that carried you and the breasts at which you nursed" (Luke 11:27). And Jesus' answer to the woman includes the second macarism of Elizabeth: "Blessed are those who hear the word of God and observe it" (11:28).[21]

Elizabeth's blessing of Mary comes right out of the pages of the Old Testament, from the stories of Deborah and Jael and Judith. Deborah blesses Jael, saying, "Blessed among women be Jael" (Judg 5:24). A similar blessing is pronounced on Judith:

---

[20] Sometimes called a "macarism" from the Greek word for "blessing"; this is the same word used for the Beatitudes (see Matt 5:3-12; Luke 6:20-23).

[21] This answer means that Mary is blessed not so much because she only has a physical relationship to Jesus but that she has a more intimate, spiritual one. She is his "mother" in that she first heard God's word and believed it. In Luke the qualifiers used of Mary are consistently the terms used of disciples. Mary hears God's word, ponders it, keeps it in her heart, brings forth its fruit (see 8:15, 19-21).

"Blessed are you, daughter, by the Most High God, above all the women on earth. . . . Your deed of hope will never be forgotten by those who tell of the might of God" (Jdt 13:18-19).

Luke tells us that the infant (John) leaped for joy at the sound of Mary's voice. This detail is also rooted in the Old Testament: the twins Jacob and Esau leaped and played in Rebekah's womb (Gen 25:22), although they would grow up to be adversaries. Elizabeth's child, however, leaps for joy at recognizing the voice of Jesus' mother. John will never be pictured as a competitor of Jesus. When he testifies to Jesus' superiority, John is not just being humble. John was well known and admired. All four Gospels make clear that John proclaims the surpassing greatness of Jesus. That is part of the answer of the Christian community to those disciples of John who might have hesitated over a choice between the Baptist and Jesus. John knows that there is no contest. He "goes before" the Lord (Luke 1:17), as the angel had foretold, acting as precursor of Jesus even from the womb. John inherited his mother's gift of prophecy, fulfilling what the angel also said: "He will be filled with the holy Spirit even from his mother's womb" (1:15).

The infancy narrative is full of phrases to express the overwhelming reaction of joy and praise sensed by its characters, who can hardly contain their enthusiasm. Four canticles are required to voice all their gratitude: Zechariah's, Mary's, the angels', and Simeon's. It seems as if the word "joy" or some synonym appears in every other line. "And you will have joy and gladness, and many will rejoice at his birth," the angel tells Zechariah (1:14). Elizabeth's neighbors and relatives rejoice with her (1:58). Mary "rejoices" in God the Savior for all God has done for her. Angels bring "glad tidings" to the shepherds, which will mean "great joy that will be for all the people" (2:10). A multitude of heavenly hosts fill even the heavens with praise, saying, "Glory to God in the highest / and on earth peace to those on whom his favor rests" (2:14). Simeon holds the child in his arms and blesses God, saying, "Now, Master, you may let your servant go in peace . . . for my eyes have seen your salvation" (2:29-30).

The atmosphere of celebration is echoed with another entrance Jesus makes as he comes into Jerusalem just before his passion. Only Luke presents that as a joyful entry (19:37). Luke's use of similar language must mean that he links the two comings.

Rather than a multitude of angels who sang of his birth, at the end, ". . . the whole multitude of his disciples began to praise God aloud with joy for all the mighty deeds they had seen. They proclaimed: / 'Blessed is the king who comes / in the name of the Lord. / Peace in heaven / and glory in the highest'" (Luke 19:37-38). Once again, it is as if the earth alone can hardly contain the sentiments of the people's praise. When the Pharisees object that Jesus ought to "rebuke" the enthusiasm of his disciples, Jesus replies, "I tell you, if they keep silent, the stones will cry out!" (Luke 19:40). That must have been what happened at Jesus' birth. Because there was "no room for them" at the inn, and Jerusalem was unreceptive, hosts of angels filled the void.

Yet Luke also warns that for all this joy on the part of Jesus' disciples, the shadow of the cross is never far away. Simeon's prophecy will make that clear. His blessing is accompanied by a prophecy to Mary when he says, "Behold, this child is destined for the fall and rise of many in Israel, and to be a sign that will be contradicted (and you yourself a sword will pierce) so that the thoughts of many hearts may be revealed" (Luke 2:34-35). Luke so often notes that the people who saw these things were "amazed" (for example, Luke 1:21, 63; 2:33, 47). This term has a double meaning. Often the chorus of bystanders were astounded and praised God all the more, but frequently their amazement is mixed with confusion and consternation. All part of the process. Luke's God is a God of surprises. Elizabeth started all this with her praise of Mary's faith and her acceptance of her own role in salvation history. As it unfolds, there still will be a lot to learn.

THE MAGNIFICAT (LUKE 1:46-55)

Just as the story of Zechariah and Elizabeth is torn from the pages of the Old Testament, so also Mary's spirituality is described by Luke as a scriptural one. Luke's portrait of Mary is enhanced by the stories and the sentiments of Old Testament saints like Sarah, Miriam, Hannah, Deborah, Jael, and Judith.[22]

---

[22] See the stories of Sarah in Genesis 18:9-15; 21:1-13; Miriam in Exodus 15:20-21; Hannah in 1 Samuel 1–2; Deborah in Judges 4–5; Jael in Judges 4:18-23; Judith in Judith 8–16.

Mary is portrayed as a young girl, a virgin, in the first scene when the angel Gabriel comes to her. A girl could be betrothed at a very young age; a young woman was often given in marriage, that is, transferred to her husband's house and care soon after she reached puberty. Thus in her first scene, the annunciation, Mary would seem to be quite young, inexperienced, almost passive. In her second scene, the visit to Elizabeth, the profile of Mary is much more complete. She is presented as someone with an extraordinary education in the Scriptures. Luke is probably using poetic license here, attributing to Mary the thoughts and spiritual expression of an array of Old Testament heroes.

The canticle of Hannah stands out as the main inspiration for the prayer Luke puts on Mary's lips, as can be clearly seen in a comparison of Mary's Magnificat with some lines from 1 Samuel 2:1-10 (see page 33).

Parallels between Mary's and Hannah's sentiments are obvious in making this comparison. In addition to the Song of Hannah, there are other Old Testament passages that could have inspired the prayer of Mary. For example, several parallels can be noted between Mary's prayer of praise and the victory song of her Old Testament namesake Miriam, sister of Moses and Aaron.[23]

Verses from several psalms drawing on an array of emotions and sentiments of the psalmist could likewise have inspired Luke's portrayal of Mary. For instance, Psalm 89 begins, "The promises of the LORD I will sing forever" (Ps 89:1). The psalmist goes on to elaborate God's own sentiments: "I have made a covenant with my chosen one; / I have sworn to David my servant" (Ps 89:4). Then, rhetorically, the psalmist asks, "Who in the skies ranks with the LORD? (Ps 89:7). "Mighty your arm, strong your hand!" (Ps 89:14). "Justice and judgment are the founda-

---

[23] Some instances are that both Miriam and Mary begin by celebrating what God has done for them personally. Miriam says, "My strength and my courage is the LORD, / and he has been my savior. / He is my God, I praise him" (Exod 15:2; see Luke 1:46-47). Both list the powerful deeds done by God's might (Exod 15:16; Luke 1:51), and both speak of God's mercy and love (Exod 15:16; Luke 1:49). Reid's longer list of the clear comparisons is impressive; see Reid, *Women in the Gospel of Luke*, 76.

Song of Mary (Luke 1:46-55)

⁴⁶My soul proclaims the greatness of the Lord,
⁴⁷my spirit rejoices in God my savior.
⁴⁸For he has looked upon his handmaid's lowliness;
behold, from now on will all ages call me blessed.
⁴⁹The Mighty One has done great things for me
and holy is his name.
⁵⁰His mercy is from age to age
to those who fear him.
⁵¹He has shown might with his arm,
dispersed the arrogant of mind and heart.
⁵²He has thrown down the rulers from their thrones,
but lifted up the lowly.
⁵³The hungry he has filled with good things;
the rich he has sent away empty.
⁵⁴He has helped Israel his servant,
remembering his mercy,
according to his promises to our fathers,
to Abraham and to his descendants forever.

Song of Hannah (1 Sam 2:1-10)

¹My heart exults in the LORD,
my horn is exalted in my God.
I have swallowed up my enemies;
I rejoice in my victory.
²There is no Holy One like the LORD;
there is no Rock like our God.

³Speak boastfully no longer,
nor let arrogance issue from your mouths.
For an all-knowing God is the LORD,
a God who judges deeds.
⁴The bows of the mighty are broken,
while the tottering gird on strength.
⁵The well-fed hire themselves out for bread,
while the hungry batten on spoil.
The barren wife bears seven sons,
while the mother of many languishes.
⁶The LORD puts to death and gives life;
he casts down to the nether world; he raises up again.
⁷The LORD makes poor and makes rich,
he humbles, he also exalts.
⁸He raises the needy from the dust;
from the ash heap he lifts up the poor . . .
⁹He will guard the footsteps of his faithful ones,
but the wicked shall perish in the darkness . . .
¹⁰the LORD'S foes shall be shattered.
The Most High in heaven thunders;
The LORD judges the ends of the earth . . .

tion of your throne" (Ps 89:15). "Truly the Lord is our shield" (89:19). In a similar way, Psalm 98 celebrates Israel's God:

> Sing a new song to the Lord,
>   who has done marvelous deeds,
> Whose right hand and holy arm
>   have won victory. . . .
> [God] has remembered faithful love
>   toward the house of Israel.
> All the ends of the earth have seen
>   the victory of our God (Ps 98:1, 3).

Mary prays with her whole being, finding strength in God rather than in her own status or merit. The parallel terms "soul" and "spirit" in the initial lines of Mary's prayer are not to be opposed to "body" or "flesh," nor do they mean to convey only a part of her. Rather, they are the poetic equivalent of self or simply mean "I." Mary's song echoes the words of many in the Old Testament who praise God for God's mighty and glorious works on behalf of the people God has chosen.

Mary sings of the justice of God, who reverses the standards of this world and supplements them with the justice of God's own kingdom. Mary epitomizes the lessons of the Beatitudes: the poor, the hungry, the weeping, those hated, excluded, and insulted are "blessed" (see Luke 6:20-23). Like them, Mary welcomes the kingdom of God, rejoicing and leaping for joy that God's kingdom and God's ways have been revealed to such as her (see Luke 10:21-22). These are the same reasons Jesus himself praises God later in Luke, as the disciples return to him with the report that they had been able to preach the Gospel with power, healing the sick and announcing the coming of God's kingdom (Luke 10:9). Like Mary, Jesus rejoices in the Holy Spirit, saying, "I give you praise, Father, Lord of heaven and earth, for although you have hidden these things from the wise and the learned you have revealed them to the childlike. Yes, Father, such has been your gracious will" (Luke 10:21).

One of Luke's images for Jesus is as a Prophet whose sentiments echo those of the great prophets of old, notably Isaiah, who reminds Judah: "For my thoughts are not your thoughts, / nor are your ways my ways, says the Lord" (Isa 55:8). Rather,

God reverses human thoughts and ways, raising up the lowly and putting down the proud of heart. God's justice is that of a kingdom not of this world. The priorities of Mary's prayer in praise of God's wondrous works anticipates the prayer her Son taught his disciples to pray: "Father . . . hallowed be your name, / your kingdom come" (Luke 11:2). Just as Jesus promised the poor that the kingdom of God would be theirs, Mary embodies the spiritual poverty and hunger and readiness to recognize and wholeheartedly welcome this kingdom. Elizabeth prophesied when she said that Mary would be blessed for all ages and by all generations because she believed that what was spoken to her by the Lord would be fulfilled (Luke 1:45). And Mary prophesied as well when she acknowledged that she stands in the great, long line of Abraham's descendants, who represent the promises of God come to those who have faith and hope.

Mary, then, symbolizes the prayers and longings of the just ones of the Scriptures who trust in God and rely on God for strength and courage and faithfulness. In fact, there is not a brand new thought among those Mary speaks; every line she says is from the Old Testament Scriptures. It is as if she was ready with those words, awaiting the moment to utter them when God's plan would be revealed to her. Yet it is not only "victory" and success that are celebrated here. Mary's prayer has also a cautionary note. There can be no arrogance or presumption, no assurance that the promises would find fulfillment without hardship. As God's servant she is lowly and without pretense. As she remembers when and how God helped Israel throughout its history, she realizes that God's "mercy" is not without cost. Mary, like Israel, would suffer even as the promises were being fulfilled.

ANNA, PROPHET AND HERALD

Suggested Reading: Luke 2:36-38

Again, the person and function of the prophet Anna are based on Old Testament models, especially her namesake,

Hannah in 1 Samuel and also Judith, Huldah,[24] Deborah. Anna, with her counterpart Simeon, participates in a tableau in the Temple consisting of two parts: Simeon and of Anna form a parallelism with the figures of Zechariah and Elizabeth and round out Luke's infancy narrative. Simeon and Anna represent the waiting and the longing of Israel. Here is how Luke presents Anna.

> [36]There was also a prophetess, Anna, the daughter of Phanuel, of the tribe of Asher. She was advanced in years, having lived seven years with her husband after her marriage, [37]and then as a widow until she was eighty-four. She never left the temple, but worshiped night and day with fasting and prayer. [38]And coming forward at that very time, she gave thanks to God and spoke about the child to all who were awaiting the redemption of Jerusalem (Luke 2:36-38).

Anna is the first Christian prophet.[25] Luke apparently has no problem stating that there were women prophets. He tells of the daughters of Philip prophesying (Acts 21:9), although he does not give us any insight into what this role in the Church meant or in what sense the term was understood. Here, as is his custom, Luke pairs men and women in his stories, featuring first Simeon and then Anna. Anna's name is the Greek equivalent of the Hebrew Hannah, the feminine derivative of the term that means "favor, grace." The name "John" (Johannah) is derived from the same word. Thus the stories of Elizabeth ("God is my favor, treasure"), John, Mary, and Anna all stress the same idea of grace.

As was the custom of the time, woman is identified in relation to man: Anna is the daughter of Phanuel, a descendant of Asher, who was the son of Jacob and Leah. This identification suggests several Old Testament connections, showing that Anna is well steeped in Old Testament traditions. In Anna's case,

---

[24] Huldah is a prophet of the Old Testament who interpreted for the king the scrolls found in the floor of the Temple (2 Kgs 22:14-20).

[25] Most translations use the term "prophetess." But here "prophet" is preferred lest we get the impression that there should be any distinction made between male and female prophets.

these connections might appear somewhat remote and strained, yet they also provide a clue to Anna's long history of waiting and longing for the Messiah who would satisfy the hopes of Jerusalem. When seen together with the ending of Luke's Gospel, these connections take on new meaning. At the end the disciples are instructed to remain in the city until the coming of the Spirit. Anna seems to represent all those who attend and await the promises of the Messiah and his kingdom. The last words of Luke's Gospel echo the life of Anna: "and they were continually in the temple praising God" (Luke 24:53).

Anna is first identified as a daughter of Phanuel. A genealogy in 1 Chronicles 4:4 speaks of a man named Phanuel, one of the descendants of Judah. Oftentimes places took on the names of tribal leaders, a practice is known as eponymy.[26] This designation would suggest that Anna lived near Jerusalem and had spent her long life awaiting the redemption promised to Jerusalem.

Another meaning of the reference might be in Genesis 32:32, where Phanuel (Penuel) is the name of a place associated with Jacob's wrestling with an angel. Here it is said that Jacob names this place Peniel (Gen 32:31), a variant of Phanuel, "Because I have seen God face-to-face." The Greek translation of the Hebrew Bible explains that Phanuel, apparently a combination of the Greek word for "appearance, face" and a Hebrew term, *el*, meaning "god," means "the face of God." This allusion could provide a hint of why Luke names Phanuel in connection with Anna, who recognizes in the child Jesus the "redemption" of Israel and so gives thanks and praise to God (Luke 2:38). There also could be a hint of warning in this reference, for Phanuel also refers to a place in the Book of Judges where the men from that place are threatened by Gideon for their refusal to feed his army; Gideon later returns there triumphantly, destroys the city and slays all the men (Judg 8:8, 17). Just as Anna speaks about Jesus to all who were awaiting

---

[26] One well-known example is the land of Judah, an area of the south where Jerusalem and Bethlehem are located, named for one of Jacob's sons. "Judah" also came to mean the name of the southern kingdom after the division of David's kingdom, soon after the death of David's son Solomon.

the redemption of Jerusalem, there are those of the city who would refuse to hear and accept Jesus and the Gospel he preached.

Anna is further identified as being from the tribe of Asher. Again, the name is later used of the place where this tribe settled. Asher lies to the north, in the region of Gilead, far from Jerusalem. Leah, Asher's mother, had named him with a play on words: "'What good fortune!' . . . 'Women call me fortunate'" (Gen 30:13; see Luke 1:42b, 48b). This location, the region of Asher, suggests that Anna was not from Jerusalem but had left her home to dedicate herself to the service of the Temple. Luke is less interested in geography than in the symbolic meaning of the extent of Anna's lifelong dedication, which involved great personal sacrifice, being displaced, being among society's poorest, most overlooked and forgotten. Her piety transcends her poverty. She has left everything of herself behind and is immersed in the identity of one who is awaiting the message she now proclaims: the coming of the One who will save/redeem Jerusalem. Our thoughts will return to Anna when, at the end of Jesus' ministry, we meet the "poor widow" who contributes her whole life *(bios)* to the Temple (Luke 21:1-4). Anna and this widow represent those who are poor and, in their need, wholeheartedly welcome the Messiah.

Anna is a transitional figure, like John, preparing Israel for its salvation in the coming of the Messiah they so longed for and hopefully expected. Anna is further described by Luke: "She was advanced in years, having lived seven years with her husband after her marriage, and then as a widow until she was eighty-four" (Luke 2:36-37). The reference to Anna's "advanced" age is the same as the expression used of Elizabeth in Luke 1:7. Anna had been married seven years; she had been, like her Old Testament predecessor, a good wife. Luke goes on to say that Anna lived "as a widow until she was eighty-four. She never left the temple, but worshiped night and day with fasting and prayer." It is unclear whether eighty-four is her total age or the length of her widowhood. As Luke is less interested in geography, so also is he less interested with exact chronology. This is probably an example of Lukan hyperbole to show the extent of her longing and waiting, just as she worshiped day and night with fasting and prayer. This description of ceaseless worship, "day and night" is also typical of Luke (see Acts 26:7). In the infancy narrative it describes Anna's participation in the prayers of the people attending daily sacrifices and prayers.

Luke concludes his description of Anna as an early witness to Jesus, saying: "And coming forward at that very time, she gave thanks to God" (2:38). Like the pregnancies of Elizabeth and Mary, Anna's arrival is in God's time, "that very time." Luke says that Anna came forward and gave thanks and praise to God. She is a witness who stands up and gives testimony to what she has experienced. Luke again joins joy and praise. Yet, though she is a prophet, Anna utters no oracle or pronouncement. Her role is as a herald spreading the news of the birth of the Messiah to others. She is in the tradition of the prophets who speak to people on behalf of God. Luke has only three verses on Anna, yet her story lives on. She is a transition figure, just like Elizabeth and Mary of the infancy narrative.

The story of Anna concludes with this observation of how she carried out her prophetic role: "[she] spoke about the child to all who were awaiting the redemption of Jerusalem" (2:38). Anna mediates between God and humans, endlessly worshiping God and interpreting events for people. So, although Anna's words are not given, the content is. She confirms the prophecy of Simeon. The tense of the verbs used in verse 38 are imperfect, suggesting an ongoing activity rather than a single past action. Anna proclaims to all those awaiting the deliverance of Jerusalem that she has seen the coming of the Savior.

The reference to Jerusalem and to Anna's witness will resonate throughout the Gospel. As Jesus nears Golgotha, where he will be crucified, he encounters women who had "come out" (just as Anna comes forward) to see him. Jesus speaks to them, saying, "Daughters of Jerusalem, do not weep for me, weep instead for yourselves and for your children" (23:28). Luke uses the literary technique called "inclusion" here, presenting Anna as a prophet who, with Simeon, will recognize that suffering will also be part of Jesus' ministry and of the followers of Jesus. The daughters of Jerusalem whom Jesus meets right before his death are likewise warned that faith involves suffering.

The city of Jerusalem is a multidimensional symbol in Luke. It is the city of fulfillment of the prophecies. It is also the city that killed the prophets. Jesus will lament that Jerusalem does not recognize the time of its visitation (see Luke 19:41-44). In the tradition of apocalyptic literature, Luke will speak of the deliverance and redemption of the faithful of Jerusalem, while also challenging those represented by this city to be converted, to change, to accept and to welcome their salvation and all that it means in their lives.

THE IMAGE AND INSPIRATION OF HANNAH (1 SAMUEL 1–2)

Our exploration of Luke's infancy narrative would not be complete without reviewing the story of Hannah found in 1 Samuel 1–2. A childless Hannah is pictured there accompanying her husband Elkanah, who went to pray at the shrine where the ark was located. Thus she is the first biblical example of one who prays privately, fervently, and relentlessly for the causes of her own heart. She did not offer sacrifice, and she did not utter audible words; she prayed silently but her lips were moving. She shed copious tears over her barrenness, crying out from the depths of her need and distress. The voices of her heart pleaded with the God she had learned to trust:

> O LORD of hosts, if you look with pity on the misery of your handmaid, if you remember me and do not forget me, if you give your handmaid a male child, I will give him to the LORD for as long as he lives; neither wine nor liquor shall he drink, and no razor shall ever touch his head (1 Sam 1:11).

The author of 1 Samuel adds, "she remained long at prayer before the LORD" (v. 12).

Upon observing her, the old priest Eli assumed that she was drunk and chided her for that, insisting that she stop making a "drunken show" of herself. Hannah explained that she did not pray out of drunkenness but was prompted by her deep sorrow and misery. Nevertheless, she returned to her quarters, ate and drank with her husband, and returned the next morning to again worship before the Lord, even though she had not yet been relieved of her sorrow nor granted her prayer. Finally her soulful pleas were heard and she conceived and bore a son, whom she named Samuel. At once she fulfilled her promise and dedicated Samuel to the service of the Temple. So she lives forever as a symbol of faithfulness and holiness. Her trust in

God was unconditional. Her story concludes with a vindication of her faith: "The LORD favored Hannah so that she conceived and gave birth to three more sons and two daughters, while young Samuel grew up in the service of the LORD" (1 Sam 2:21). In God's justice, faithfulness is rewarded with great abundance, exceeding every expectation or human hope. Hannah's prayer is answered not only in Samuel but also in the other children, who represent many more blessings God gives to her. Hannah remains a symbol of steadfast trust and faith.

The stories of all three women—Elizabeth, Mary of Luke's infancy narrative, and Anna—are in someway modeled on the story of Hannah in the Old Testament. Elizabeth, like Hannah, was barren and beyond the age of childbearing. Hannah provides the sentiments for Mary's glorious Magnificat. And Anna shares her name and her great generosity in living in dependence upon God and in her fidelity. But for Luke, Elizabeth, Mary, and Anna are more than a fulfillment of Old Testament figures such as Hannah. They are examples of God's gracious will acting in human lives. They are heralds and models of a new community of faith based in Jesus and the coming of his kingdom. The stories of these women are relived and recelebrated in many other people who draw inspiration from their memory and example as the Gospel continues and lives on.

2. Women Changed by Jesus/ Healed by Jesus

INTRODUCTION

On the whole, women are portrayed in a positive light in the Gospels. The characters we hear about are people remembered by the oral tradition of the Church. We cannot assert with certainty that this memory of certain people meant that they became disciples and remained as members of the Church; but it is more than interesting to note that no woman approaches Jesus in the Gospels without faith, and none goes away from Jesus unchanged. And that change is noted, often in praise of the woman's faith. The idea of change suggests that a person leaves behind one situation or condition and replaces it with another. The women Jesus encounters move into the Church's memory from an environment that barely distinguishes them as shadows.

As we shall see, often the Gospel stories that feature women are not really about the women at all. Rather, the stories recorded by the evangelists are about Jesus and about how the kingdom of God he proclaims affects all people. Women, like men, are changed as a result of their encounter with Jesus. Miracle stories are one of the means used by the early Church to express a change that a person can undergo when touched by Jesus. And even though these women's stories are not the focus of the evangelist, what is said does give us insight into the situation of women in the society of Jesus' day.

Many of the women mentioned in the Gospels are first introduced in terms of disabilities: one has been hemorrhaging for twelve years, another has been badly bent over, crippled for eighteen years. If women are further described, it is most often in relationship to a man: for example, the daughter of Jairus, the mother of Jesus, or the mother of Zebedee's sons. Sometimes women are referred to as coming from a certain place, such as the widow of Nain or simply the Syrophoenician woman. A few are even named, such as Mary of Nazareth, Mary of Magdala, and Martha and Mary of Bethany. When we hear the stories of these women, we are struck by how very different is Jesus' interaction with them than what was expected of him or of them.

No change could be more dramatic or powerful than death: from the resurrection perspective of New Testament writings, death precedes life, not vice versa. In the Old Testament we note a different view of illness than the modern one. Illness is a prelude to death; those who are ill are a step closer to dying. Not a doctor but a prophet may be summoned. It is hoped that healing might be had through this holy person acting as God's agent, interpreting for the ill person and her family what is required to keep living. The prophet may be able to channel God's power for healing (and often for the conversion) of the suffering person. So even though there are not many examples of illness in the Old Testament (we hear of people afflicted with leprosy, and we learn of the sorrow of infertile women; we could also interpret Saul's disturbed spirit as a kind of mental illness; we hear of Elijah's and David's depression), it is not the doctor who is sought out but the prophet, who advises the suffering person to ask in prayer that God will have a change of heart and will that the person live, not die. Prophets, in the tradition of Elijah and Elisha who speak to people on God's behalf are interpreting the will of God. But more, the word of the prophet is efficacious—it effects what it says.

A basic Old Testament image of Jesus used to illustrate the meaning of the kingdom he comes to announce is that he is a prophet. One of the features of this image is his power to perform miracles. There are basically two types of miracles stories in the New Testament: nature miracles, such as the calming of a storm, and healing miracles. Our discussion in this chapter of women changed by Jesus will lead us to consider miracle stories featuring women. But miracle stories are not new or unique to the New Testament. The culture of the ancient world, and especially of the biblical world, included the expectation of miracles. People were so needy. God is a God of history, intervening directly in human lives. Sin, natural disasters, human frailty, illness, and death—these are all signs of the need for God. And the God of Israel is, above all, compassionate. God acts on behalf of human beings even when the situation is so desperate that no words can describe it, even when people can only manage a wordless groaning to express their pain, as in the case of the Israelites in Egypt when God resolved to free them, or of the widow of Nain, who appears voiceless and defenseless, unable even to form her prayer for help.

Miracles are related to faith, as well as to the Gospel's claims about who Jesus is. Like the parables, they are a teaching tool, and part of their purpose is to distinguish believers from unbelievers. Miracle stories have three elements: (1) a serious, even insurmountable problem, (2) an intervention, a word or action by Jesus, and (3) some evidence that the miracle has taken place. Thus, for example, the Gospels will tell us that a woman was suffering a malady for many years and had seen doctors who could not help her. This serves as the first element of a miracle: a problem or illness or dilemma that seems to defy remedy.

The second element is usually expressed in the form of a word or action of Jesus. It may be expressed as a simple command such as "Arise!" Or it may take the form of some action such as touching or making clay with spittle. In every case a miracle transforms a person. A widow's young son already on his way to burial is restored to his mother; a young girl who has died can now sit up and eat.

Finally, there is some verification of a miracle. For instance, a person who could not see or walk or talk is now able to do so. Often the reaction of bystanders is part of this verification. Some may object to the circumstances of the miracle, a hint that even though they are unbelievers, they cannot deny the miracle's authenticity. While some object, others may respond more positively. They chorus their praise of God, expressing their delight and astonishment at what has taken place; they are in awe and may ask questions about the meaning of this event. Although some miracles are told very simply and one or another of these elements is embellished, the basic form is repeated in the miracles (John calls them "signs") present in all four Gospels. Readers are encouraged to discern those three basic elements as we discuss the various miracles featuring women in the Gospels. Let us see how the lives of some women Jesus encountered were dramatically changed by that experience.

"A great prophet has arisen in our midst!" (Luke 7:16).

WIDOW OF NAIN

Suggested Reading: Luke 7:11-17

> [11]Soon afterward he journeyed to a city called Nain, and his disciples and a large crowd accompanied him. [12]As he drew near to the gate of the city, a man who had died was being carried out, the only son of his mother, and she was a widow. A large crowd from the city was with her. [13]When the Lord saw her, he was moved with pity for her and said to her, "Do not weep." [14]He stepped forward and touched the coffin; at this the bearers halted, and he said, "Young man, I tell you, arise!" [15]The dead man sat up and began to speak, and Jesus gave him to his mother. [16]Fear seized them all, and they glorified God, exclaiming, "A great prophet has arisen in our midst," and "God has visited his people." [17]This report about him spread through the whole of Judea and in all the surrounding region.

We can trace the basic miracle story in verses 12-15, where the three elements of a miracle form are present. In this instance the young man is dead and almost buried, clearly an insurmountable problem for his widowed mother. He appears to be beyond hope. There is an intervention by Jesus, who is moved with compassion. Jesus simply touches the coffin and speaks. The young man sits up and speaks, and is given back to his mother. This is ample evidence that some great, efficacious, and powerful change has taken place. The crowds are awestruck. There is no question that this miracle reveals Jesus' identity. The crowd proclaims the meaning of this wonder: "A great prophet has arisen in our midst," and "God has visited his people." And Jesus' fame spread far and wide as a result of this event.

This story is unique to the Gospel of Luke, yet he probably relied on at least two sources for its composition. In writing his Gospel, Luke apparently had access to at least two sources, Mark and Q. Most commentators agree that Luke, writing around 85 A.D., used the Gospel of Mark, which had been composed some twenty or so years earlier (around 65–70 A.D.) and was already known in the early Church. In addition, Luke (and Matthew) seem to have had another source, probably oral, containing mostly sayings of Jesus; this source is known as "Q," most likely from the German word *Quelle,* which simply means "source." Both these sources, Mark and Q, might have served as inspiration for this Lukan story of the raising of the widow's son.

The Q source appears to have played a major role in the construction of the entire section of Luke from the Sermon on the Plain through Jesus' testimony about John (Luke 6:20–7:35). Although Q contains *sayings* of Jesus for the most part, it does contain one miracle story—that of the cure of the centurion's servant (see Luke 7:1-10).[1] That story has several similarities with the Lukan episode of the raising of the widow's son.

We have already noted Luke's technique of "step parallelism," a kind of study in contrasts in which Luke will draw his audience into a comparison of events, encouraging them, as it were, to see the heightened significance of the subsequent event. This characteristic might be observed here where Luke complements the story of the cure of the centurion's servant (in 7:1-10) with that of the raising of the widow's son (in 7:11-17). This technique escalates the Gospel's claims about the power of Jesus, which reaches even beyond curing a person who is seriously ill. Jesus can also restore a person to life and "save" not only a son but his grief-stricken mother as well.

Just prior to his account of the cure of the centurion's servant, Luke included the Sermon on the Plain (Luke 6:17-49),

---

[1] This healing story appears also in Matthew (8:5-13) but not in Mark, a defining characteristic of Q. It is interesting to note that John (4:43-54) also includes this story.

illustrating that Jesus is powerful in both word and deed. Mark had presented Jesus as a teacher who taught with "authority" or power. So, for example, in response to Jesus' first miracle in Mark, the people said to one another, "What is this? A new teaching with authority" (Mark 1:27). Mark stresses that Jesus' teaching is illustrated by his power to perform miracles, like the prophets of old.

Luke makes it even more clear that Jesus is a prophet and more. Following the story of the widow and her son, Luke says that some of John's disciples come to Jesus with questions about his identity (Luke 7:18-35). Jesus tells them to go and report to John what they have seen and heard. In his inaugural address (see Luke 4:16-30), Jesus had described his mission as working on behalf of the poor, the sick, the blind, the lame. He challenges his listeners with the words, "Today this scripture passage is fulfilled in your hearing" (4:21). Now in chapter 7, Jesus adds "the dead are raised" (7:22) for John's disciples to tell their imprisoned leader. This is not merely an anticipation of the raising of Jairus's daughter nor even of Jesus' own resurrection. According to Luke, these disciples are to tell what they have witnessed. If they do as they are told, they will be acknowledging that Jesus is at once a prophet and more than a prophet. He is the promised Messiah.

The Markan story of the raising of the daughter of Jairus (Mark 5:23-34) could also have served as inspiration for Luke's story of the raising of the son of the widow of Nain. We have taken note of Luke's tendency to "pair" stories of men and of women, as if to insist that both are equally included in the blessings of the messianic kingdom of God. When describing the resuscitation of the young girl in the story he has from Mark, Luke alone adds that she is the "only" daughter of Jairus. In our story it is noted that this widow is burying her "only son." Mark, followed by Matthew, tells of the single resuscitation of this young girl, while John, who does not include this story of Jairus's daughter, also tells of a single resuscitation, that of Lazarus (John 11:1-44). These are clearly miracles in the extreme. The resurrection of these people is a prelude to the Christian belief in the resurrection of the dead. This faith is based not only on Jesus' prophetic power but on his own resurrection.

Luke describes Jesus on a journey accompanied by a large crowd (7:11). Luke develops the Markan idea that the course of Jesus' life can be represented as a journey from Galilee to Jerusalem, from power to powerlessness, from miracles to the cross. Luke introduces this story with a note that Jesus is traveling around the cities and villages of Galilee to the north. Luke emphasizes Jesus' huge following. The crowd is friendly and receptive, willing to follow Jesus the wonderworker, apparently curious and eager to see if he will perform any spectacular events.

Although Luke portrays Jesus as more than a prophet, Jesus is in a direct line with the prophets of old, as Luke will repeatedly emphasize. Luke tells the story in such a way as to evoke the prophet Elijah's resuscitation of the son of the widow of Zarephath in 1 Kings 17:8-24. We should remember that Luke referred to this same widow already when he announced his mission in chapter 4 (see v. 26). There are several significant points of comparison between the story of Jesus and the one about Elijah. Jesus approaches a town just as the prophet Elijah did; in Jesus' case it is the town of Nain. Elijah comes to the town of Zarephath. Both meet a bereaved widow at the "gates of the city," and both are moved by the distress she experiences. In both cases the deceased is the "only son"[2] of the widow; in both stories the young man is restored to life. But there is also a significant difference between these stories. Elijah had to stretch himself out over the boy three times; Jesus raises the widow's son with an oral command. Finally, the most obvious connection between these stories is made when Luke quotes 1 Kings 17:23 verbatim, saying that Jesus, like Elijah, "gave him to his mother." In doing so, both the son and his mother are given back their lives.

Luke's obvious reliance on the Old Testament story illustrates his belief that Jesus fulfills the role of prophet. The prophet heals. He speaks God's saving word. Jesus is called prophet in 24:19. He is explicitly identified with Elijah and

---

[2] Many children are a great blessing, but when there is an "only" child, the possibilities for disaster multiplied. A widow whose only son died is poor indeed.

Elisha in 4:24, 27. This identification is also reflected in the nature of his ministry on behalf of the poor and destitute, the weak and overlooked. The crowd recognizes that in Jesus, "God visited his people." This phrase harks back to the infancy narrative,[3] when Zechariah praised God and all the people celebrated with joy at the births of John and of Jesus.

Although Luke presents Jesus as a prophet, and here even casts Jesus in the role of Elijah, Jesus will reject this role for himself. In fact, in the following event, as he gives testimony about the role of John the Baptist, Jesus will show that not he but John is Elijah. John is the last and the greatest of the prophets.

Jesus and his huge entourage encounter a widow burying her "only son." The image of a widow as a symbol for the poor who are completely dependent on God is more developed in Luke than in any other Gospel.[4] Although there is a crowd of mourners around her, she appears isolated in her sorrow and despair. The jostling crowds present a stark contrast to the palpable loneliness of the widow. Her only son was the more beloved because he was her only hope. But he was dead. He was being carried outside the village. It was all over but the burial.

Along with the orphan, the widow becomes, in the Old Testament tradition, a powerful symbol of the limits of human justice and the need for God's help. Despite the commandment "Thou shalt not kill," many wars created many widows and orphans. The development of various laws provided for the rights of men and of those women and children who were in men's care. Such is the legal basis of a patriarchal society. But the figure of a childless widow, like that of a parentless child, signifies one outside the pale of law, without recourse or defenses. So, for example, when God reluctantly allowed Israel to have a king, it was stipulated that the king should act on God's behalf in defense of the widows and orphans. The prophets

---

[3] See Luke 1:68, 78; Acts 15:54.

[4] Other "widows" in Luke's Gospel include Anna (2:36-38), the woman of Jesus' parable who demands justice from the unjust judge and is satisfied (18:1-8), and the widow who gave her whole livelihood to the Temple (21:1-4). God shows special care for the widow (e.g., Exod 22:23); the childless widow represents the extreme example of defenselessness.

would excoriate king and people when these special groups were neglected, taken advantage of, or ignored. For example, we read, "I will draw near to you for judgment . . . Against those who defraud widows and orphans, / those who turn aside the stranger" (Mal 3:5). In fact, concern for the widows and orphans became the measurement of a person's "righteousness."

A woman was passed on from her father's to her husband's to her son's care. Women could not inherit unless they had no brothers. They could not act as witnesses. They did not pronounce any vow in marriage, nor could they initiate proceedings of divorce. It was a great shame to be divorced, as it was to be widowed without children. A woman without father, husband, or son to care for her was destitute and without any means of support. Thus Luke can describe a truly desperate person when he says that this widow from Nain was met as she was burying her "only son."

In marriage it was particularly important to have a son, hopefully many. Then, if widowed, a woman would have a means of income as well as ongoing physical protection. Her sons were a source of prestige for a mother. Leah, for instance, rejoiced when she had sons; her former shame at being barren receded in proportion to the great number of sons she bore her husband Jacob. Her joy and satisfaction were great when she became the mother of six strong boys.[5]

Burial is the final step in the process of dying; it meant that the life of the deceased was truly over. While there is always hope even when a person is gravely ill, burial means that all hope of life is gone. The responsibility for burying someone rests with the family, although burial is also a communal affair. Oftentimes mourners accompanied the body to the gravesite. These would be further witnesses to the fact of the person's death. The practice of washing and dressing the body also served as an indication that the person had truly died. Jewish rituals emphasized the grief of the mourners and their obligation to carry out certain practices and say certain prayers in memory of the deceased. Since belief in an afterlife is not universal to Jews nor clearly stated in the Old Testament Scriptures,

---

[5] Gen 29:31-35; 30:14-21.

death means for many the end of life and therefore of hope for the deceased.

In our story the young man is already dead and to the point of being carried to burial. This is stressed so that there is no question about the reality of his dying, as there might be, for example, in the story of Jairus's daughter. As evidence of the reality of the resuscitation, Luke says that the young man sat up and began to speak.[6] Although Luke does not indicate what he said, his speaking is itself a sign that he is fully alive.

The episode about the raising of the son of the widow of Nain is really not about a woman, yet it so well describes the situation of women, especially in the time of Jesus. The woman does not speak; she makes no plea of Jesus. She simply is there with the lifeless body of her son. She appears devoid of meaningful expression, unable even to formulate her needs or prayer. The widow is like the Israelites in Egypt, so weighed down by their misery that they could only groan in wordless pain (Exod 2:23-24). It is God who remembers the covenant and acts on Israel's behalf. Similarly, in Luke's story there is no mention of faith; Jesus does not ask for it nor does the woman offer it. The initiative to raise the young man comes from Jesus.

After the miracle the woman still does not utter a sound. There is no thanks, no proclamation of faith. Faith is not mentioned, not demanded of the widow or her son, neither before, during, or after the miracle. Luke is careful to say that Jesus himself is moved with compassion. He is not swayed by another who intercedes for the woman. Nor does she make a request for herself or for her son. The focus is on Jesus and what his actions mean for his identity. This miracle is attributed to the compassion of "the Lord," the benefactor of the people. It elicits a fundamental Christological affirmation from the crowd: Jesus is a "great prophet." In Jesus, God has visited the people. Luke describes Jesus as "Lord," a title attributed by his culture to benefactors of the people. Jesus is moved by compassion and commands the grieving mother, "Do not weep." Dramatically Luke focuses on this encounter, as if only Jesus and the woman

---

[6] This sign of life appears only here and in Acts 9:40, in the story of Tabitha.

are present, united by their sad emotions—hers of sorrow, his of compassion.

Although this story is included in this commentary on women in the New Testament, the beneficiaries of Jesus' action here go beyond both the woman and her son. Luke's real purpose in telling this story is Christological. Luke's audience is invited to join in the reaction of the crowd, which, upon seeing this miracle, exclaims, "A great prophet has arisen in our midst," and "God has visited his people" (Luke 7:16).[7] A great awe seized them all. The crowds glorify God and recognize Jesus as a prophet. They give voice to a positive reaction to a miracle: they testify that God has come. For Luke this is the point of a miracle story. He implies a challenge to his readers: What verdict do you render about Jesus as a result of witnessing this miracle?

"This report" or word (that is, *logos*) went out from that small village and spread like wildfire, Luke concludes (Luke 7:17). He speaks of Jesus' "reputation" (*pheme* in Greek). Here is another example of Lukan style. He tends to exaggerate the swift and efficient reception of the Gospel. Luke already referred to the spread of the Gospel throughout all the land in Luke 4:14, where "news of him spread throughout the whole region." At the same time, Luke will show typical restraint, following this story of resuscitation of the widow's son with the query of the Baptist languishing in prison and concerned that Jesus is taking too long to get the message out. It is as if Luke wants to convey two apparently contradictory ideas at the same time. Believers will give testimony to their experience of Jesus and tell others who will also believe. But faith requires perseverance. It is not a one-time thing, and we are prone to become discouraged, a dangerous "trial," according to Luke. We must profess our faith over the long haul, despite hardship and disappointment. The "fame" of Jesus spreads beyond where Jesus is physically; others believe on the basis of the faith of witnesses.

---

[7] See Luke 19:44, where, in contrast, Jesus mourns over Jerusalem, "you did not recognize the time of your visitation."

"My daughter has just died. But come, lay your hand on her,
and she will live" (Matt 9:18).

THE RAISING OF JAIRUS'S DAUGHTER

Suggested Readings: Mark 5:21-24, 35-43; Matt 9:18-19, 23-26;
Luke 8:40-42, 49-56 (see Appendix, pages 264–265)

In the synoptic Gospels, the story of Jairus's daughter is
combined with the story of the woman with a hemorrhage.
Matthew and Luke both follow Mark in this regard. Mark has a
tendency to use intercalation, that is, to insert or "sandwich"
one story within another, as in this case. Mark begins by telling
of Jairus's coming to Jesus to report the serious illness of his
daughter and to request that Jesus come and heal her. Jesus
agrees and sets off with the synagogue leader. A great crowd ac-
companies them. But their journey is interrupted by a woman
who approaches Jesus surreptitiously, hoping to be able to get
close enough to touch him and be cured of her own malady.
After confronting her and healing her, Jesus again resumes his
journey to Jairus's house. This so-called sandwich technique of
Mark implies that the two stories can be better understood in relation to each other. That one interprets the other. Therefore,
even though we can and will discuss them separately, it ought
to be remembered that these two stories of women restored by
Jesus form a unit in all three synoptic Gospels.

There are several links connecting these two stories with
each other. Obviously, both have to do with women; the influential father of one intercedes for her, while the other must approach Jesus from behind, fearfully and in secret. The term
"daughter" recurs; Jairus describes his daughter's grave illness, and Jesus addresses the woman as "Daughter." Jairus's
daughter is "twelve years old," the same length of time the
other woman has suffered hemorrhages. The women's circumstances render them unclean; the young girl becomes a
corpse, and the woman's issue of blood makes her continuously unclean and untouchable. Both are "as good as dead."[8]
Both are restored by the "touch" of Jesus.

---

[8] Reid, *Women in the Gospel of Luke,* 141.

These cures are very public affairs, witnessed by many people. At the same time, the cure and the resuscitation are also inward and private, and they both are met with mixed reactions from bystanders. The stories of these two women share the same theme: the opposite options of faith and fear (Matt 5:32). Jesus makes this explicit in response to Jairus's initial request: "Do not be afraid; just have faith." Readers are left to ponder their own response to these events.

We will focus first on the story of Jairus's young daughter, the story that envelops the account of the woman with the hemorrhage.

This story is about the raising of a young girl who is not given her own name but takes her identity from her father. According to the custom of the day, a girl only acquires a name of her own when she has a son; until then she is identified as related to some other man—first her father and later her husband. Girls could not be given in marriage before the age of puberty. They usually were transferred from their father's to their husband's house soon after reaching the age of puberty, around twelve years of age. This was so because of the importance of preserving the husband's family in a patriarchal society. Children were highly valued, especially sons.

Since the death of women in childbirth as well as the infant mortality rate were comparatively high, while life expectancy was low, it was important that girls marry as soon as it was possible for them to bear children. Girls did not have the right to inherit. If a man had no sons to be heirs, his name would die out. Therefore marriage was considered an obligation, a contract between families, a way to achieve immortality in the lives of descendants. That there was only hesitant belief in an afterlife beyond death among some Jews reinforced this practice.

It is possible that the Gospels' unusual notation of the age of the girl is an indication that Jairus's sorrow may be compounded by the fact that his daughter has reached the normal age for marriage. Marriages were arranged between families. A year-long initiation into marriage was usually begun and sealed with the offering of a *mohar,* or bride price, offered by the husband-to-be to the family of the bride to compensate them for the loss of her services.[9] Thus the father may have faced financial loss as well as social disgrace, in addition to the personal sorrow of his daughter's illness and death.

Jairus is described as one of the leaders of the synagogue, the main teaching institution of Israel since the time of the return from exile in the sixth century B.C.E. Mark notes that many of the Jewish leaders, some Pharisees, Herodians, scribes, and Sadducees took issue with what Jesus said and did, and some even determined to put him to death from the earliest days of his preaching (Mark 3:6). Yet here is a Jewish leader who seeks out Jesus because he recognizes that Jesus has healing prophetic powers.

The prominence of her father Jairus as well as her own coming of age may have redounded to the increased value of the daughter. Yet we ought to take notice not only that a man of such stature approaches Jesus with some degree of faith and hope but that he intercedes on behalf of one who is little valued by the society of the day. Matthew and Luke have a story not found in Mark of Jesus' healing the male servant of the centurion who intercedes for him. It is yet more remarkable that in our story this important man would request a cure for someone whom society so took for granted as a young girl. In fact, we should note the extraordinary visibility of women in this passage: the two who are cured, the mother of the girl, and the mourners, probably professional female mourners.[10]

---

[9] Theodore Mackin, "The Primitive Christian Understanding of Marriage," in *Perspectives on Marriage: A Reader,* ed. Kieran Scott and Michael Warren (New York: Oxford, 1993) 24–29, at 27.

[10] See Jer 9:16-17; Ezek 32:16. The text of Jeremiah 9:19 suggests that this was a trade or profession that women taught their daughters. Matthew adds a reference to the flute players. Rabbis required that at least two flutes and one female wailer be present at the poorest of funerals; (m.Ketub. 4:4); see Daniel J. Harrington, *The Gospel of Matthew,* Sacra Pagina 1 (Collegeville: The Liturgical Press, 1991) 132. Funeral associations may have been one of the voluntary associations open mainly to women; this possibility provided a means for women to organize and work together on a project of mutual, ongoing interest. This is significant, since maintenance of a proper memorial for the deceased was seen as a kind of immortality.

Miracles are worked by a holy person, a prophet, someone seen as a channel for the power of God. Many of the witnesses "laugh" at the claim that the girl is alive. Jesus is treated by the mourners as a foolish person before it is shown that it is they who are foolish. They "know" that she is dead, but that is erroneous. She sits up, is restored to her family, and is given something to eat. These actions are evidence that, indeed, she is alive. Jesus heals the girl with a word, commanding death to leave her. It is also remarkable that he "touches" her, just as the hemorrhaging woman had touched him. There is power in this contact with Jesus and "immediately" she is enlivened.

Earlier in Mark, Jesus' own family, his mother and his brothers, think that he is out of his mind and wish to take him away, presumably to mollify and quiet him. He is causing disturbances. His enemies have a similar reaction to his exorcisms, falsely accusing him of casting out demons by the power of Beelzebub. In contrast, there is the witness of Peter, James, John, and the parents of the girl, who all "go in" with him to where the lifeless child lies. She is restored to life quietly, in private, while the public din of the mockers continues "outside." Now it is they who look and act foolishly.

The references to a "house" and to "eating" may suggest that this story was remembered and recounted in a liturgical setting in the early Church. Jesus often teaches and heals in a house, whereas his preaching in synagogues is often met with disputes and rejection. Early Christian communities were formed and grew in the setting of households in the Greco-Roman world.

THE STORY'S CONTEXT IN MARK

Mark inserts these miracle stories between the parable chapter and the note of rejection by Jesus' own in chapter 6. Mark's chapter 4 is called the "parable chapter"; here Jesus teaches in several parables, the longest and probably most important being the parable of the sower and the seed. In the section following this parable (Mark 4:35–5:43), Mark presents a number of miracles designed to distinguish between the rocky ground and the good earth. The latter are those who are healed.[11]

---

[11] John Keenan, *The Gospel of Mark* (Maryknoll: Orbis, 1995) 145.

This section of several miracles of different types (the stilling of the storm, the cure of the Gerasene demoniac, and these stories of the two women healed by Jesus) is followed by the account of Jesus' rejection by his own townspeople. It seems that he is at the same time "too much for them" and also too familiar to the people of Nazareth, who point out that they know him and his family too well.

Mark notes that Jesus left the crowds outside, whereas he takes the three disciples and the girl's parents "inside" (Mark 5:37). We are reminded of what Jesus says about speaking in parables in chapter 4 of Mark. Parables distinguish insiders from outsiders. To those who are "inside," who have faith, who accept the parables and their implications for conversion and healing is entrusted the "mystery of the kingdom of heaven." But to those who are outside, everything remains a parable or a riddle whose meaning remains hidden and obscure (Mark 4:10-12).

One of Mark's designations for Jesus is "Teacher," and that is how the delegates from Jairus's house refer to him in 5:35. From the beginning Mark has asserted that Jesus' teaching is "with authority" or "power." Mark's Jesus does not speak much, but he teaches with powerful deed, demonstrating that he acts with the authority and power of God. And this, the crowds in Mark also note, is in contrast to "their leaders." After Jesus' very first miracle, the cure of a demoniac in Capernaum, Mark notes, "All were amazed and asked one another, 'What is this? A new teaching with authority [the Greek word *exousia* can also mean "power"]. He commands even the unclean spirits and they obey him'" (1:27).

In his Gospel, Mark surprisingly appears to undermine the identification of Jesus as a miracle worker. Jesus even appears somewhat foolish in these stories. In the story of the menstruous woman he is confused, and in the story of Jairus's daughter, people laugh at him. Mark records the Aramaic words of Jesus almost as if they appear to have some magical power. In the end Jesus commands people not to tell what he has done. This is an impossible order to obey, and it appears almost nonsensical. It is certainly illogical. What are the mourners to do when they see the dead girl sitting up, walking, and eating?

The command to tell no one, found in various forms often in Mark, serves his purpose of insisting that only at the cross is

Jesus' true identity revealed. Early in the Gospel, for example, Jesus gives a self-contradictory command to a leper he has just healed: "See that you tell no one anything, but go, show yourself to the priest and offer for your cleansing what Moses prescribed" (1:44). The man appears ungratefully disobedient as Mark goes on to say, "The man went away and began to publicize the whole matter. He spread the report abroad so that it was impossible for Jesus to enter a town openly" (1:45). After healing a deaf man on another occasion, Jesus commands him, "not to tell anyone. But the more he ordered them not to, the more they proclaimed it" (7:36).

What's going on here? It seems that Mark is using a theological device meant on the one hand to assert Jesus' power to perform miracles that simply defy silence, and on the other hand to warn of the inadequacy of miracles to reveal the true nature of Jesus' identity and mission. Only the centurion, a foreigner, correctly confesses that Jesus is the "Son of God," and that only when Jesus dies (Mark 15:39). For Mark this is the first time a human being has been able to correctly identify Jesus.

In Mark, when Peter asserts that Jesus is the Messiah, Jesus commands him not to tell this to others (Mark 8:27-30). Mark's meaning is somewhat clarified when in the very next verses Peter shows that he cannot accept the idea of the suffering of the Messiah (8:30-31). For Mark, the cross is the key to faithful discipleship. The disciples are dull and weak, full of doubt and without understanding throughout the Gospel. Mark leaves us wondering even at the very end, when he notes that the women ran away from the tomb and told no one, for they were afraid (16:8). Faith for Mark must go beyond the hope and expectation of miracles and perceive the meaning of the cross. For the struggling Markan community, facing the persecutions and martyrdom, belief in the miracle-working power of Jesus is not enough. Thus, even while Mark asserts Jesus' miracle-working powers, he undermines this aspect of Jesus' ministry in order to ground faith on a much deeper level.

Mark directs the reader to look beyond the wonderworker, but at the same time to see in Jesus the power of God and to respond to this power with faith. At a deep level Mark is weaning his readers away from hope that Jesus will preserve them from harm through miracles. That he performs miracles is not what Jesus wants people to say about him. Jesus does work by the power of God. But faith is not to be dependent on miracles. Nor are miracles a way Mark would recommend in order to discover and know who Jesus is. In fact, people are confused by miracles, according to Mark. Miracle-faith is far too fragile and conditional.

In the telling of this and other miracle stories, Mark differentiates between two truths. He asserts on the one hand that Jesus is a wonderworker, a healer, capable even of raising the dead. Mark also progressively asserts that faith in Jesus must go beyond the primitive expectation that God will work in our lives in the ways we expect and demand, through "signs" that function as proof for us.

ADAPTATION OF MATTHEW AND LUKE

Matthew and Luke draw on their source, Mark, but make editorial changes consistent with the emphases of their respective Gospels. Matthew was writing for a primarily Jewish-Christian audience, in about 85, at a time when Christianity was trying to understand its relationship to Judaism. It was a painful time for both religious groups. Rome represented a threat to both. After the Temple had been destroyed in 70, the Jews were intent on preserving the Law. They used the synagogues to develop their teaching about how to maintain tradition in the midst of hostility and persecution, which they saw as coming not only from Rome but also from the new Christian sect that claimed to have its roots in Judaism. It was a tense atmosphere, and we should read the New Testament with an awareness that Christian claims about Jesus and especially a certain Christian critique of some traditions related to the Law were very threatening to the Jews.

This historical context helps mitigate damage to relationships with Jews and an erroneous fundamentalism in our approach to texts that are potentially so destructive of understanding and tolerance. Jesus is not against Judaism in the Gospels.[12] He himself is a pious and an observant Jew, as are

---

[12] In fact, we probably should speak not about "Judaism" but about "Judaisms" of the first century. Judaism was not and is not monolithic.

his immediate followers. But some of Jesus' opponents, for instance the Pharisees, who were synagogue leaders, and the Sadducees, who were a powerful group in Jerusalem during the first century, do represent certain interpretations of the Law that were different from the one that Jesus advocated. In the Gospels, then, the Pharisees and Sadducees act as antagonists whose views on matters help the evangelists give expression to the differences in Jesus' teaching.

Matthew heightens the faith of Jairus by noting that he already knew that his daughter had died when he came to Jesus. Matthew describes Jairus as "doing homage" as he approaches Jesus, a technical phrase Matthew uses to express a proper reverential attitude (see Matt 2:2, 8, 11; 8:2). Matthew's new context for this story as part of the clustered miracles in chapters 8–9 highlights his emphasis on discipleship. Jairus's attitude is in stark contrast to those in his home who mock and laugh at Jesus when he tells them that the girl is only asleep.

It is Matthew, who among the Synoptics most closely identifies the crucifixion with the resurrection, notes that at the moment Jesus died, the bodies of saints rose up from their tombs and appeared to many in Jerusalem (Matt 27:51-53). Conversely, Matthew also tells us that at Jesus' resurrection, the guards sent to assure that Jesus would remain dead in the tomb, themselves became like "dead men" (28:4). That the story of Jairus's daughter anticipates Jesus' own resurrection is reinforced when Matthew uses the standard term for resurrection in 9:25, "and the little girl arose." Further, Matthew concludes his account of the resurrection with a note that the guards, in collusion with the Pharisees, circulated a story that the disciples stole Jesus' body as the guards slept (28:11-15).

Clearly there were several forms of Judaism before the destruction of the Temple, as we can see even from the limited groups we meet in the New Testament (e.g., the Pharisees, the scribes, the Zealots, John the Baptist and his followers). After 70, Judaism may have been most influenced by the rabbis, but still there were various emphases and beliefs coming from many different perspectives. No single interpretation or line of interpretation ever dominated. Christian feminism needs to avoid anti-Judaism, as if to imply that Christianity represents emancipation of women oppressed in Judaism. Presumptions of both elements of that comparison are false.

Matthew says finally, "And this story has circulated among the Jews to the present [day]" (28:15). Matthew has a similar note to end the story of the resurrection of Jairus's daughter: "And news of this spread throughout all that land" (9:26). Matthew contrasts the reaction of "the Jews" to that of believers.

As he often does, Matthew ignores Mark's comment that Jesus commanded them not to speak of what he had done. Matthew's editorial changes are meant to highlight his own themes of faith in Jesus and the right interpretation of the Law. Matthew shows Jesus as fulfilling, not abolishing, the Law (5:17-20). The Law's purpose is to give access to God and God's righteousness (justice). The young girl, like the hemorrhaging woman, was considered outside the boundaries of cleanness and of holiness. But they are now included in the righteousness that is found by faith in Jesus.

According to Luke, just when the cured woman Jesus now calls "daughter" goes off in peace, a messenger from the house comes to say that Jairus's daughter has died. Luke adds to Mark's story that this young girl was Jairus's "only" daughter, a notion that underscores the idea of "well beloved." Some commentators note that the Johannine tradition refers to Jesus as the "only son" of God (see John 1:14, 18; 3:16, 18).[13] This is the mirror story to the raising of the widow's only son. Luke, as we have noted, tends to pair stories of men and women. When we read the two stories together, one lasting impression is that Jesus demonstrates that girls as well as boys are to be cherished.

Even though it does not function as well in his own version of the story as it does in Mark, Luke keeps the command of Jesus not to tell of this miracle. This vestige is one of the indications for the judgment that Luke probably had access to Mark and used Mark in the composition of his Gospel. He leaves clues to his source, even when Mark's comments do not serve Luke's purpose. This admonition to silence is in contrast to the "open" and public profession of the hemorrhaging woman, who, in the Lukan account, told the "whole truth" of the miracle she had experienced in the full presence of all the people.

---

[13] E.g. Reid, *Women in the Gospel of Luke*, 137.

"Daughter, your faith has saved you.
Go in peace and be cured of your affliction" (Mark 5:34).

THE WOMAN HEALED OF A HEMORRHAGE

Suggested Readings: Mark 5:25-34; Matt 9:20-22; Luke 8:43-48

Again we should remember that the synoptic Gospels combine this story of a unnamed woman identified by the illness that ostracizes her with the story of the raising of Jairus's daughter. Both stories bring out the opposition between faith and fear. Both women are introduced in terms of their extreme religious and social poverty. One is a young girl on the verge of dying, and she does die. The other has a condition that leaves her physically, spiritually, financially, and socially empty and alone. The status of both is changed by their encounter with Jesus. The isolation and sadness of their families are transformed into joy and celebration when the women are restored to them. Both stories reflect a degraded status of women and how this is rejected by Jesus.

During the life of Jesus and afterward, most women in Palestine were restricted almost exclusively to domestic duties, perhaps more so than at any other time in Jewish history. But this was due less to Judaism than to the defensive posture official Judaism was forced to take as it struggled with self-definition during a long period of great hostility against it. Ever since the sixth century B.C.E., when the Jews returned from the terrible experience of a fifty-year exile in Babylon, they sought to strengthen their religion and their sense of identity through the local synagogues, which served as the main forum where Judaism could be taught and learned. It was here that the teachers emerged as experts on Jewish law and tradition. The influence especially of the rabbis (teachers) grew, and they endeavored to "build a fence around the Law" to protect it. In this atmosphere the oral teaching tradition passed on by the rabbis came to have authority equal to the written tradition they ascribed to Moses. The focus of the rabbis' teaching was how to make the Law applicable and alive in any situation. Above all, Judaism is a family-oriented religion.

The main duty of parents is to "teach this to your children," handing down from generation to generation the precious gift of Torah that had been entrusted to them.

The development of rabbinic legal tradition heightened the inequality that existed between men and women. A man and woman, even husband and wife, were not to speak on the street if they wandered out together. The first-century Jewish philosopher Philo, a Pharisee, says that women are best suited to the indoor life and should not stray from the house, "within which the middle door is taken by the maidens as their boundary, and the outer door by those who have reached full womanhood."[14] He adds later, "A woman then should not be a busybody, meddling with affairs outside her household concerns, but should seek a life of seclusion. She should not show herself off like a vagrant in the streets before the eyes of other men, except when she has to go to the Temple." Josephus, also writing in the first century, gives a demeaning picture of women with this judgment: "The woman, says the Law, is in all things inferior to the man. Let her accordingly be submissive, not for her humiliation, but that she may be directed; for the authority has been given by God to the man."[15] We get a different reaction from Jesus in the Gospels.

Both the story about the woman who suffered a hemorrhage for twelve years and the one about the daughter of Jairus bring up the issue of ritual "cleanness" and "uncleanness." It is truly significant that Jesus said and did what he said and did in order to liberate us. And that is also why the Gospels recount Jesus' words and deeds. These are not only history but salvation. Yet to understand how the Gospel can liberate today, we sometimes need to discuss its historical and cultural contexts. Part of this context affecting our understanding of the story of the woman with a hemorrhage involves the laws re-

---

[14] Philo, *Special Laws*, 3.169, trans. Loeb Classical Library, 7.581; quoted in Donald P. Senior, *Jesus: A Gospel Portrait* (Dayton: Pflaum, 1975) 74–75; also in Carolyn Osiek and David L. Balch, *Families in the New Testament World: Households and House Churches* (Louisville: Westminster/John Knox, 1997) 44.

[15] See Senior, *Jesus: A Gospel Portrait*, 74–75.

lated to the circumstances that render a person unclean. Such circumstances include contact with blood or contact with a corpse. Since the combined stories of the daughter of Jairus and the hemorrhaging woman involve these forms of uncleanness, we need to investigate this issue.

Mark 5:25-34

[25]There was a woman afflicted with hemorrhages for twelve years. [26]She had suffered greatly at the hands of many doctors and had spent all that she had. Yet she was not helped but only grew worse. [27]She had heard about Jesus and came up behind him in the crowd and touched his cloak. [28]She said, "If I but touch his clothes, I shall be cured." [29]Immediately her flow of blood dried up. She felt in her body that she was healed of her affliction. [30]Jesus, aware at once that power had gone out from him, turned around in the crowd and asked, "Who has touched my clothes?" [31]But his disciples said to him, "You see how the crowd is pressing upon you, and yet you ask, 'Who touched me?'" [32]And he looked around to see who had done it. [33]The woman, realizing what had happened to her, approached in fear and trembling. She fell down before Jesus and told him the whole truth. [34]He said to her, "Daughter, your faith has saved you. Go in peace and be cured of your affliction."

Matthew 9:20-22

[20]A woman suffering hemorrhages for twelve years came up behind him and touched the tassel on his cloak. [21]She said to herself, "If only I can touch his cloak, I shall be cured." [22]Jesus turned around and saw her, and said, "Courage, daughter! Your faith has saved you." And from that hour the woman was cured.

Luke 8:43-48

[43]And a woman afflicted with hemorrhages for twelve years, who (had spent her whole livelihood on doctors and) was unable to be cured by anyone, [44]came up behind him and touched the tassel on his cloak. Immediately her bleeding stopped. [45]Jesus then asked, "Who touched me?" While all were denying it, Peter said, "Master, the crowds are pushing

and pressing in upon you." ⁴⁶But Jesus said, "Someone has touched me; for I know that power has gone out from me." ⁴⁷When the woman realized that she had not escaped notice, she came forward trembling. Falling down before him, she explained in the presence of all the people why she had touched him and how she had been healed immediately. ⁴⁸He said to her, "Daughter, your faith has saved you; go in peace."

We focus now on an unnamed woman, identified only by her multiple disabilities. She is financially, physically, and socially bankrupt. She is ill because of an unnatural flow of blood, weak because she has had this condition for twelve years. She is continuously "unclean," ostracized and isolated because of religious connotations of the bleeding that plagues her. Further, she has been impoverished at the hands of impotent doctors, unable to help her. She has gone from bad to worse. Although she is a social outcast, she has "heard about Jesus." Her situation has made her fearful and suspicious of false claims. But she has hope.

Unable to really communicate with anyone else, she is described as shoring up her confidence by talking to herself. She has no one to run interference for her, no one to intercede on her behalf as Jairus did for his daughter. So she approaches Jesus secretly, from behind. She gathers the courage to push herself through the crowd in hopes of getting close enough just to touch Jesus' clothing. She may be unsure of herself, but she is clearly confident about Jesus.

Jesus is pictured as somewhat confused. Although he "felt power" leave him, he appears not to understand where this power went or who has it now. He seems to wonder aloud, also talking to himself: "Who has touched my clothes?" (Mark 5:30). Now it is their turn to be confused, but his disciples humor him, "How can you ask who touched you in this packed crowd?" Jesus persists in his questioning, as if giving the woman an opportunity not only to identify herself but to acknowledge the change she has experienced. Jesus hesitates, looking around, waiting.

The drama continues as now the woman's initial courage seems to leave her, replaced with "fear and trembling." Her response is to prostrate herself before Jesus. But these are not marks of timidity; rather, they are the attitudes and postures of a believer. She pours out the "whole truth." The woman finally has an identity, knowing herself now not only as someone in need of mercy and healing but as one who has received these. Her body and her spirit attest to what Jesus has done for her. And Jesus confirms that she has been transformed by this encounter with him. He affirms her new identity, as one born of faith. Jesus says to her, "Daughter, your faith has saved you. Go in peace" (Mark 5:34).

THE WOMAN'S UNCLEANNESS

Judaism, as well as the other ancient Near East cultures, considered a menstruant woman taboo. Rachel Biale explains:

> Undoubtedly the taboo is so common since many cultures share the same basic psychological components: fear of bleeding, discomfort with genital discharge, and bewilderment especially on the part of men, at the mysterious cycle of bleeding and its connection to conception and birth. Despite the lack of understanding of the precise physiology of menstruation and conception, many societies came to associate menstruation with death because the lack of menstruation meant conception and life. [16]

The relationship of cleanness or purity to holiness has to do with the mysteriousness of God. Blood and death are in the realm of the mystery of God. Part of the reasoning here has to do with the conception of the divine as holy and the required awe or reverence in approaching the divine. Strict boundaries separate the holy from the impure or contaminated. So, for example, a veil covers the Holy of Holies, the sanctuary where the ark of the covenant is kept. Only the high priest entered once a year into this innermost holy space.

We can compare the thinking on another topic that was debated in the first century, especially as Judaism dealt with challenges posed by the early Christians, namely, which books

---

[16] Rachel Biale, *Women and Jewish Law: An Exploration of Women's Issues in Halakhic Sources* (New York: Schocken Books, 1984) 147.

were sacred and belonged to the canon of the Scriptures. Toward the end of the first century, after the Temple had been destroyed, Jewish leaders struggled with such issues as part of their effort to define themselves in relation to the hostilities of Rome and the new situation they faced without the Temple. Further, Christian reading of the Scriptures forced them to take stock of exactly which texts ought to be considered sacred. Jews phrased the question, "Which books render your hands unclean?" This is obviously uncleanness in the symbolic sense of ritual purity; paraphrased, "Which books render ordinary human beings unworthy to touch them without undergoing a purification rite to signify that they are coming into contact with holiness?"

The language of purity was reserved for the realm of the holy, a concept almost synonymous with purity or cleanness. Here the physical and the symbolic meet. Terms for purity included unstained, unblemished, clean, innocent, blameless, as well as holy. On the other hand, terms for pollution included unclean, spotted, stained, defiled, blemished, common, profane.[17]

Rituals involve making and maintaining boundaries. The ordinary or the profane were not to get mixed up with, violate, or penetrate the veil on the world of the holy. Some ritual had to be performed for a person to cross over from the realm of the profane or ordinary to the realm of the sacred or holy. For the sake of preserving order and protecting the holy, these rituals were to be strictly kept. So, for example, ritual washings and sexual abstinence were signs that a priest was purifying himself to prepare to participate in the holy act of offering sacrifice in the Temple. Similar thinking required a woman to bathe herself in a *mikveh* after her menstrual cycle was completed. A longer term of purification was required after childbirth. Again there was a comparable way of certifying that a person who had had a disease such as leprosy might be healed. The healed person presented himself to a priest for verification of his healing and then made an of-

---

[17] See J. Neyrey, *Paul in Other Words: A Cultural Reading of His Letters* (Louisville: Westminster/John Knox, 1990) 54–55.

fering of thanks for his healing. After this ritual he could cross over into the realm of the ordinary, having been freed of the taboo that ostracized him in a kind of social and spiritual limbo.

The period of purification after childbirth was double when the child was a girl. Women were considered "less clean" than men and "a perceived threat of pollution to men."[18] A double standard existed regarding women when it came to observing religious laws and duties. Women were not required to go to the Temple, for example, where they were not permitted full access anyway. Their religious obligations were like those of slaves. The reasoning seems to have been that women, like slaves, were not responsible for their own time.[19] They had duties that depended on the will of their husbands and family. Nevertheless, women were held responsible for keeping laws regarding ritual purity, such as remaining in seclusion during their menstrual period or undergoing the rituals of purification after the birth of children. Yet again, explanations for why these laws had to be strictly observed focused mainly on preserving the purity of men.

For seven days, considered the time of a normal female period, a woman was secluded, which means she was also ostracized or excluded from regular interactions with others. During this time she was considered "unclean." A woman hemorrhaging for twelve years would be permanently unclean. She had not been able to perform the prescribed *mikveh*, which would have allowed her to return to normal social interaction. Her illness was not only physical but had enormous social implications. If unmarried, she would not be able to marry. If married, her condition would be grounds for divorce. She would be expelled from her home, cut off from her family. We are struck by the loneliness of her situation, much like the stark isolation and despair of the widow of Nain. Ironically, both women meet Jesus in the midst of a huge crowd. The irony heightens the drama. And their restoration to social

---

[18] Joanna Dewey, "The Gospel of Mark," in *Searching the Scriptures,* 470–509, at 481.

[19] See Senior, *Jesus: A Gospel Portrait,* 75.

status, including a return to their families, is an integral part of the story.[20]

Because healing has taken place, the woman can now offer her thanks offering; she prostrates herself before Jesus. She knows that she is in the presence of holiness. She crossed over into the realm of the holy through the required "fear and trembling." She is not profaning the holy but expressing her awe. Without a word, she acknowledges the "whole truth" about who she is and who Jesus is.

In a subtle but powerful way Mark identifies this woman with Jesus. The phrases "suffered greatly" and "afflicted" (5:25-26) describing her torture are used by Mark in Jesus' passion predictions to describe the outcome of his journey to Jerusalem (see 8:31; 10:34). Mark notes that the woman spoke the "whole truth" (5:33). Similarly, Jesus is recognized even by those seeking to entrap him as "a truthful man . . . not concerned with anyone's opinion. You do not regard a person's status but teach the way of God in accordance with the truth" (12:14). Some commentators have noted that the language suggests that "Mark dared to identify her suffering with Jesus."[21]

The power of Mark's identification of this woman with Jesus himself is softened by Luke, who avoids the use of these phrases. But Luke also gives us food for thought about this story. Luke says that this woman openly confessed why she had touched Jesus and how she had been immediately healed, "in the presence of all the people" (Luke 8:47). Witness to faith is the basis of true discipleship, according to Luke. He concludes this story with high praise for the woman and reassurance from Jesus: "Daughter, your faith has saved you; go in

---

[20] The son of the widow is restored to life and given back to his mother; the twelve-year-old girl is raised and given back to her parents. Her restoration to her own people is not mentioned in the story of the woman with the hemorrhage, but the Gospels say that she is "completely healed," which has social implications.

[21] Quoted in Dewey, "Gospel of Mark," 481; also see Hisako Kinukawa, *Women and Jesus in Mark: A Japanese Feminist Perspective* (Maryknoll: Orbis, 1994); Marla J. Selvidge, *Women, Cult and Miracle Recital* (Lewisburg: Bucknell University Press, 1990); Reid, *Women in the Gospel of Luke,* 142.

peace" (8:48). Faith is the key to salvation, the basis of peace. Although the witness of women is not valid in Judaism and the women's testimony is not accepted by the Christian male leaders, such as Peter (see Luke 24:10-11), the witness of this woman is confirmed by Jesus himself.

Matthew clusters this miracle with others in chapters 8–9, changing their context to use them as part of his reflections about mission and discipleship. The woman's inner thought processes, "If only I can touch . . ." (Matt 9:21), are captured by Matthew as the reverse of Jairus's statement "Come, lay your hand on her" (9:18).[22] Jairus may assume that Jesus has some magical power. But Matthew reinforces the idea that the woman's faith is integral to her cure. This and the other miracles in these chapters of Matthew are part of the preparation for the sending of the disciples (chapter 10) to do the same work of healing as they have seen Jesus do. Such works as these are also part of Jesus' self-description when confronted by the Baptist's disciples in Matthew 11:4-6.

"[Jesus] touched her hand and the fever left her" (Matt 8:15).

THE HEALING OF SIMON'S MOTHER-IN-LAW

Suggested Readings: Mark 1:29-31; Matt 8:14-15; Luke 4:38-39

We turn now to a relatively short, apparently insignificant miracle. A woman suffers from an everyday illness. She is not a wealthy or influential person and seems not to have a very important job. Afterwards she gets up and carries on as usual. Why is this woman's story important enough to be included in the Gospel? What is so memorable about a cure that enables a person to go about her life, as if nothing at all ever happened? Perhaps a closer reading, including the contexts of this story in the synoptic Gospels, will help us answer this question.

---

[22] Harrington, *The Gospel of Matthew,* 131.

Mark 1:29-31

[29]On leaving the synagogue he entered the house of Simon and Andrew with James and John. [30]Simon's mother-in-law lay sick with a fever. They immediately told him about her. [31]He approached, grasped her hand, and helped her up. Then the fever left her and she waited on them.

Matt 8:14-15

[14]Jesus entered the house of Peter, and saw his mother-in-law lying in bed with a fever. [15]He touched her hand, the fever left her, and she rose and waited on him.

Luke 4:38-39

[38]After he left the synagogue, he entered the house of Simon. Simon's mother-in-law was afflicted with a severe fever, and they interceded with him about her. [39]He stood over her, rebuked the fever, and it left her. She got up immediately and waited on them.

Here we have the story of an unnamed woman who is identified in the customary way—in relation to a man: she is the mother-in-law of Simon. Perhaps she had no sons, since we would expect her to be named in relation to males in her own family. Since her society was patrilocal, it is a possibility that she is a widow living with her daughter's family.[23] But our text does not say that she lived there, only that she was ill there.

This woman came down with a fever. When his disciples alerted him to this situation, Jesus came to her, took her by the hand and lifted her up. And the fever left her. As proof of the immediacy and completeness of her cure, this woman arose from her sickbed and served her family and visitors. Actually this is hardly a story about the woman at all; it is more about Jesus and about discipleship. She does not speak for herself, nor is there any report about faith being demanded of her.

We might get a better understanding of why this story was included in the Good News by examining first its setting in the earliest Gospel, Mark. It is near the beginning, in Mark 1:29-31,

---

[23] See Bruce Malina and Richard L. Rohrbaugh, *Social Science Commentary on the Synoptic Gospels* (Minneapolis: Fortress Press, 1992) 181.

among several miracles that Jesus performs in Capernaum, as if to demonstrate the power of God's kingdom which is at hand. Mark opens his Gospel with the figure of John announcing the coming of the Messiah. Jesus appears in the wilderness and is baptized by John. He is recognized as God's Son and is then tempted by Satan. After his ordeal Jesus is ministered to by angels, Mark says (1:13).

The first words of Jesus proclaim the inauguration of the kingdom of God (Mark 1:14-15). Jesus then calls two sets of two brothers, Simon and Andrew, James and John (1:16-20). These disciples or learners will be witnesses to the mighty works Jesus performs as he demonstrates the power and the priorities of God's kingdom. This first part of Mark's Gospel features Jesus' ministry in Capernaum. Five miracles are worked here: the cure of a demoniac (1:21-28), the healing of Simon's mother-in-law (1:29-31), the cleansing of a leper (1:40-45), the healing of a paralytic (2:1-12), and the restoration of a man with a withered hand (3:1-6). It is remarkable that Jesus' first three miracles in particular are worked on the lowliest, even the outcasts, of society: a demoniac, a woman, and a leper. In Mark the term "immediately" appears twice in the three verses of this short story. A healing like this is part of Jesus' frenetic activity to jump-start his ministry in Galilee. It is an attention-getter, just like the cure of lepers and exorcising demons.

These events provoke different reactions on the part of those who witness them. Some people are struck by a difference in Jesus' teaching; it is done with authority, with power. Some "immediately" follow Jesus, leaving everything behind. Others are suspicious of Jesus' lifestyle and challenge him because his disciples do not fast. Still others openly plot to destroy him, as if rejecting him outright, before he even got started on his mission, without regard for the good he has done.

Part of the Gospel's claim is that what Jesus did was out of the ordinary, not what at least some "expected" of the Messiah. For example, rather than fast and require fasting of his disciples, Jesus went about attending to the sick and the crippled, speaking more about the forgiveness of sins than about how to achieve significance in the eyes of the righteous. Some people then and now welcome surprises and are delighted with an opportunity to reexamine their own presumptions and expectations. Others find it harder to change their minds and hearts. After all, many have awaited a Messiah for a long time and feel sure that they are right in what they want and expect. So in what way might they (and we) be gracefully caught off guard when the second miracle Jesus does is on behalf of a woman whose reaction is that she "got up and ministered to them"?

The setting of this miracle is the house of Simon (and Andrew), apparently their patriarchal homestead. Mark and Luke make clear that Jesus moved from the synagogue ("he left the synagogue") and "he entered the house." This is more than an indication that Jesus went from a formal to a cozy setting. The early Church was formed and nurtured within the Greco-Roman household, using it as a model for much of the Church's organization. Christians, for example, spoke of one another as "brothers and sisters." They shared table fellowship, much like members of a family do. The synagogue, unlike the household, did not serve as a useful model for describing the Church. For one thing, although practice varied from place to place, women were usually segregated from men in the synagogue and did not have any official duty to go there. But the home is the traditional domain of women; in fact, in the first century, women were mainly confined to domestic circles. In the language of the social scientists, women were mistresses of the private domain symbolized by the household, while men functioned as leaders in the public domain.

We know from a number of New Testament texts that the place and roles of women in the Church were a matter of controversy. This may have been less an issue for Mark than for Luke, who gives us a more developed picture, especially in Acts, of women in the Church. But we know that Paul, who wrote his letters before the composition of Mark's Gospel, had his own views on the subject of women. And it was a subject that continued to be debated as the Church grew. Mark may have had apparently more pressing concerns, writing in the late sixties or seventies, when Rome was making life difficult for all Christians as well as Jews. But Mark's description of the early Church does include some intriguing hints that women and their proper role in the new order of things were a subject that could not be ignored.

So the woman's illness is brought to the attention of Jesus by his disciples. He responds without hesitating over the fact that she is a woman. He enters the room where she is in bed; in so doing, Jesus defies custom. Jesus further ignores propriety when he "grasped her hand, and helped her up" (Mark 1:31). As testimony to the extent of his cure, she "waited on them," enabled to resume her daily life as if nothing had happened.

The idea of ministry (the verb is *diakonein*, the noun *diakonia* in Greek; a servant is called a *diakonos*) as the response of the woman has stimulated a lot of debate, especially in the past thirty years. In the Gospels Jesus is often the one who ministers to others, but he is not often said to be the object of ministry in the Gospels. In 1:13 Mark says that angels ministered to Jesus after his temptation; in 15:41 Mark refers to the presence at the cross of the women who had "followed him and ministered to him."

It is not clear that the idea of "ministry" or "service" means only performing domestic duties, such as cooking or waiting on tables, or includes other services that might be of the public domain. We can note that in Acts, for example, the Jerusalem community was forced to recognize a new form of ministry in the distribution of goods, and this involved a certain leadership position (Acts 6:1-6). Acts describes the male deacons recognized by a "laying on of hands" by the presbyters and leaders of the Church. The first named Christian deacon is Phoebe, recommended by Paul in his letter to the Romans and further described as a patron who has helped many, including Paul himself.[24] The early Church began developing various ministries as needs arose, and both women and men filled most if not all these ministries. The fact that these roles were called "services" appears not to be accidental, since Jesus uses himself as a model of "one who serves" others.[25]

---

[24] Yet, while Mark and Luke say, "she ministered to them," Matthew says, "She ministered to him." Mark uses the verb four times (in 1:13, 31; 10:45; 15:41), the noun twice (9:35 and 10:43).

[25] The only ministry that appears to be gender specific is that of the "widow," described in 2 Timothy and Titus. The role of these women was to share their experience as Christian wives and mothers with younger women. This ministry suggests that the need arose out of the controversy

There is at least one danger in understanding "service" as the exemplary Christian response in that it may reinforce an insidious, harmful prejudice against women. Service is not the same as subservience. Feminist writers in particular have noted that we need to take care in interpreting texts such as this. Elisabeth Schüssler Fiorenza, for example, points out that a theology of service has different implications for women than for men.

> When women are socialized to "be for others," and when, because of their gender, they have been assigned and/or assumed subservient tasks in the church, to speak of ministry as service causes women to internalize and legitimate the patriarchal-hierarchal status quo in theological-spiritual terms.[26]

Sometimes it is argued that service is liberating when it is freely chosen. But this is true only for those who have the power and the freedom to choose. In the present patriarchal structure women do not have such freedom. Thus, to speak of ministry as service does not empower women.[27] A parallel could be drawn with what missionaries to this country used to tell slaves about their Christian calling. They quoted Paul as saying that if you are a slave, do not seek your freedom. You should not try to change the status you had when you were called, that is, when you became a Christian (see 1 Cor 7:21-22). This is a reading of Paul intended to justify rather than challenge an unjust social structure. It is an example of using the Gospel as "bad news" and cannot be supported. In this way Christianity functioned as a maintenance argument even for slavery for way too long.

It certainly would be harmful and wrongheaded to read our story as if the woman's service of Jesus and his disciples in her home were the only possible response she could have made

---

about whether Christian women should marry and then whether they should bear children. This ministry seems to presume that the experience of older women who had successfully maintained their own families would provide good role models for younger women.

[26] Elisabeth Schüssler Fiorenza, quoted in Reid, *Women in the Gospel of Luke*, 102.

[27] Ibid.

to her cure. Remember that part of a miracle story is that it ends with testimony to the reality and sometimes the extent of the cure that has taken place. Many miracles restore a person to a more liberated condition than simply eliminating disease. So a paralytic cannot only walk but carry his bed; a dead man sits up and starts speaking; a dead girl walks around and eats. In this case we have an indication of the thoroughness of the cure when the woman can resume her daily life. She has been, like the widow of Nain's son and Jairus's daughter, restored to her family.

But if she had not been changed by her encounter with Jesus, what is the use of recounting this story? There is another avenue of reflection that may help us to see why this little vignette about Simon's mother-in-law is included in the Gospel. Gerd Theissen was among the pioneers in showing how a social science perspective can help us interpret the text. He refers to the nascent Christian community in its initial stages as the Jesus movement.[28] Although aspects of his presentation have since been challenged, he describes a dynamic in that movement that has implications yet to be more fully mined. Thiessen distinguishes between those he calls "local sympathizers" and others he calls the "itinerant preachers" among Jesus' followers. Not everyone was expected to be like Paul, who journeyed from city to city preaching the Gospel. Such itinerants depended upon receiving hospitality from believers in the cities they visited. When they left, they appointed leaders from within the local community. Or leaders emerged from among the heads of the households where Christians gathered to worship, to instruct, to encourage one another, to "break bread," and to serve the community in various ways. Our story shows that this woman's service was condoned by Jesus and by the evangelists. If, by the time the Gospels were written, some questioned whether women could be deacons, Peter's mother-in-law and other stories, drawing on Jesus' authority, confirm that they could.

---

[28] Gerd Theissen, *Sociology of Early Palestinian Christianity* (Philadelphia: Fortress Press, 1978).

Jesus tells his disciples to go out and preach the Gospel, carrying no money or staff or shoes, staying with those who welcome them. This command must have survived in the oral tradition because some practiced this radical way of life. If these itinerants had not been received and supported in the houses of "local sympathizers" who fed and clothed them, how would they have been able to survive or be sent on their way to the next city? We can well imagine that sometimes tensions developed between the itinerants and their hosts. In fact, couldn't the story of Martha and Mary be a reflection of just such tensions? It certainly is an indication that tensions did in fact exist in the early Christian community about which roles a woman could legitimately claim and which ought to be "taken from her." In appealing to Jesus' authority to solve this issue, Luke pictures him defending both the role of host and that of hearer and preacher of the word.

According to the Gospels, some women apparently left their families and followed Jesus wherever he went (for example, Mary Magdalene, Joanna, and Susanna: see Luke 8:1-3). That's how they got from Galilee to Jerusalem. That's how they came to be standing and watching at the cross and ultimately at the tomb from which Jesus was raised. That's how they were there to hear and to tell the message of the resurrection to the male disciples. But it was also necessary that some women (and men) stayed where they were, providing the means for the Church's prospering by opening their homes to the travelers. For example, Mary of Jerusalem seems to have provided lodging, food, and comfort to the itinerants. She is remembered gratefully by the early Church for doing so (see Acts 12:12; 13:13).

The response of Simon's mother-in-law does not diminish her place in salvation history but opens up a world of possibilities to future generations of believers. That is why she is included in Mark's account from the beginning as a symbol of her newly gained importance. Before this event she may have been an ordinary woman. Now she is immortalized as the first woman convert to Christianity, according to all three Synoptics. She represents an example of living the Christian life in the world, as a woman with a family and a home. Like other women we have studied, she is restored to her family, and that is praiseworthy.

Luke reworked Mark's story to include yet another dimension. It should be noted that, according to Luke, prior to this healing, Simon has no relationship with Jesus. Simon is only called in the next chapter, in Luke 5:1-12, *after* the healing of his mother-in-law. Her cure "lays the foundation" for Simon's call.[29] We are reminded of stories in Acts where whole households were converted along with the head of the household. This happened, for example in the case of Paul's jailer in Philippi, after the earthquake that destroyed the prison where Paul was incarcerated (Acts 16:29-34). But it had already happened in the same town in the case of a woman named Lydia, who met Paul under less dramatic circumstances and opened up her home to him (Acts 16:14-15, 40). Hers became the first house church of Philippi, and Paul considered her to be so important that he refused to leave town until he had said goodbye to her and all the believers who met at her house. Her conversion was the occasion for many others to believe. People are drawn to Jesus through the testimony of women as well as men; the story of the Samaritan woman makes this clear. Luke presents the story of Simon's call and his acceptance as one of the consequences of his mother-in-law's cure.

And Matthew's rendition of the same story provides yet another insight along the same lines. Matthew presents this as one of the series of miracles he links together in chapters 8–9 with Jesus' comments on discipleship. When these miracles are followed by a discourse on mission in chapter 10, the three chapters form a unit on the nature and high cost of following Jesus. The healing of Simon's mother-in-law becomes, under Matthew's pen, a "call story with a healing motif."[30] Matthew's account is shorter even than Mark's or Luke's. Matthew's account has the same form elements as the story of the call of Matthew (9:9), a good example of a "call story." In both, Jesus takes the initiative; he "sees" one he calls, there is a description of the one called, a word or action of Jesus, and the person's response. The focus is on Jesus in both. The woman simply "waits on him" as Matthew the tax collector "followed him."

---

[29] Reid, *Women in the Gospel of Luke*, 102.
[30] Ibid., 101.

---

*"This daughter of Abraham, whom Satan has bound for
eighteen years now, ought she not to have been set free on
the sabbath day from this bondage?"* (Luke 13:16).

A CRIPPLED WOMAN CAN STAND ERECT

*Suggested Readings: Luke 13:10-17; see Mark 3:1-6; Luke 6:6-11;
14:1-6; Matt 12:9-14*

This story incorporates two different literary forms we find
typical of the Gospels: a healing story and a controversy. The
healing of the woman becomes the occasion for the debate
about the Law, specifically the Sabbath observance. The woman
is described as so crippled that she cannot stand erect; she is
bent over. Consistent with the beliefs of the times regarding ir-
regular medical conditions, her disability is attributed to a
"spirit." Luke gives this version of events.

> [10]He was teaching in a synagogue on the sabbath. [11]And a
> woman was there who for eighteen years had been crippled
> by a spirit; she was bent over, completely incapable of stand-
> ing erect. [12]When Jesus saw her, he called to her and said,
> "Woman, you are set free of your infirmity." [13]He laid his
> hands on her, and she at once stood up straight and glorified
> God. [14]But the leader of the synagogue, indignant that Jesus
> had cured on the sabbath, said to the crowd in reply, "There
> are six days when work should be done. Come on those days
> to be cured, not on the sabbath day." [15]The Lord said to him in
> reply, "Hypocrites! Does not each one of you on the sabbath
> untie his ox or his ass from the manger and lead it out for wa-
> tering? [16]This daughter of Abraham, whom Satan has bound
> for eighteen years now, ought she not to have been set free on
> the sabbath day from this bondage?" [17]When he said this, all
> his adversaries were humiliated; and the whole crowd re-
> joiced at all the splendid deeds done by him (Luke 13:10-17).

This story is found only in Luke. But it has parallels in his
source, Mark, and in Matthew. Except for the fact that it is a
woman who is the recipient of Jesus' cure, this is fairly typical
of the kinds of healings and the types of controversy we find

in many instances in the synoptic Gospels. There are a number of episodes in the Gospels that are occasions for Jesus to make a pronouncement about a controversial issue; in this case, the issue was Sabbath observance and who has the authority to define what is allowed and what is prohibited in order to "keep" the Sabbath as the Law states. From Mark (3:1-6), Luke has a story of a man with a withered hand who is cured in a synagogue on the Sabbath. In Mark this man is almost a setup: "they watched him closely to see if he would cure him on the sabbath so that they might accuse him" (3:2). The outcome was that "the Pharisees" colluded with "the Herodians" about how to destroy him (3:6). For Mark this miracle prompts the argument over the Sabbath, which in turn concludes with a deadly conspiracy to kill Jesus. This background helps us understand how Luke adapts such a combination story to his own audience and purpose.

Luke adapts the Markan story in two other places. In chapter 6 he gives his version of the Markan story, following Mark rather closely, just as Matthew does. In all three Gospels this story follows a pronouncement of Jesus that "the Son of Man is lord of the Sabbath." That is to say that Jesus, as the Son of Man, claims the authority to decide the justice of a Sabbath work and to do it. The miracle, in this instance, is an expression of his "authority" or power. Christians were debating about how to appropriately keep the Sabbath and observe other religious laws. The Synoptics draw on Jesus' saying to authorize the practices of the Christians.

As is his custom, Luke parallels a story featuring a man which he found in his source, Mark (see 3:1-6; Luke 6:1-6; 14:1-6), with one focusing on a woman (Luke 13:10-17). Parallelism is found especially in the fact that this cure happens in a synagogue, on the Sabbath, and prompts a debate between Jesus and his adversaries about work on the Sabbath. Luke has yet another story parallel to that of the man healed on the Sabbath, but in the second instance the cure takes place in the house of a "ruler of the Pharisees" (Luke 14:1). The upshot is the same in all these stories. Jesus confronts his adversaries about whether it is lawful to help an animal that had fallen into a well (for example, a sheep [Matt 12:11], an ox [Luke 14:5], or even a son [Luke 14:5]) on the Sabbath.

The reaction to Jesus' rhetorical question is the humiliation of his adversaries and the jubilation of "the crowds." The woman and the people appear liberated, while his opponents are more entrenched than ever against Jesus. Sometimes in an effort to see the power and uniqueness in Jesus' dealings with women, he and his actions are compared with the opinions and actions of "the Jews," as if the latter held a single, universally held common view. But this is not so. First-century Judaism, as now, represented myriad forms, and there were many different ways to be Jewish and practice Judaism. The Gospels should not become a tool for intolerance. Yet they need to be understood in their historical context in order to avoid this abuse. Because he was regarded as a teacher, Jesus came into conflict with other teachers of the Jewish law. Questions of interpretation were posed to him, and his answers sometimes presented dilemmas for the religious people of his day. For example, we know from the Gospels that there were differing opinions regarding the grounds for divorce and whether there was an afterlife and/or a resurrection of the dead. There were also many views on how to preserve the holiness of the Sabbath, a crucial aspect of Jewish religious faith. There were legitimate bases for differences on such issues.

Jesus debates with the religious leaders, especially the Pharisees, who were so prominent in the synagogues, about what constitutes keeping the Sabbath. As in Mark, Luke often designates the "synagogue" as the setting for these debates. Yet it is also significant that Jesus holds a similar discussion in the "house" of a "ruler of the synagogue." Luke seems to be implying, then, that these issues were not only subjects of debate among Jews and Christians but within the church (the "house") as well. This story of the healing of the crippled woman could have been included by Luke as a reflection on baptism. One conclusion is that the value of the woman is as great as that of a man. In this instance the woman is healed, and she "at once stood up straight and glorified God" (Luke 13:13). The fact that this occurs in the synagogue and her right to be there is not disputed means that it would have been acceptable to have a woman there, a woman with a voice.

When Luke says that Jesus looked around and called the bystanders "hypocrites," he was not speaking of the Jews or

even of the Pharisees. The "leader of the synagogue" had refused to confront Jesus directly. Instead, he addressed the
crowd, saying that they could "come and be healed" on any
other day but the Lord's. Jesus' reply includes anyone who
would be swayed to believe that the Sabbath is not a day for
God's work. The story immediately follows Jesus' call for repentance and religious reform. The barren fig tree, a symbol of
Judaism, is given time to "bear fruit." The time is now. There is
an urgency about the tone of this story. All the people can be
affected and cured as a result of what they have witnessed in
the healing of this daughter of Abraham.

The woman is said to be "crippled by a spirit." In the synoptic Gospels, possession by a spirit is closely linked to illness,
although the two are not identified (see Luke 7:21; 13:32).
Medical knowledge was rudimentary. The causes of many illnesses and disabilities remain mysterious. Various afflictions
are connected with a spirit, especially in Luke: possession
(8:29), something like epilepsy (9:39), an inability to speak
(11:14), an inability to walk (13:11), even the delirium of a fever
in the case of Simon's mother-in-law (3:29). The close link between possession and illness could explain why Luke says that
Jesus "rebukes" the fever, a verb often found in exorcism (for
example, Luke 4:35; 9:42). Sometimes the spirits cause natural
disasters, such as the storm at sea; thus Luke says that Jesus
"charged" the winds to be calm (see Mark 4:34; Luke 8:24).

Although attributed to a "spirit," who may be "unclean" or
even evil, such physical symptoms are not, however, usually
associated with Satan. They do not indicate moral depravity.
But in this instance Luke makes a close connection, without
actually identifying the illness and Satan. It strikes us as odd
that Luke says that "Satan" has kept this daughter of Abraham
"bound" for eighteen long years. Apocalyptic literature may
explain the background for this connection. Jesus is locked in
a life-and-death struggle with evil. The battleground is the
world; humans are being used as pawns of the evil one. There
is symbolism in the language of the woman's being "locked
up" by Satan and Jesus' indignant challenge to the people. The
religious leaders claim the authority to "bind and to loose" the
requirements of the Law and the people as well. In fact, this
came to be a technical phrase the Pharisees used, especially in

the synagogues, to describe their own authority to interpret the Law and teach its implications. Jesus' anger is provoked because more is being done to "bind," to fetter, obstruct, and "tie up" the children of Abraham rather than to free them to worship God. Jesus claims the authority to free this woman and others. He is challenging the synagogues and the leaders with this claim.

That Jesus' views of illness and even death were very different from those of many of his contemporaries is evidenced in his reaction to the question of his disciples when they encountered a man born blind: "Who sinned, this man or his parents?" (John 9:2). Jesus answered, "Neither he nor his parents sinned; it is so that the works of God might be made visible through him" (9:3). A similar reaction is given to the news that Lazarus was very ill. Jesus says that "this illness is not to end in death, but is for the glory of God, that the Son of God may be glorified through it" (John 11:4). Thus, although she suffered many things for a very long time, the woman of our story, like Lazarus, is set free from her bondage. Her immediate reaction is not to stop and consider whether or not it is the Sabbath; it is a day to give praise and thanks to God and she knows it.

"O woman, great is your faith! Let it done for you as you wish"
(Matt 15:28).

THE SYROPHOENICIAN WOMAN

Suggested Readings: Mark 7:24-30; Matt 15:21-28

In the context of Mark's Gospel, this story presents a marked contrast between the faith of the woman and the rejection Jesus has experienced among his own. The preceding episode in Mark told of the challenge to Jesus about the boundaries between the sacred and the ordinary, or between the holy and the unclean. As if wearied with the casuistry, Jesus wanders away to a region supposed to typify disbelief and paganism at its worst. There he encounters a wonderful faith in a very unlikely source.

Mark 7:24-50

²⁴From that place he went off to the district of Tyre. He entered a house and wanted no one to know about it, but he could not escape notice. ²⁵Soon a woman whose daughter had an unclean spirit heard about him. She came and fell at his feet. ²⁶The woman was a Greek, a Syrophoenician by birth, and she begged him to drive the demon out of her daughter. ²⁷He said to her, "Let the children be fed first. For it is not right to take the food of the children and throw it to the dogs." ²⁸She replied and said to him, "Lord, even the dogs under the table eat the children's scraps." ²⁹Then he said to her, "For saying this, you may go. The demon has gone out of your daughter." ³⁰When the woman went home, she found the child lying in bed and the demon gone.

Matthew 15:21-28

²¹Then Jesus went from that place and withdrew to the region of Tyre and Sidon. ²²And behold, a Canaanite woman of that district came and called out, "Have pity on me, Lord, Son of David! My daughter is tormented by a demon." ²³But he did not say a word in answer to her. His disciples came and asked him, "Send her away, for she keeps calling out after us." ²⁴He said in reply, "I was sent only to the lost sheep of the house of Israel." ²⁵But the woman came and did him homage, saying, "Lord, help me." ²⁶He said in reply, "It is not right to take the food of the children and throw it to the dogs." ²⁷She said, "Please, Lord, for even the dogs eat the scraps that fall from the table of their masters." ²⁸Then Jesus said to her in reply, "O woman, great is your faith! Let it be done for you as you wish." And her daughter was healed from that hour.

In our story Jesus wanders into Gentile territory, perhaps wanting to retreat from all the debates and opposition he had encountered, or maybe even to find a different audience among the Gentiles. He heads toward the Mediterranean, toward the infamous cities of Tyre and Sidon. This is territory unfriendly to the Jews and known to us from the Old Testament as a symbol not only of wealth and commerce but of seduction to false gods and hostility to the Jewish people. Although it is part of the territory that had been assigned to the tribe of Asher, one of the sons of Jacob, it was never occupied by the Israelites.

Cedars of this far away region had to be imported to help build and furnish the Temple.

But the danger of becoming too friendly with these outlying districts is very well illustrated by the story of the Phoenician princess Jezebel, who was married to Ahab, the king of the northern kingdom of Israel. Jezebel imported devotion to the god Baal, and Ahab looked the other way rather than remain true to Yahweh. Jezebel opposed and persecuted Elijah the prophet. She later paid for her sins with a gruesome death at the command of Ahab's successor, Jehu.[30a] That was the end of amicable relations with the region of Tyre and its sister city, Sidon. The cities are often mentioned together in the Old Testament. The psalmist asks God's assistance against such hostile places as Tyre (Ps 83:8). The prophets excoriate these cities as symbolizing all the evil and sin that pagans do.[31]

Yet there is a saying of Jesus in judgment against his own people, comparing them negatively to Tyre and Sidon with the words,

> For if the mighty deeds done in your midst had been done in Tyre and Sidon, they would long ago have repented in sackcloth and ashes. But I tell you it will be more tolerable for Tyre and Sidon on the day of judgment than for you (Matt 11:21-22; see also Luke 10:13-14).

From the beginning of his ministry, people from Tyre and Sidon had flocked to hear Jesus and to witness his miracles (see Mark 3:8; Luke 6:17). These pagan regions represent an extension of Jesus' mission and the overwhelming acceptance of the Gospel by outsiders, contrasted with its rejection by Jesus' own.

Still, it is no wonder that we are somewhat confused by this story in Mark. Jesus goes off toward that foreign region, but his purpose is unclear. Mark inserts the "secrecy" motif here, saying that Jesus "wanted no one to know" that he is there (Mark 7:24), as if he is hiding. Mark's parenthetical phrase

---

[30a] See the story of Jezebel in 1 Kings 16:31-33; 19:1-3; 21:1-26.

[31] See Barbara Reid, "Tyre and Sidon," in *The Collegeville Pastoral Dictionary of the Bible* (Collegeville: The Liturgical Press, 1996) 1028–1030.

serves to heighten the drama of the inconvenience of the woman's interruption and also the strength of her faith and persistence. It also helps us understand Jesus' apparent impatience when importuned by this woman.

Although she is a pagan from a faraway place and probably has been fully absorbed by the care of her child, she has "heard about" Jesus. From the earliest days of Jesus' mission, Mark had said previously, people from Tyre and Sidon had flocked to hear and see him (see Mark 3:8). Perhaps neighbors, seeing her distress, have told her about him and about his clandestine visit nearby. On the basis of what she has heard, she seeks Jesus out. This meeting happens because the woman's mind is made up. She wants justice and wholeness for her child. She leaves her child and sets out, apparently alone, and single-minded. She appears as a nuisance to Jesus and, Matthew adds, to his disciples. She throws herself down in front of Jesus, begging him to cure her little girl.

In 7:26, Mark specifies that this is a Greek woman and a Syrophoenician by birth. After the fourth century B.C.E. and the conquest of Alexander the Great, the Jews referred to non-Jews as "Greeks." Other synonyms for Gentiles are pagans, the nations, or peoples, sinners, even "dogs." This last reference is reflected in Jesus' own response to the frantic mother of our story. This female outsider conjures up another well-known biblical woman, the infamous Jezebel, mentioned above. She was a Phoenician princess who came to represent all of the horrific possibilities of marrying outside Israel. In fact, Ahab, the king of Israel, married her. Israel was the nation to the north once the Davidic dynasty was divided after the death of Solomon. It was Jezebel who opposed the prophet Elijah and pursued him relentlessly. He became a fugitive and lived in a cave trying to escape her.

Ahab's capital of this northern kingdom was Samaria, another region that stirred long feelings of hostility among "the Jews," whose own name is probably derived from the land of Judah to the south. The capital was Jerusalem, the "holy city," the place where the Temple was built. But the region of the north persisted in the belief that its own shrines and holy places were older and more important than even the Temple. Most Jews avoided traveling to any of these areas, which represented a kind of heretical thinking and certainly a long history of animosity toward them.

The daughter of the Syrophoenician woman is possessed by an "unclean spirit." Mark has a predilection for exorcisms; further, spirit possession was a generic way of speaking about illness that was scarcely understood. Perhaps the woman had heard that Jesus had cured a man possessed by a "legion" of demons. That man had been so ill that he was chained, living among the tombs. He was outside the village of Gedara, another pagan place.

Jesus' answer appears almost like a proverb. It is a more vulgar form of the adage "Charity begins at home." He speaks of limits and priorities, hardly what this frantic mother wanted to hear. He appears to be unmoved by her desperation. "It is not right to take the food of the children and throw it to the dogs." Jesus' answer to the woman implies that she is one of those whom some Jews call "dogs." This on the lips of Jesus sounds shocking. Yet in this context the woman must know she is unwelcome on several counts. She is interrupting something. She has no credentials for approaching Jesus. She must have steeled herself before coming here. She had to know that this cure wasn't going to come easy.

That epithet sounds startlingly strange, especially coming from Jesus. But it is indicative of the centuries of animosity between people of this region. The reference to Tyre and Sidon, to a Syrophoenician or Cannanite, and to a woman coming alone to visit a man, no matter what her mission, already designated her as an unlikely beneficiary of this traveling Jew's good deeds. This woman is unflinching in her response to Jesus. As if pride and self-pity never occurred to her, she replies, "Even the dogs under the table eat the children's scraps." She implies that she has been waiting her turn. The children, the Jews, have had an opportunity to accept or reject Jesus. Now that he has appeared in her neighborhood, she gambles on getting something for her family from him.

Her faith is rewarded, although she cannot know yet how true to his word he is. So faith is still required. Mark makes it clear that she had left the child at home. If she is to verify that the cure she sought has been done, she must be willing to trust some more. Jesus cures her daughter from a distance. The woman leaves, a believer.

The description of the woman and her conversation with Jesus are significantly longer than the cure, which is so briefly reported. Mark seems to imply that this miracle is really an opportunity to address the mission to the Gentiles, an issue that greatly concerned his Church. The discussion between Jesus and the woman means more than Jesus' healing being extended to a single little girl. The Church remembered and repeated this story because it is Jesus' authorization for the Gentile mission to proceed unimpeded. Jesus' praise of the woman's great faith represents a challenge: "Go, therefore and make disciples of all nations," as the closing "Great Commission" of Matthew's Gospel will confirm (see Matt 28:19).

Luke does not report this story, but Matthew does. Matthew follows Mark rather closely, making a few significant changes (see Matt 15:21-28). For example, Mark's "Greek, Syrophoenician woman" is referred to as a "Canaanite" in Matthew, a more ancient reference to the pagans. Her request for her daughter is put into prayer form, a request the woman directly addresses to Jesus as "Lord, Son of David" (see the prayer of the two Jewish blind men in Matthew 9:27). The woman repeats her request, kneeling before Jesus and simply imploring him, "Lord, help me." Jesus appears to twice spurn her prayer, saying first, "I was sent only to the lost sheep of the house of Israel" (15:24) and, in reply to her prayer for help, "It is not right to take the food of the children and throw it to the dogs" (15:26). Jesus' praise of the woman in Matthew is more direct and exuberant than in Mark: "O woman, great is your faith! Let it be it done for you as you wish" (15:28). The woman's faith is only implied in Mark, but Matthew makes it explicit.

The woman's faith expressed in prayer and her kneeling posture link this with other Matthean stories. The Jewish official "came forward, knelt down before [Jesus], and said 'My daughter has just died. But come, lay your hand on her, and she will live'"(Matt 9:18). Just then the hemorrhaging woman stole up to Jesus from behind, her faith overcoming her enormous fear. As in the story of the Canaanite woman, Jesus praised the faith of the bleeding woman with the efficacious word, "Courage, daughter! Your faith has saved you" (9:22). Then Matthew adds, "And from that hour the woman was cured." As with the Canaanite woman's daughter, the healing is instantaneous (9:22; 15:28).

The faith of the Canaanite woman crossed long-standing socioreligious boundaries and was reaffirmed even in the face of rejection by Jesus and his disciples. Her faith was great indeed—greater than Peter's, whom Jesus chided in the previous chapter for his doubt and "little-faith" (14:31). This is the more surprising in that Matthew usually upgrades Mark's evaluation of the Twelve, especially Peter.[32]

Matthew's double phrase, "the woman came and did him homage," expresses for him the proper attitude and posture with which to approach Jesus. It is used of the Magi who traveled from afar to Bethlehem in search of Jesus (2:2, 8, 11). It describes the demeanor of the leper, whose individual healing is the first one Matthew recounts (8:2). The father of the dead girl displays this attitude (9:18), as do "all in the boat" after Jesus calms the storm (14:33). This double expression appears in Matthew's account of the parable of the unforgiving servant as the kind of conduct that won his temporary reprieve (18:26). Matthew uses the combination again of a woman, the mother of the sons of Zebedee, who makes a request of Jesus for her sons (20:20). And finally, it is the same combination of verbs "come" and "do homage" that appears when the women went to see the tomb and met Jesus on their way to proclaim to the other disciples the resurrection message (28:9). For Matthew, the Canaanite woman exhibits all the right stuff.

---

[32] For example, Mark pictures Peter's answer to Jesus "You are the Messiah" (Mark 8:29) followed by Jesus' instruction for the disciples not to tell anyone (8:30). Immediately afterward, Peter "rebukes" Jesus for speaking of his impending suffering and death, to which Jesus responds with his own "rebuke" to Peter: "Get behind me, Satan" (8:33). Matthew, however, embellishes Peter's confession of Jesus' identity, "You are the Messiah, the Son of the living God," and has Jesus answer with a blessing, "Blessed are you, Simon son of Jonah. . . . I will give you the keys to the kingdom of heaven" (Matt 16:16-17, 19).

3. More Women Changed by Jesus

Chapter 2 dealt with women changed by miracles worked as a result of their encounter with Jesus. In this chapter we will consider women changed by contact with Jesus or with the Gospel, but not through miracles. There are ordinary women like the one who went out for water and met him at the well. Maybe not so ordinary is the one who was rousted from her home as a suspect in a case of adultery. But the encounter does not involve miracles save the amazing power of understanding, of forgiveness, of acceptance.

―――――――――

"He told me everything I have done" (John 4:39).

THE SAMARITAN WOMAN

Suggested Reading: John 4:4-42

The Samaritan woman provides such an interesting contrast to Nicodemus, the Jewish leader who came to Jesus at night (John 3). When he meets this woman, Jesus, we are told, is on a journey. He appears tired and thirsty. He stops at the well of Shechem[1] in Samaria. With his disciples off buying provisions, Jesus requests a cup of water from a townswoman. Here's how John tells the story.

―――――――――

[1] Also called Sychar, as in the New American Bible translation. Shechem appears in some manuscripts.

91

[4]He had to pass through Samaria. [5]So he came to a town of Samaria called Sychar, near the plot of land that Jacob had given to his son Joseph. [6]Jacob's well was there. Jesus, tired from his journey, sat down there at the well. It was about noon. [7]A woman of Samaria came to draw water. Jesus said to her, "Give me a drink." [8]His disciples had gone into the town to buy food. [9]The Samaritan woman said to him, "How can you, a Jew, ask me, a Samaritan woman, for a drink?" (For Jews use nothing in common with Samaritans.) [10]Jesus answered and said to her, "If you knew the gift of God and who is saying to you, 'Give me a drink,' you would have asked him and he would have given you living water." [11][The woman] said to him, "Sir, you do not even have a bucket and the cistern is deep; where then can you get this living water? [12]Are you greater than our father Jacob, who gave us this cistern and drank from it himself with his children and his flocks?" [13]Jesus answered and said to her, "Everyone who drinks this water will be thirsty again; [14]but whoever drinks the water I shall give will never thirst; the water I shall give will become in him a spring of water welling up to eternal life." [15]The woman said to him, "Sir, give me this water, so that I may not be thirsty or have to keep coming here to draw water."

[16]Jesus said to her, "Go call your husband and come back." [17]The woman answered and said to him, "I do not have a husband." Jesus answered her, "You are right in saying, 'I do not have a husband.' [18]For you have had five husbands, and the one you have now is not your husband. What you have said is true." [19]The woman said to him, "Sir, I can see that you are a prophet. [20]Our ancestors worshiped on this mountain; but you people say that the place to worship is in Jerusalem." [21]Jesus said to her, "Believe me, woman, the hour is coming when you will worship the Father neither on this mountain nor in Jerusalem. [22]You people worship what you do not understand; we worship what we understand, because salvation is from the Jews. [23]But the hour is coming, and is now here, when true worshipers will worship the Father in Spirit and truth; and indeed the Father seeks such people to worship him. [24]God is Spirit, and those who worship him must worship in Spirit and truth." [25]The woman said to him, "I know that the Messiah is coming, the one called the Anointed; when he comes, he will tell us everything." [26]Jesus said to her, "I am he, the one who is speaking with you."

[27]At that moment his disciples returned, and were amazed that he was talking with a woman, but still no one said,

"What are you looking for?" or "Why are you talking with her?" [28]The woman left her water jar and went into the town and said to the people, [29]"Come see a man who told me everything I have done. Could he possibly be the Messiah?" [30]They went out of the town and came to him. [31]Meanwhile, the disciples urged him, "Rabbi, eat." [32]But he said to them, "I have food to eat of which you do not know." [33]So the disciples said to one another, "Could someone have brought him something to eat?" [34]Jesus said to them, "My food is to do the will of the one who sent me and to finish his work. [35]Do you not say, 'In four months the harvest will be here'? I tell you, look up and see the fields ripe for the harvest. [36]The reaper is already receiving his payment and gathering crops for eternal life, so that the sower and reaper can rejoice together. [37]For here the saying is verified that 'One sows and another reaps.' [38]I sent you to reap what you have not worked for; others have done the work, and you are sharing the fruits of their work."

[39]Many of the Samaritans of that town began to believe in him because of the word of the woman who testified, "He told me everything I have done." [40]When the Samaritans came to him, they invited him to stay with them; and he stayed there two days. [41]Many more began to believe in him because of his word, [42]and they said to the woman, "We no longer believe because of your word; for we have heard for ourselves, and we know that this is truly the savior of the world." (John 4:4-42).

It seems that we have here a very ordinary scene, a commonplace event. A male traveler asks a native woman for a cup of water. Travel is difficult, even today, in the Middle East, but especially at midday when the weather is warm. It was much more so in Jesus' time. So Jesus stops to rest, and his disciples all go off in search of food. But there are several extraordinary elements about this seemingly ordinary scenario. For example, the woman comes alone to the well, at high noon. This is unusual. It would be customary for women to gather water in groups, early in the morning or later in the day, around dusk. Jesus initiates a conversation with her, beginning with a request, or rather a command, "Give me a drink" (John 4:7). Even spouses did not talk with one another in public. The woman challenges his manners, as much on the grounds that he is a Jew as that he is a man. (This, by the way, is the single time Jesus is referred to as a Jew in the Gospels.) Jesus does not rise to the bait but assures her that he could give her living water. She misunderstands this to mean "flowing water," such as would be required for purification rites, or a *mikveh*. She is being sarcastic when she asks if he thinks he is greater than Jacob, who is associated with the well where they have met.

This is no mere banter or one-upmanship. The conversation proceeds, with both Jesus and the woman leading each other from a concrete level to an increasingly more spiritual, meaningful, theological level. Jesus and this female stranger become engaged in deep reflection. She shows a knowledge of the history that has long separated the Samaritans from the Jews and caused so much hostility between them. She also shows her understanding that they share a longing and a hope for a Messiah. Jesus prods her to an even deeper level. He already "knows" her, and she accepts that, although she is puzzled how.

The conversation is lengthy. We can notice two distinct parts to it: verses 7-15 are characterized by misunderstanding; in verses 16-30 the woman shows herself open and receptive to Jesus' revelation. She herself becomes a witness for others to the truth he has revealed to her.

Here we have John at his best. Yet, if we read it only at a superficial level, we may finish the chapter wondering why this encounter made such an impression on the evangelist that he includes it in his Gospel when even he admits that he cannot include everything that Jesus said and did (see John 21:25). There is no miracle or parable here. Why is this meeting and this conversation included in John? This Samaritan woman will be remembered because she was changed from an outcast shunned by others to a witness whom others heard and through whom others believed because they also came to know Jesus.

The Samaritans were age-old enemies of the Jews and especially of the Jerusalem Temple, which came to symbolize the tensions between them. The patriarchs Abraham, Isaac, and Jacob lived in the north. The shrines of Bethel, Shechem, and Mount Gerizim attested to their religious experiences there and lived in the memory of the Samaritans as sacred places. This northern area was anti-monarchy; the period of the united kingdom, with its capital in Jerusalem to the south, lasted a mere hundred years under Saul, David, and his son Solomon.

The people to the north located their capital in Samaria when the kingdom was divided. According to the Samaritans, their own traditions reached much further back than the monarchy and were much more important.

In Shechem, Abraham and Jacob had both built altars to mark the places of their encounters with God. Jacob's well, featured in our story, is in Shechem, and the "holy mountain" (presumably Mount Gerizim) mentioned by the woman, is nearby. Shechem was a major religious and political center, second only to Jerusalem. The city of Shechem was for the Samaritans what Jerusalem was for the Jews.[2] A Samaritan temple had been located nearby overlooking the city. But this had been destroyed in 107 B.C.E. by John Hyrcanus, the Hasmonean Jewish ruler who governed the south. During the Roman period, Shechem and Jerusalem competed with one another, if not to gain Rome's favor, at least to be spared Rome's wrath.

Jesus and his disciples were returning from Galilee to Jerusalem, about thirty-five miles to the south, when this encounter took place. When John says that Jesus "had to pass through Samaria," he is referring to a theological necessity. Many Jews took a longer route, on the other side of the Jordan, to avoid the land of the Samaritans, whose general opposition to Jews is attested in all the Gospels. So Jesus is in hostile territory here. Samaritans were regarded as heretics and unclean by the Jews. Jews would ordinarily avoid handling any vessel or utensil touched by a Samaritan. Certainly Jews would not want to drink from a cup offered by a Samaritan. Thus the woman asks sarcastically, "How can you, a Jew, ask me, a Samaritan woman, for a drink?" (4:9).

But the woman can identify with Jesus, for she, too, is an outcast. She comes alone to the well at noon because she is ostracized by more respectable women. She has had five husbands; everyone would know that about her. They make a fine pair, Jesus and this woman. Both find themselves shunned by religious leaders. Yet they discuss together the true nature of spirituality and truth. They confront the history of their respective

---

[2] La Moine F. DeVries, *Cities of the Biblical World* (Peabody, Mass.: Hendrickson, 1997) 236.

religious traditions and seek to find common ground that transcends their tensions. And they share their own deep faith.

The woman proves herself to be a worthy student. She knows both her own traditions and those of the Jews. For example, she knows that the Jews await a Messiah who will restore the hopes of the kingdom of David, including Jerusalem and the Temple. This woman appears to be without guile or defensiveness, ready and eager to have her own religious hopes fulfilled. When Jesus tells her that she is living with one who is not her husband, she shows no anger. When Jesus says that salvation will come from the Jews, she remains open-minded and attentive. During their conversation, Jesus leads the women to an ever deeper level of understanding, not only of the history both represent but of the nature of God and of Jesus' own mission. She progresses in her address of Jesus, discarding her apparent initial disdain of him as a "Jew." Intrigued by what he is saying, she calls him "Sir," a title of respect. She moves on to recognize that Jesus is "a prophet." Later she is receptive when he affirms that he is the Messiah, and this is what she tells others. Finally, many Samaritans come to believe that, in fact, he is "the savior of the world" (4:42).

When their conversation is interrupted by the returning disciples, the woman undertakes her own missionary responsibilities. She is not sidetracked by their sexist protests that Jesus is talking to her; she neither excuses nor accuses them. Rather, she hurries back to her own, risking also their rejection. She appears not to have always been so interested in religion and could have wondered whether they would laugh at her. Her witness is simple: "Come see a man who has told me everything I have done" (4:29). Her life is laid open, and she shares what she has experienced and now believes. They follow her.

The outcome unveils the reason why John inserts this encounter among the limited number of events he could include in his account. The Samaritan woman represents all that the Gospel is about. She believes on her own experience, and she tells others so that they can "see" for themselves and believe. The Samaritans begin to believe, not only because she has told them of Jesus but on the basis of their own experience. As John concludes his Gospel, he explains, "These (things) are written that you may [come to] believe that Jesus is the Messiah, the

Son of God, and that through this belief you may have life in his name" (John 20:31).

John uses the literary device of *misunderstanding* to guide the conversation and the readers to a new level of spiritual reflection. For example, the woman's lack of comprehension even of the physical or literal meaning of Jesus' questions serves as an opportunity for Jesus to teach her more, to open her up to more revelation. When he asks her for a cup of water and she answers haughtily, Jesus responds by saying that he could give her living water. After he tells her to go and get her husband, she truthfully answers that she does not have one. Then Jesus further affirms that "true worshipers . . . worship . . . in Spirit and truth" (4:23).

Another technique John uses is *irony*. There are several instances of it in our story. For example, Jesus asks the woman for a drink but then goes on to say that "everyone who drinks this water will be thirsty again." But Jesus himself can give water that will become "a spring of water welling up to eternal life" (4:14). A great irony is that John shows how Jesus was rejected by his own but accepted by the Samaritans. John had just described the Jews' rejection of Jesus with the cleansing of the Temple (2:13-25); and then Nicodemus appears at night to question him but shows an unwillingness to accept and understand the meaning of baptism (chap 3). In contrast, the Samaritan woman engages Jesus and becomes a believer as a result of talking with him. She then goes and tells her townspeople, and many who are likewise open to him. They ask him to "stay with them," another Johannine theme (4:40).

Discovering Jesus, listening to him, is only the beginning. The really hard and more important part is "remaining" with him. Indeed, this idea is raised to a theological level in John. It is the sum and essence of Jesus' command to his disciples, those he comes to call "friends," as he addresses them for the last time before he died. Jesus compared their relationship with him as the branches to the vine, saying,

> Remain in me, as I remain in you . . . . Whoever remains in me and I in him will bear much fruit, because without me you can do nothing. . . . If you remain in me and my words remain in you, ask for whatever you want and it will be done for you. . . . As the Father loves me, so I also love

you. Remain in my love. If you keep my commandments,
you will remain in my love . . . . This is my commandment:
love one another as I love you (John 15:4, 5, 7, 9, 10, 12).

Jesus warns his friends that this sounds simple, but will be difficult, not because of pressure or hostility from outsiders, but because we are in union not only with Jesus but with "one another."

Just as the women who were healed by Jesus were returned
to their families, so this Samaritan woman returns to her people.
Jesus "remains" not only with her but also with them. For
John, the high point of mysticism is communal; loving Jesus
means loving "one another" and remaining in that love. It
never gets any harder or any easier than this.

Like Nicodemus, the Samaritans search Jesus out, but unlike him, they come to believe.[3] It is also ironic that while his
disciples are off in search of food, the woman takes care of
Jesus' needs and gives him water. When the disciples return,
they are scandalized that he is speaking with a woman, but
she goes off to do their missionary work for them!

John is very interested in *symbolism,* one of his favorite theological tools. We are meant to go beyond the literal meaning to
the deep level of symbolism. There is symbolism in the fact that
Nicodemus came at night, while the woman encounters Jesus at
high noon. There is symbolism in the darkness that did not accept Jesus and the light. Water also has a great deal of significance in John's Gospel. Water has been an essential part of the
stories of Cana, of Nicodemus, and of the Samaritan woman. At
Cana, water was transformed into wine, another symbol. In the
episode of Nicodemus, water is a symbol for rebirth. Jesus is
speaking about baptism, even though Nicodemus does not
understand his meaning. John implies that Jesus might have
been leading him on: the term *anothen* in 3:3, 7, 31, which
Nicodemus takes to mean born "again," could also mean born

---

[3] The willingness of the Samaritans to accept Jesus is also developed
by Luke, for example, in the parable of the good Samaritan (Luke 10:29-
37). The Samaritans are contrasted with Jesus' own people, who reject
him, according to all four Gospels. Nicodemus is pictured as indecisive in
John 3; he appears to have become a disciple by the time of Jesus' burial
when he brings the spices required to anoint Jesus "according to the Jewish burial custom" (John 19:39-40).

"from above." John deliberately uses a term with a double meaning. In any case, Nicodemus takes Jesus' words literally, asking how a grown person can reenter the womb. Finally, the woman in our story is led from thinking about "flowing water" literally to an understanding that Jesus is the revealer of God. John ends her lesson when Jesus reveals that "God is Spirit, and those who worship him must worship in Spirit and truth" (4:24). The woman ultimately accepts the symbolism of the water, and it is on her word that others are brought to faith.

It is also characteristic of John to show that Jesus replaces former Jewish feasts and practices. Jesus is the revelation of God, the intimate child of God, and the surest way for us to come to God. As such, Jesus replaces all Jewish feasts and in-stitutions, all other means of access to God, and makes them irrelevant. Neither Mount Gerizim nor Mount Zion, where Jerusalem is located, is important. Jesus is the way, the truth and the life. He is the living water. He is the revelation that supersedes any temple made by hands.

John makes it clear that we are in the debt of the Samaritan woman. Like the other people Jesus encounters who are recep-tive to him, she is an apostle (the term means "sent") for us. She brought out Jesus' meaning for us, leading him in dia-logue and asking our questions. Later in John, Jesus will bless disciples such as she is for their faith. Perhaps more impor-tantly for us, Jesus will bless us through them, saying in prayer to his Father, "I pray not only for them, but also for those who will believe in me through their word" (John 17:20).

"Go, [and] from now on do not sin" (John 8:11).

A WOMAN JUDGED FORGIVEN

Suggested Reading: John 7:53–8:11

Jesus is seated in the Temple when a woman accused of adultery is brought to him by "scribes and Pharisees." His seated posture portrays him as a teacher of the Law. Even his opponents, although they seek to entrap him, recognize him as such. Jesus' "judgment" is not a condemnation of the woman but an invitation to a totally new life free of sin. The encounter between Jesus and the woman is an opportunity for her to begin a new life "from now on."

> [53]Then each went to his own house, [1]while Jesus went to the Mount of Olives. [2]But early in the morning he arrived again in the temple area, and all the people started coming to him, and he sat down and taught them. [3]Then the scribes and the Pharisees brought a woman who had been caught in adultery and made her stand in the middle. [4]They said to him, "Teacher, this woman was caught in the very act of committing adultery. [5]Now in the law, Moses commanded us to stone such women. So what do you say?" [6]They said this to test him, so that they could have some charge to bring against him. Jesus bent down and began to write on the ground with his finger. [7]But when they continued asking him, he straightened up and said to them, "Let the one among you who is without sin be the first to throw a stone at her." [8]Again he bent down and wrote on the ground. [9]And in response, they went away one by one, beginning with the elders. So he was left alone with the woman before him. [10]Then Jesus straightened up and said to her, "Woman, where are they? Has no one condemned you?" [11]She replied, "No one, sir." Then Jesus said, "Neither do I condemn you. Go, [and] from now on do not sin any more" (John 7:53–8:11).

This synoptic-like story appears as an intrusion in John. The incident plays no role in Jesus' visit to Jerusalem for the feast of Tabernacles. This story apparently floated around in the tradition in written form until it finally settled here in John's Gospel without much context.[4] Here we have a striking account of an event that "probably has its roots in the ministry of Jesus."[5] Christian scribes would not have wanted to leave it out but seemed to have been in a quandary about where to insert it. It finally nestled here in the Gospel of John, although it sounds a lot more like a Lukan story and has noticeable Lukan characteristics.[6]

---

[4] It appeared at various places: after John 7:36; 7:44; 52 or 21:25 and also after Luke 21:38. See Francis J. Moloney, *The Gospel of John*, Sacra Pagina 4 (Collegeville: The Liturgical Press, 1998) 259.

[5] Ibid.

[6] For example, Jesus isolates himself, alone at prayer before this teaching scene; see Luke 4:42; 6:12; 9:18; 11:1; 21:37-38; 22:39-46.

There are a number of factors that attest to the historical basis for this story and for its consistency within the Christian tradition. For example, Jesus' reaction to his opponents and to the woman in this story are like his interactions with such people in many other stories (e.g., Mark 12:15; Luke 10:25; Matt 22:35-36). We learn of the punishment for adultery not only from the Old Testament but from other Gospel texts, such as Mark 10:2. There is, depending on the circumstances, a double standard of punishment for men and for women. Jesus opposes certain authoritative defenders of the Mosaic tradition. Especially in the Synoptics these are called "scribes and Pharisees."[7] One of the charges against Jesus that is of particular concern to his opponents is that he forgave sin on his own authority. All these elements of our story contribute to its historicity, that is, to the likelihood that it could have happened during the time of Jesus' earthly ministry, and probably did.

The synoptic Gospels frequently make clear that Jesus is an observant Jew but that his interpretation of the Law put him at odds with certain *leaders* of Judaism with different interpretations. John is often more problematic for the modern reader, since ordinarily John indiscriminately refers to Jesus' opponents as "the Jews." One explanation for this might be that when John wrote, near the end of the first century, many of the Jewish groups that provided diversity during Jesus' life in the thirties (e.g., the Sadducees, the Essenes, the zealots, the Herodians, as well as the Pharisees) had been weakened or eliminated under the Romans, especially during the Jewish-Roman wars of 66–72. The dominant party in a restructuring of Judaism after the destruction of the Temple were the Pharisees, the teachers, who strongly influenced the direction of the synagogues. As Christianity was defining itself as open to Gentiles and developing in house churches, it also identified "Jews" with those who were not accepting Jesus as the Messiah nor the Gospel he preached.

The story of the woman caught in adultery appears as a controversy story, but there is more to it than controversy. The point is not the defeat of Jesus' opponents who exit, bowed but

---

[7] See Mark 2:16; 7:1, 5; Matt 5:20; 12:38; 15:1; 23:2, 13-15; Luke 5:21, 30; 6:7; 11:53; 15:2.

not broken. The whole point is in the encounter between Jesus and the woman who are left alone, center stage. But first we need to set the stage.

The structure of the story betrays the fact that it seems to have "floated" around, unanchored to this or any other specific context. There is an introduction in 7:53–8:2, which first has Jesus at prayer, alone. Everyone else went to his or her own home. The setting of Jesus' prayer, the Mount of Olives, across the Kedron Valley from the Temple Mount, is another reminder of the Synoptics, especially of the night Jesus was arrested (see Mark 14:32; Matt 26:36; Luke 22:39). He spent that night in prayer, the Synoptic writers tell us. According to Luke (21:37), Jesus lodged on the Mount of Olives the last days before he died.

Then suddenly the scene completely changes. Jesus is in the Temple, surrounded by a large group of people. And Jesus is teaching them. This scene provides the backdrop for the story. This is a public forum. The drama unfolds as his opponents try to catch Jesus in a conflict with the Law of Moses.

The grouping of Jesus' opponents as "scribes and Pharisees" occurs in the Synoptics, but only in this section of John. They bring before him a woman "caught" in the act of adultery; their intention is to use her to "get" Jesus. For most of the story she is but a prop, an object used in the story. This only changes when Jesus speaks to her directly. These teachers challenge Jesus, "What do you say about her," that is, this obvious sinner? Their question is not designed to see if he knows what Moses says but to see if he will answer with something they can use against him. This is another situation that reminds us more of the Synoptics than of John.

It would seem at first that since it occupies most of the telling, the confrontation between Jesus and his opponents is the main concern of the story. The woman is passive and facing certain death. The tension is strong, and Jesus and the woman seem to be grossly outnumbered. The crowds make the situation explosive; the Temple setting solemnizes the drama. But Jesus turns away and begins to draw with his finger on the ground. Some have speculated about what he wrote. The sins of the accusers? Some alternative quotations to the ones these lawyers and learned people were using to indict the woman? It is impossible to know. But we do have Jesus in a posture that would seem to take him out of the picture entirely, as if bored with these proceedings, maybe even as if doodling to show his disinterest. Jesus turns away and ignores them all.

They persist in their questioning about the dilemma they have presented to him. The woman remains an object. So Jesus stands up, as if to enter the debate. Readers can almost feel the tension mounting again. The opponents are hopeful that they will now "get to" Jesus. But then Jesus reverses the roles, taking charge of the situation with his own challenge: "Let the one among you who is without sin be the first to throw a stone at her." Normally witnesses are the first to throw the killing stones. The accusers also serve as the executioners. Jesus' words about throwing the first stones are not the most surprising part of this story.

But then, Jesus again turns away, as if more interested in the dust than in his opponents' practiced attempts at entrapment. This is probably the moment that intrigues many readers the most. John simply notes that, "in response, they went away one by one, beginning with the elders." What happened here? Just previously, it seemed they tasted sure victory. Interestingly, some manuscripts even added, "Because of their consciences." This supplies a presumed reason for their change of heart; they had to face their own consciences and convict themselves of sin.

We might even reason that they were admitting to setting up the woman and her sexual partner, in order to "catch" her and thus to use her to get to Jesus. After all, how is it that they were able to witness her sin? Further, they may even have realized their own double standard; how is it that they caught the woman and not her partner? Can they honestly execute her and not the man she was with? While fascinating questions, these are not the ones the text is concerned about. Jesus' challenge is that the accusers can only participate in the execution of a sinner if they know that they themselves have not sinned. But, as they are experts in the Jewish Scriptures, that is not possible. All have sinned and all are in need of God's mercy. That is fundamental to any biblical spirituality. This is an anecdote to illustrate the truth of the command, "Stop judging, that you may not be judged."

Finally, in the last two verses, the point of this story is presented. Nothing is said of what happened to "all the people." It seems that they, too, have been confronted with their own sin and have vanished. In any case, Jesus is left alone with this woman. Up to this point she has been completely passive, exposed and defenseless because she is guilty. She does not say a word, neither defending herself nor asking for mercy. Jesus again stands and confronts her, inquiring, "Has no one condemned you?" These are the first words addressed to the woman. Jesus personalizes her, inviting her to take an active part in her own story, to respond. She is transformed.

The Law says that witnesses are needed, and they have all gone away. She answers, "No one, *kyrie* (i.e., sir)". And Jesus says, "Neither will I condemn you." Finally we have a Johannine statement. It reminds us of the testimonial on the meaning of baptism in chapter 3, supposedly on the lips of Jesus but really the reflection of the evangelist, who said, "For God so loved the world that he gave his only Son, so that everyone who believes in him might not perish but might have eternal life. For God did not send his Son into the world to condemn the world, but that the world might be saved through him" (John 3:16-17). In Jesus, God "judges" the world, according to John, but his judgment is salvation, not condemnation.

Jesus confirms his judgment of the woman with a command, "Go, and from now on, do not sin any more." His judgment offers the gift of a new life, free from sin. For John, there are only two moments: before faith and after faith. The woman was sinful, condemned, facing death, exposed, humiliated, treated as an object. Then she encounters Jesus. She is personalized and given life. Her accusers, who were also Jesus' opponents, wanted to take away even her physical life. Now these have left the scene, banished by their own judgments, and Jesus invites her to share in the eternal life he offers the world. This is why he came, or better, why he was sent. Although we do not know of what happened to her after that, her story is remembered in the Church because she was transformed by her encounter with Jesus. This is a turning point for her; she ought not return to the way of sin that leads to death.

"Do you see this woman?" (Luke 7:44).

THE WOMAN WHO SHOWED GREAT LOVE[8]

Suggested Reading: Luke 7:36-50

We group this story with three others (the Samaritan woman, the woman judged forgiven, and the daughters of Jerusalem) in this chapter because they are examples of "women changed by Jesus." The emphasis of this "change" is on what these women have become as a result of this encounter. In the story presented in Luke 7:36-50, Simon is challenged by Jesus to really "see this woman" for who she is and thus to understand the motivation for her actions. She anoints Jesus out of her great love.

Too often already the title of the story given in various Bible translations presupposes that the woman is to be seen as a sinner, probably a prostitute. But that is certainly not Luke's point in recounting this story. The fact that she had been a sinner and the nature of her sin is irrelevant. Indeed, concerns about these things are really at the heart of why Luke incorporates the story the way he does. He wishes to dispel such concerns once and for all. Here Luke explains that a woman who had been a sinner is now transformed into a person whose gratitude and love inspire all her actions.

> [36]A Pharisee invited him to dine with him, and he entered the Pharisee's house and reclined at table. [37]Now there was a sinful woman in the city who learned that he was at table in the house of the Pharisee. Bringing an alabaster flask of ointment, [38]she stood behind him at his feet weeping and began to bathe his feet with her tears. Then she wiped them with her hair, kissed them, and anointed them with the ointment. [39]When the Pharisee who had invited him saw this he said to himself, "If this man were a prophet, he would know who and what sort of woman this is who is touching him, that she is a sinner." [40]Jesus

---

[8] This title is borrowed from Barbara Reid. Its significance will be explained in the following commentary: see Reid, *Women in the Gospel of Luke*, 107–123.

said to him in reply, "Simon, I have something to say to you." "Tell me, teacher," he said. ⁴¹"Two people were in debt to a certain creditor; one owed five hundred days' wages and the other owed fifty. ⁴²Since they were unable to repay the debt, he forgave it for both. Which of them will love him more?" ⁴³Simon said in reply, "The one, I suppose, whose larger debt was forgiven." He said to him, "You have judged rightly." ⁴⁴Then he turned to the woman and said to Simon, "Do you see this woman? When I entered your house, you did not give me water for my feet, but she has bathed them with her tears and wiped them with her hair. ⁴⁵You did not give me a kiss, but she has not ceased kissing my feet since the time I entered. ⁴⁶You did not anoint my head with oil, but she anointed my feet with ointment. ⁴⁷So I tell you, her many sins have been forgiven; hence, she has shown great love. But the one to whom little is forgiven, loves little." ⁴⁸He said to her, "Your sins are forgiven." ⁴⁹The others at table said to themselves, "Who is this who even forgives sins?" ⁵⁰But he said to the woman, "Your faith has saved you; go in peace" (Luke 7:36-50).

Our story is often confused with other accounts of women anointing Jesus found in the other Gospels (Mark 14:3-9; Matt 26:6-13; John 12:1-8). Yet there are significant differences in these accounts, which may suggest either that they are based on different anointings or that they are based on the same event, but adapted by the Gospel writers for distinctly different reasons. One account is found at the beginning of the Passion story in Mark, whose account Matthew closely follows. An unnamed woman anoints Jesus' head. Another story is found in John, who tells us that Mary, the sister of Lazarus and Martha, anointed Jesus when he visited their home in Bethany, on the Mount of Olives, just across the valley from Jerusalem. In the accounts of Mark, Matthew, and John, this woman anoints Jesus for his burial. She uses expensive ointment. Some witnesses object that this is a waste and that the money could better have been spent on the poor.

Our discussion of this story told as an introduction to the passion of Jesus by Mark, Matthew, and John will appear later in chapter 5. In the present chapter we are focusing on Luke's version of this story and his portrayal of the changes in this woman as a result of her encounter with Jesus. We can summarize the differences in the accounts, using a table of comparison.

Luke 7:36-50	Mark 14:3-9/Matt 26:6-13	John 12:1-8
unnamed woman, known as a sinner	unnamed woman	Mary, sister of Lazarus and Martha
house of Simon the Pharisee	house of Simon the leper	house of Martha and Lazarus
in Galilee	Bethany	Bethany
washed feet with tears, wiped them with kisses, hair	anointed head with expensive ointment	anointed feet with expensive ointment
objection: by Simon— if he were a prophet, he would know that woman is a sinner	by "some" that money wasted could have gone to the poor	by Judas that money wasted could have gone to the poor
Response of Jesus: parable about 2 debtors— she has been forgiven; she loves much	Leave her alone— she has done a good thing anointing in anticipation of Jesus' burial	anointing in anticipation of Jesus' burial
They asked themselves, "Who is this who even forgives sins?"		
Jesus said to the woman, "Your faith has saved you, go in peace."		

These differences in the telling, together with its setting in the course of Jesus' ministry rather than near the end, as an introduction to the Passion, indicate that Luke clearly has a different purpose than the other Gospel writers in including this story.

Luke likes to contrast the people of his stories; for example, only in Luke do we hear about the differing prayers of the Pharisee and the publican, the "righteous" person and the tax collector, a known sinner (Luke 18:9-14). Pharisees were respected teachers in the synagogues, the local Jewish centers of liturgy and study that had gained in prominence especially since the exile in Babylon six hundred years before Jesus' birth. The Pharisees are so important because at the time of the writing of the Gospels,[9] the Temple had been destroyed. Its leadership was largely replaced by the synagogues, where rabbis (that is, teachers) were the recognized authorities. The Pharisees were the dominant group that was giving shape to the Mishnah (a rabbinic commentary on the Law) and, eventually, the Talmud.

The Law and its interpretation became all the more important in the absence of the Temple. Thus the teachings of the rabbis, or Pharisees, provided the foil or backdrop against which the evangelists presented and contrasted the teachings of Jesus and the early Church. The Gospels make it clear that one of the reasons Jesus was rejected was that he did not conform to the expectations of the Jewish leaders, the most powerful of whom were the Pharisees. In the case of our story, the Pharisee named Simon is contrasted with the unnamed woman who anoints Jesus. She becomes the model of hospitality, another important Lukan theme, while Simon, the host who had invited Jesus to his home, neglects even the fundamentals of hospitality.

The name "Pharisees" means "separated or pious ones." As teachers of the Law, they also were public practitioners of the Law. They "separated" themselves from the unrighteous. They had strict ideas about the boundaries that exist and must exist between the holy and the ordinary, between the clean and the unclean. For example, Paul the Pharisee had been known for outstripping all his contemporaries in his zeal for the Law (See Gal 1:13-14). Pharisees by definition did not associate with sinners or other unclean people.

But this woman is described as a "sinner," and Simon will challenge Jesus' very identity because he allows the woman to touch him. As the story unfolds, Luke will make it clear, however, that this woman was no longer a sinner; she performed this loving act of anointing precisely because she had been "forgiven." She had been changed, apparently by some previous encounter with Jesus, although we do not hear about this encounter. Why else would Jesus be the recipient of her act in such lavish gratitude?

---

[9] Mark's around the end of the Second Temple (65–70 C.E.), Matthew's and Luke's around 85, and John's sometime in the 90s.

This woman is described not only as a sinner but as someone who is known to be a sinner. Many presume that this is a euphemism for saying that she is a prostitute. But there is nothing in Luke's story to suggest this. As Barbara Reid argues, in the ancient Middle East, especially in the small towns of Galilee, everyone knew everyone else's business.[10] People were "known to be sinners" for many reasons; if they were in an occupation that brought them into contact with Gentiles who were considered unclean, for example. Thus, tax collectors were considered sinners, not only because they were despised for taking people's money but because they interacted with the Romans. Reid adds that the woman need only to have been ill or disabled or have contact with Gentiles to be "known" as a sinner. In contrast, Simon's remark in verse 39 suggests that her appearance did not indicate that she was a sinner; in fact, Jesus would have had to be a prophet to know that she was a sinner.

Other elements in Luke's story may seem to be responsible for the impression that the woman's reputation as a sinner was gained through prostitution. These include the banquet setting, the alabaster jar of ointment, and the woman's presumably long, loosened hair. Is this woman using her "glory" (as Paul calls women's hair in 1 Corinthians 11:15), that is, is she employing her physical attractions just as she did in her former profession? Luke's allusion to the kisses she gave Jesus' feet might also have a sexual connotation, some assume. But we need to reread this story with fresh eyes to "see" the woman as Jesus invites us to see her rather than as we have been conditioned to see her because of certain prejudices.

We cannot surmise that because, uninvited, she entered the banquet place where men were eating means that she was a prostitute.[11] Although a banquet might be a likely setting for prostitutes to come, neither the language used to describe her nor her clothing nor her demeanor suggests that she is sexually promiscuous. "Banquets" is one of the characteristically Lukan themes and settings. The fact that Jesus shares table fellowship

[10] *Women in the Gospel of Luke,* 116.

[11] Reid mentions that "it is surprising how many modern commentators reinforce Simon's initial perception of the woman and never move beyond that." Ibid., 112–113.

with known sinners subjects him to criticism by the Pharisees and scribes. That is the situation in chapter 15, for example, where Luke tells us that Jesus is at table and "tax collectors and sinners were all drawing near to listen to him" (15:1). At this, the Pharisees and scribes complain that "this man welcomes sinners and eats with them." The criticism provides the context for Jesus' response, which is to show the magnanimity of God's love in searching out and welcoming the poor and the lost and the overlooked. Here is where Jesus illustrates the generosity and prodigal nature of God's love with three parables: the strayed and returned sheep, the lost and found coin, and the dead but now reconciled and alive son.

No one jumps to the conclusion that when Luke says "tax collectors and sinners drew near to him" and the righteous "Pharisees and scribes" objected that Jesus "welcomes sinners and eats with them" that the "sin" of all these people is prostitution. To further illustrate the sexual bias that plagues this story of the woman who anoints Jesus, Reid refers to the call of Peter in Luke's account and the objection of Peter, "Depart from me, Lord, for I am a sinful man!" (Luke 5:8). No one accuses Peter of prostitution![12]

It would be a leap to say that the alabaster jar of ointment is a sexual prop and its expense an indication that prostitution is the source of the woman's means to buy it. Besides, the cost of the ointment is an issue in the other Gospels, but not in Luke's version of this story. Again, the ointment is an element of Luke's emphasis on hospitality rather than on sexuality. Ointment was sometimes used in banquets as a kind of soothing balm for guests and as a perfumed way of dispelling unpleasant odors. Similarly, guests were often greeted with a kiss, a gesture of respect and welcome as much as of affection. Jesus notes that Simon offered neither of these signs of hospitality.

The woman's hair is similarly used to express her loving care of Jesus as yet another personal tool to be put at his disposal. There is no indication that she is being flirtatious or calling attention to herself; rather, she is focusing on Jesus. In fact, although Jesus finally "turns to her," he speaks to his host,

---

[12] Ibid., 115.

Simon, asking, "Do you see this woman?" (Luke 7:44). Jesus himself only addresses the woman at the end (7:50), neither challenging nor correcting her, but affirming her, saying, "Your faith has saved you; go in peace."

There is only one passage in all of the New Testament that serves the speculation that Jesus associated with prostitutes; namely, Matthew 21:31-32. But even that text is inadmissible. There Jesus addresses the chief priests and elders, warning that tax collectors and prostitutes will enter the kingdom of God ahead of them. And, Jesus adds, "When John came to you in the way of righteousness, you did not believe him; but tax collectors and prostitutes did." Matthew is contrasting the self-righteousness and smugness of the religious leaders with those considered least likely to be righteous. Matthew has Jesus warning the leaders against their own arrogance, not describing the actual historical people who made up his band of followers. The point is that if Luke had meant to specify that the woman who anoints Jesus was a prostitute, he would have said so, using one of the many terms for that lifestyle available to him.

The woman of our story is sometimes also confused with Mary Magdalene. There may be some reasonable explanation for this. In the very next passage, Luke will name three women who follow Jesus from Galilee, and one of these is Mary of Magdala, "from whom seven demons had gone out" (Luke 8:2). Mary Magdalene's is a healing story, no less so than the Gadarene demoniac; no one connects that poor man chained to the tombs in the desert with prostitution! (see Mark 5:1-10). These same three women from Galilee surface again at the crucifixion and the resurrection. In the popular imagination, people might make the leap of association between the anointing and Jesus' death and resurrection.[13]

But in Luke's account, this anointing event happens as part of Jesus' earthly ministry and is consistent with other things Luke says about the unlikely people who, in fact, persevere in following Jesus and remain with him until the end. Also,

---

[13] To make it more complicated, Mary of Bethany also anoints Jesus (John 12:1); she, too, is sometimes confused with Mary Magdalene.

Luke's readers who are not limited by anti-woman biases can see that this woman's action represents hospitality, in contrast to the inhospitable neglect of Jesus' host, Simon the Pharisee. More, this woman has the marks of the ideal disciple.

The nature of her former sinfulness and the fact that she "was" (i.e., had been) a sinner are both unimportant, except to the misinformed, like Simon. He is the only one Jesus feels the need to correct. Jesus does so by challenging Simon, "Do you see this woman?" What this woman used to be is specified in verse 37; that she had been forgiven before this dinner is clear from verse 47. Jesus uses the past tense, saying, her "sins have been forgiven." We do not hear that Jesus had encountered her before, but the Gospels make clear that his authority and claim to forgive sins are considered blasphemous. If she had not been forgiven by Jesus, why are her expressions of gratitude directed toward Jesus? Even those who sit around the table come to recognize that she is forgiven, for they ask themselves, "Who is this who even forgives sins?"[14]

Luke seems to have a heightened liturgical sense and, within the context of first-century house churches, a table would be a most appropriate setting for lessons in the Christian community about reconciliation, forgiveness, and *agape*-fellowship. To their Temple or synagogue services, early Christians added gatherings including Gentiles for the "breaking of bread." We know from Paul and Acts that there were questions about how much, if any, of the Jewish Law ought to be observed by Gentiles (who were known sinners) in order to be fully accepted into the Church. No doubt some "righteous" people objected that certain others could not be welcomed because they were sinners. Some argued that faith in Jesus' messiahship was not sufficient in order to be saved.

That faith is indeed sufficient is the primary lesson Jesus teaches as he sits around a table. Jesus' own authoritative statement is found in the story of the woman who was transformed from a sinner into a lover. This is meant to settle this issue for good. It is faith that saves. Luke concludes our story with Jesus'

---

[14] Another story that raises this question is the healing of the paralytic in Mark 2:1-12.

gentle, affirming words to the woman, the same words said to the woman healed of her bleeding affliction of twelve years: "Your faith has saved you: go in peace" (see Luke 8:48; also Mark 5:34). Salvation and peace are often linked as blessings brought by the Messiah. Luke pictures Jesus as saying that these women experience these messianic blessings because of their faith. Faith makes them whole (*shalom*, commonly translated "peace," also means integrity). Luke makes it clear that it is totally irrelevant what she used to be, what sins she used to commit, what ailments used to afflict her. She is changed. Jesus' words about her great love, her faith, her salvation, and her peace explain why she is worthy of remembrance.

"Daughters of Jerusalem, do not weep for me; weep instead for yourselves and for your children" (Luke 23:28).

DAUGHTERS OF JERUSALEM

Suggested Reading: Luke 23:26-31, 48

Luke tells us that along the way to the cross, a "large crowd of people followed Jesus, including many women who mourned and lamented him." Jesus addresses these as "Daughters of Jerusalem." Luke immortalizes these women by marking Jesus' words to them. In the process Luke challenges us to reflect on the experience of the women's transformation.

> [26]As they led him away they took hold of a certain Simon, a Cyrenian, who was coming in from the country; and after laying the cross on him, they made him carry it behind Jesus. [27]A large crowd of people followed Jesus, including many women who mourned and lamented him. [28]Jesus turned to them and said, "Daughters of Jerusalem, do not weep for me; weep instead for yourselves and for your children, [29]for indeed, the days are coming when people will say, 'Blessed are the barren, the wombs that never bore and the breasts that never nursed.' [30]At that time people will say to the mountains, 'Fall upon us!' and to the hills, 'Cover us!' [31]for if these things are done when the wood is green what will happen

when it is dry?" . . . ⁴⁸When all the people who had gathered for this spectacle saw what had happened, they returned home beating their breasts (Luke 23:26-31, 48).

Luke's source, Mark, has only a single transitional sentence between the soldiers' mockery of Jesus and his crucifixion: "They pressed into service a passer-by, Simon, a Cyrenian, who was coming in from the country, the father of Alexander and Rufus, to carry his cross" (Mark 15:21). Here, without further comment, Mark refers to a man named Simon from Cyrene, who is enlisted to help Jesus carry his cross. Cyrene was the capital city of Cyrenica, a Roman province on the north coast of Africa. Simon was probably Jewish, since the Roman executioners forced him to help Jesus. The Romans showed themselves to be particularly heavy-handed during feast days as a way of reinforcing their mastery of the people they conquered. Many Greek-speaking Jews lived in Cyrene. Possibly Simon had come to Jerusalem for the Passover. As he describes Jesus' execution, Luke says that they made Simon "carry [the cross] behind Jesus" (Luke 23:26).

It is possible, although we cannot know for sure, that Mark's further identification of Simon by including his sons' names implies that this family became numbered among Jesus' own disciples. Naming people could indicate that the addressees of the Gospel were familiar with such persons. Mark's mention of Simon triggers Luke's addition of several elements characteristic of his style. Luke develops a more dramatic sense, including attributing dialogue to his characters. We can see Luke's use of inclusion here, tying this story with his account of Jesus' birth. Luke has stressed the journey theme he found in Mark, showing how travel with Jesus requires faith and involves suffering. Luke has demonstrated that Jesus' message is received more by outsiders than by insiders, although Luke is also softer than Mark in his treatment of Jesus' disciples. Finally, but not last, Luke includes women among the witnesses who accompany Jesus along the way and persevere with him to the end, going beyond Jerusalem and even beyond the cross. They are present at the tomb and at the resurrection and even go beyond that. They remain faithful to him as they await the spirit and their mission to go out to the ends of the earth.

Luke inserts a more dramatic sense of the "way of the cross." It is characteristic of Luke to add dialogue and dramatic contrast. For example, from Mark's simple notation that two revolutionaries were crucified with Jesus (Mark 15:27), Luke adds that one of the criminals derided him while the other expressed faith in Jesus (see Luke 23:39-43). Thus Luke is able to show once again the significance of "witnessing." The two robbers both experience the same reality, but only one prays, "Jesus, remember me when you come into your kingdom" (23:42).

In the case of the funeral procession to the cross, Luke's additions restructure the entire scene. The end result is that in Luke the cross is in the center of the picture. On each side is a trio of witnesses. Before the crucifixion we see three sympathetic groups: Simon of Cyrene, the large crowds, including many women who mourned and lamented Jesus, among whom were the weeping daughters of Jerusalem. After Jesus' death, again there are three groups of witnesses: the centurion, who testifies that Jesus was "an innocent man," the crowds who return home beating their breasts, and all his acquaintances, including the women from Galilee, who stand and watch all these events (23:47-49).[15]

Luke uses *inclusion* here, making us think of the beginning of his Gospel. There we were introduced to Simeon's prophecy, we heard of events in Jerusalem, we learned of men who doubted and of women who believed. At Jesus' death we read of another Simon, who helped fulfill the words of Simeon's prophecy that Jesus and his own would suffer. These events happen just beyond the city of Jerusalem which Jesus lamented. And among the witnesses are women who believed, although the men found them to be unreliable. And Luke had noted that when Jesus was born, many Jews received him favorably. Think of Anna and Simeon and the shepherds, for example. Luke will show that the same is true when Jesus died; many bystanders pondered the meaning of these events and were changed by

---

[15] This idea of a "triptych" with the cross at the center is beautifully explained by Raymond E. Brown in "The Gospel According to Luke," *An Introduction to the New Testament* (New York: Doubleday, 1997) 225–278, at 259.

them. Those who "gathered for this spectacle," for instance, went home "beating their breasts" (Luke 23:48). Some Jews received Jesus at his birth; now at Jesus' death there are outsiders like Simon and the women as well as the centurion who represent the Gentiles.

Only Luke has this developed account of Jesus' journey to the place of execution and those who accompanied him. It is an extension of the journey to Jerusalem which Luke, more than the other Synoptics, has already stressed and elongated (in Mark the journey is recorded in 8:27–10:45; in Luke it stretches from 9:51–19:28). In fact, a "journey" is an image that Luke also uses as he develops the sequel to the Gospel in Acts. The Church as described in Acts is also on a journey. Luke refers to the community of believers as followers of the "Way." Throughout the Gospel, Luke reiterates that "large" crowds accompany or follow Jesus. After the resurrection they continue to "follow him."

Luke is softer and kinder, too, to Jesus' disciples. Luke omits Mark's comment about Jesus' disciples that "they all left him and fled" (Mark 14:50) from the Garden. That omission allows Luke to insert the ambiguous note that Jesus' "acquaintances stood at a distance" from the cross. They may be passive and unresponsive, but Luke is unwilling to condemn them or accuse them of fleeing altogether. Perhaps Luke is thinking of the psalmist, who, in a personal lament to God for so much suffering, comments that "my neighbors stand far off" (Ps 38:12). So great and embarrassing to others is the unexplainable suffering of just people that they can complain to God, "Because of you my friends shun me" (Ps 88:9). In any case, Luke rescues the image of the original disciples, at once warning his own audience of how hard it is to persevere and at the same time challenging them to remain with Jesus, despite their fears and weaknesses. Luke leaves open the question of their success; it is up to them.

And always there are the women. Mark and Matthew and John admit that women were there at the end, but Luke tells us how they got there, in the company of Jesus, ministering, listening to him, supporting his mission. It is characteristic of Luke to mention along the way that there were many women following Jesus.

As we have seen often, in miracles and parables for example, Luke typically pairs stories of men with stories of women; thus his allusion to Simon may suggest that he insert here the women who also accompanied Jesus on his way of the cross. The women mourn and lament what is happening to him. This note reminds the reader of the other Simeon's prophecy to Jesus' parents at the beginning of this story: "this child is destined for the fall and rise of many . . . and you yourself a sword will pierce" (Luke 2:34). Jesus' words at the Last Supper also come to mind: turning to his disciples, Jesus said, "It is you who have stood by me in my trials" (22:28).

As he makes his way to Golgotha, Jesus addresses the "daughters of Jerusalem." This could be another of Luke's allusions to the fulfillment of Judaism, since the phrase "daughters of Jerusalem" or its equivalent occurs fairly often in the Old Testament.[16] Yet frequently it has a positive and joyful connotation there. For example, Zephaniah says, "Shout for joy, O daughter Zion! . . . Be glad and exult with all your heart" (3:14). Likewise in Zech 9:9 we read,

> Rejoice heartily, O daughter Zion,
> shout for joy, O daughter Jerusalem!
> See, your king shall come to you;
> a just savior is he,
> Meek, and riding on an ass,
> on a colt, the foal of an ass.

But in Luke 23:28 the phrase has a much different connotation; it carries the tone of Jesus' sadness about the daughters of the city where he meets his own destiny (Jer 9:19-20). Jesus echoes, this time more strongly, his lament of the city known for killing the prophets (see 19:41-44). With his execution the fate of the city is sealed, despite some who are sympathetic. The generation after Jesus will see disasters in Jerusalem. Of the Synoptics, only Luke has Jesus speak at this time and at the crucifixion. It is as if his commentary gives bystanders one more opportunity to see and to hear and to finally understand and accept through the testimony of faith. Luke's combination of drama

---

[16] See, for example, Song 3:5; 8:4; Isa 37:22; Zeph 3:14; Zech 9:9.

and dialogue provides one more example of the recurring theme of giving witness.

The daughters of Jerusalem weep. These women act as the replacement for the professional mourners prescribed in Jewish custom to accompany a corpse to burial. So, for example, we saw the loneliness of the widow of Nain despite being surrounded by a crowd of wailers. As Joseph Fitzmyer indicates, these "daughters of Jerusalem" are distinguished from the "women of Galilee" mentioned in Luke 23:49.[17] The former are not necessarily disciples, but, devout and sympathetic, they may have come out to bewail the execution of a human being. It is not known whether this is customary[18] in the case of a condemned man in Roman times. Jesus turns the tables and bewails the fate of Jerusalem in anticipation of what is to happen there when the Temple is destroyed by the Romans, during their war against the Jews (66–72). Luke challenges the women to draw a lesson from his own fate. They cannot be sure that the forces of evil that have brought him to this hour of darkness are not going to have an effect on their own lives.[19]

Luke pictures Jesus praying often during his life. Once, after they had witnessed Jesus at prayer, his disciples asked, "Lord, teach us to pray" (Luke 11:1-4). Jesus' answer was to teach them the "Lord's prayer," which closes with the most urgent request of all: "do not subject us to the final test." Facing his destiny, Jesus counsels the women of Jerusalem not to weep for him but for themselves and their children. The sense of this warning seems to be that if only they knew what was coming, they would really weep.

For Luke, suffering is inevitable for the followers of Jesus, but it is also an enormous trial, a temptation against faith. The sting of suffering is the strain it puts on faith. In the midst of suffering, it is difficult to resist the temptation either to blame God or to question our own friendship with God. Suffering threatens to break the slender thread that binds us to a merciful

---

[17] J. A. Fitzmyer, *The Gospel According to Luke*, Anchor Bible 28A (New York: Doubleday, 1985) 1496.

[18] Ibid.

[19] Ibid., 1495.

and just God. In the throes of suffering, it is hard to have faith. The coming fate is so terrible that people will consider childlessness a blessing. Jesus is speaking like the prophet he is here. Perhaps Luke is drawing on Isaiah 54:1, which says: "Raise a glad cry, you barren one who did not bear . . . you who were not in labor." It may be better not to have children and be spared seeing them tortured and put to death. This may also be an allusion to Hosea 10:8: Israel of old cried out for mountains and hills to fall on them. The people of Jerusalem will feel the same way. Jesus already spoke about this when he prophesied the destruction of the Temple and its connection spiritually with the "end of the world" (see Luke 21). Jesus said,

> When you see Jerusalem surrounded by armies, know that its desolation is at hand. . . . for these days are the time of punishment when all the scriptures are fulfilled. Woe to pregnant women and nursing mothers in those days, for a terrible calamity will come upon the earth and a wrathful judgment upon this people (Luke 21:20, 22-23).

On the way to the cross, Luke has Jesus pronounce a "blessing" which, like other beatitudes, speaks of a reversal of values. But it is out of intense suffering that people will say, "Blessed are the barren, the wombs that never bore and the breasts that never nursed" (Luke 23:29). A woman had previously "blessed" Jesus and his mother positively, using almost the same words: "Blessed is the womb that carried you and the breasts at which you nursed" (11:27).

Finally Jesus makes an ironic statement, comparing his own confrontation with evil as "green wood," and the situation of later Jerusalem as "dry wood." The meaning of this parablelike saying is disputed; the contrast proceeds from lesser to greater. Fitzmyer suggests that it could mean, "If God allows the innocent Jesus to suffer this fate at the hands of Jerusalem, how much more suffering will Jerusalem's fate involve?" Luke could be thinking of Proverbs 11:31, which says,

> If the just man is punished on earth,
> how much more the wicked and the sinner!

The prophet Ezekiel warned that God was kindling a fire "that shall devour all trees, the green as well as the dry" (Ezek 21:3);

fire is God's punishment, God's indignation and fiery wrath. "You shall be fuel for the fire, your blood shall flow throughout the land," Ezekiel adds in 21:37. Another possibility is a contrast between the wood on which Jesus is crucified, which is not consumed by flames, and the wood of Jerusalem, which will be consumed by flames.[20]

Luke suggests that some will heed Jesus' prophetic warning. Some of this same crowd witness the crucifixion. Luke mentions that people "had gathered for this spectacle," much like crowds gathered to see Jesus' miracles. They are depicted as curious rather than interested. But Luke adds that after they "saw what happened, they returned home beating their breasts" (23:48). Only Luke adds this note of repentance on the part of the people. In Luke 18:13 the tax collector's gesture of "beating his breast" is a clear indication of guilt and contrition. Repentance and forgiveness are two more themes characteristic of Luke. They add a touch of hope to this powerful scene.

Luke stresses the inevitability of suffering as a by-product of "following" Jesus. Although Luke often refers to the "large crowds following" Jesus, he will also show that prayer is necessary if people are to persevere in being his disciples. Indeed, "following" Jesus and persevering have a theological connotation. At the beginning of the Gospel, Jesus calls disciples with the words, "Follow me" (see Mark 1:17; 2:14; Luke 5:11, 27). Throughout the Gospel, Luke pictures Jesus as accompanied by a large following (Luke 6:17; 7:11-12; 8:4; 9:37; 11:29; 19:3). He often reminds these men and women of the high cost of discipleship, of the need not only to undertake the journey but to remain faithful despite obstacles. And the road will involve huge and myriad personal sacrifices. Luke stresses the hardships of following Jesus, saying,

> If anyone comes to me without hating his father and mother, wife and children, brothers and sisters, and even his own life, he cannot be my disciple. Whoever does not carry his own cross and come after me cannot be my disciple (Luke 14:26-27).

[20] See Fitzmyer, *The Gospel of Luke*, 1498; also see Isa 10:16-19; 1 Pét 4:17-18.

Jesus says much the same thing in another place: "If anyone wishes to come after me, he must deny himself and take up his cross daily and follow me" (9:23). Of the early days of Jesus' journey to Jerusalem, Luke writes:

> As they were proceeding on their journey someone said to him, "I will follow you wherever you go." Jesus answered him, "Foxes have dens and birds of the sky have nests, but the Son of Man has nowhere to rest his head. . . . No one who sets a hand to the plow and looks back to what was left behind is fit for the kingdom of God" (Luke 9:57-58, 62).

In sending out his seventy disciples, Jesus warns them of the dangers that await them:

> [Jesus] said to them, "Go on your way; behold, I am sending you like lambs among wolves. Carry no money bag, no sack, no sandals" (Luke 10:3-4).

The Gospel destination for Jesus is Jerusalem. Luke noted already in chapter 9 that Jesus "resolutely determined to journey to Jerusalem" (9:51). Luke is careful to show that Jesus died, however, outside Jerusalem. He was crucified in a place called Golgotha. It seems that Luke wishes to demonstrate that Jesus fulfilled all the prophecies, all of Judaism. His execution outside the city that Jesus called "killer of prophets" (13:34) means that Jesus has now gone beyond Jerusalem. For Luke, the time of the prophets and of Israel is completed with the ministry of Jesus. The time of the Spirit is at work in the Church of both Jews and Gentiles. Now is a time of universal salvation.

At the end of his Gospel, Luke pictures Jesus addressing his disciples, saying, "Thus it is written . . . that repentance, for the forgiveness of sins, would be preached . . . . to all the nations, *beginning* from Jerusalem" (Luke 24:46-47). At the start of Acts, Jesus will say to his disciples, "You will be my witnesses, in Jerusalem, throughout Judea and Samaria, to the ends of the earth" (Acts 1:8). In Acts, Luke portrays the journey of the Church as spreading out from the closed doors of the Upper Room in Jerusalem (1:13) to Rome, where Luke leaves us with the enduring picture of Paul under house arrest (28:30-31). But Luke insists even at the very end of Acts that nothing could stop the spread of the Gospel—not the execution of the leaders, Peter and Paul, nor the suspicion of the Jews nor the hostility of Rome. The very last line of Acts insists, "without hindrance he proclaimed the kingdom of God" (28:31). For Luke, Jerusalem is the place of the fulfillment of the promises made to Israel; but this is only the beginning of the age of the Spirit which was poured out on the Church.

4. Women of Prominence

Celsus, a second-century pagan writer, derided Christianity, claiming that it deliberately excluded educated people. He added that it was only attractive to the "foolish, dishonorable and stupid, and only slaves, women and little children" joined its ranks.[1] But that judgment is not supported by other non-Christian writers, nor does it seem justified by evidence from the New Testament. The diversity of social backgrounds of Christians is notable, for example, if we compare Peter, the Galilean fisherman, with Paul, the well-educated Pharisee from Tarsus. But this diversity might be even more significant in the profiles of women who became Christian. And far from lowering our evaluation of the impact of Christianity on the world because it did attract women, we are more and more impressed with their contribution the more we get to know them.

The women introduced to us in the New Testament are of mixed social, economic, racial, and ethnic backgrounds. We come to know aristocrats (though they are in the minority, it is true) and slaves, women who owned their own homes and had their own businesses, mothers, wives and single women, widows and women with connections. In this chapter we will consider what the New Testament says about some women of prominence: women like Pilate's wife, who had the ear of the Roman governor, and women like the mother of James and John, who

---

[1] Celsus's judgment is quoted in Wayne A. Meeks, *The First Urban Christians: The Social World of the Apostle Paul* (New Haven: Yale University, 1983) 51.

had the ear of Jesus. We read again the story of how Herodias used her influence to get the head of John the Baptist, and how Priscilla used her learning and skills to teach the eloquent Apollos a thing or two about Jesus. The New Testament women do not fit a single profile. They are too versatile for that.

"Herod feared John, knowing him to be a righteous and holy man" (Mark 6:20).

HERODIAS AND HER DAUGHTER

Suggested Reading: Mark 6:14-29; Matthew 14:1-12; Luke 9:7-9

Here we have a story that conforms to some popular images of women and their potentially destructive influence on men. It is important to note that neither Herodias nor her daughter (whom Josephus, the Jewish general turned Roman historian, identifies as Salome) encounter Jesus. Herodias may not even have met John the Baptist either. But her hatred of him is very strong in any case. Herodias used her influence to bring down John because he dared to fulfill his role as prophet in challenging the Jewish leader, Herod Antipas.

Mark 6:14-29

[14]King Herod heard about it, for his fame had become widespread, and people were saying, "John the Baptist has been raised from the dead; that is why mighty powers are at work in him." [15]Others were saying, "He is Elijah"; still others, "He is a prophet like any of the prophets." [16]But when Herod learned of it, he said, "It is John whom I beheaded. He has been raised up."

[17]Herod was the one who had John arrested and bound in prison on account of Herodias, the wife of his brother Philip, whom he had married. [18]John had said to Herod, "It is not lawful for you to have your brother's wife." [19]Herodias harbored a grudge against him and wanted to kill him but was unable to do so. [20]Herod feared John, knowing him to be a righteous and holy man, and kept him in custody. When he heard him speak he was very much perplexed, yet he liked to listen to him. [21]She had an opportunity one day when Herod, on his birthday, gave a banquet for his courtiers, his military

officers, and the leading men of Galilee. [22]Herodias's own daughter came in and performed a dance that delighted Herod and his guests. The king said to the girl, "Ask of me whatever you wish and I will grant it to you." [23]He even swore [many things] to her, "I will grant you whatever you ask of me, even to half of my kingdom." [24]She went out and said to her mother, "What shall I ask for?" She replied, "The head of John the Baptist." [25]The girl hurried back to the king's presence and made her request, "I want you to give me at once on a platter the head of John the Baptist." [26]The king was deeply distressed, but because of his oaths and the guests he did not wish to break his word to her. [27]So he promptly dispatched an executioner with orders to bring back his head. He went off and beheaded him in the prison. [28]He brought in the head on a platter and gave it to the girl. The girl in turn gave it to her mother. [29]When his disciples heard about it, they came and took his body and laid it in a tomb.

Matthew 14:1-12

[1]At that time Herod the tetrarch heard of the reputation of Jesus [2]and said to his servants, "This man is John the Baptist. He has been raised from the dead; that is why mighty powers are at work in him."

[3]Now Herod had arrested John, bound [him], and put him in prison on account of Herodias, the wife of his brother Philip, [4]for John had said to him, "It is not lawful for you to have her." [5]Although he wanted to kill him, he feared the people, for they regarded him as a prophet. [6]But at a birthday celebration for Herod, the daughter of Herodias performed a dance before the guests and delighted Herod [7]so much that he swore to give her whatever she might ask for. [8]Prompted by her mother, she said, "Give me here on a platter the head of John the Baptist." [9]The king was distressed, but because of his oaths and the guests who were present, he ordered that it be given, [10]and he had John beheaded in the prison. [11]His head was brought in on a platter and given to the girl, who took it to her mother. [12]His disciples came and took away the corpse and buried him; and they went and told Jesus.

Luke 9:7-9

[7]Herod the tetrarch heard about all that was happening, and he was greatly perplexed because some were saying, "John has been raised from the dead"; [8]others were saying, "Elijah

has appeared"; still others, "One of the ancient prophets has arisen." [9]But Herod said, "John I beheaded. Who then is this about whom I hear such things?" And he kept trying to see him.

The story of the death of John the Baptist and the collusion of Herodias and her daughter in that death appear as a flashback in the Gospel of Mark, followed by Matthew. Luke only alludes to the death of John under Herod, without telling of any role in this tragedy for the women in Herod's life. Herod thinks that Jesus is John *redivivus*, returned to life. Clearly Herod's conscience is bothering him. The Gospels agree with Josephus in this respect; Herod was wrong to have executed John. Josephus assigns a political reason for his having put John to death. Mark ascribes his death to the machinations of Herodias. Matthew lays the blame at the feet of a weak, dishonorable leader while downplaying the roles of Herodias and Salome. Luke gives only theological reasons for John's execution: John is a prophet like Elijah. Herod couldn't bear the prophet's honesty. Herod killed his conscience.

We have very few sources outside the New Testament to support the information we have there. Only two non-Christian writers appear to be roughly contemporaneous with some of the events we hear about in the New Testament. Philo was an Alexandrian Jewish philosopher whose writings help us better understand New Testament times. Like the Christian Apollos, as he is described in Acts 18:24, Philo is interested in relating Judaism to Greek philosophy. Another non-Christian first century writer named Josephus gives us another window into life then. Josephus was a Jewish general who defected to Rome sometime before the Jewish-Roman wars of 66–72. Josephus appears very eager to ingratiate himself with Rome and to show how sincere and complete was his conversion. That makes some of his information suspect because it is obviously so self-serving. But Josephus, taken with a grain of salt, does provide some very interesting information that we would not otherwise know.

Gospel readers remember Herod the Great from Matthew's infancy narrative (see Matt 2:1-19). Herod was a particularly cruel person whose credentials were suspect. He was from Idumea, a region to the south, and he had been schooled among

Romans. He was granted the title "king of the Jews" by the Roman senate in 40 B.C.E. apparently because they wanted to give the impression that the people of Palestine could govern themselves. But Herod was despised by the Jews. He put his own sons to death out of jealousy over their popularity. Matthew's story of the slaughter of the innocents captures some of the flavor of Herod's maniacal paranoia. When Herod died around 4 B.C.E., his kingdom was divided among his remaining sons, who were known as "tetrarchs," a title meaning "ruler of a fourth." Among Herod the Great's sons were Herod Antipas and Philip, who each ruled over a part of Galilee at the time of Jesus.

Mark and Matthew mistakenly identify Herodias as the former wife of Philip, whom she abandoned to marry Herod Antipas. Actually, as Josephus notes, Herodias had been married to Herod Antipas's paternal half uncle, whom she discarded for the nephew. Later, it seems, Salome, daughter of Herodias, would marry Philip, her own half uncle. Mark erroneously identifies Herod Antipas as "king," a misnomer Matthew at first corrects in Matthew 14:1, referring to him as Herod the tetrarch. But in 14:9, Matthew reverts to the title "king" of his source, Mark. Perhaps this is so because the rowdy palace party described as the setting for this miscarriage of justice is reminiscent of Esther's appearance before her husband the king, and Matthew often draws on the Old Testament, stressing the notion of "fulfillment" (Esth 5:3-6).

Josephus attributes the execution of John to Herod's political envy and fear. John was a popular prophet. Herod Antipas is competing on many fronts to stay in power. If the Romans suspect that he cannot control the Jewish people, they could replace him as they did his brother Archelaus, who had ruled briefly in Jerusalem. The Romans banished Archelaus and replaced him with a Roman governor, of whom Pilate was one. It is Luke who adds the note in the passion story that when Pilate heard that Jesus was a Galilean, that is from the region of Herod's jurisdiction, Pilate sent Jesus to him (see Luke 23:5-12). Luke adds further that Herod was curious to see a miracle, but when that did not happen, he returned Jesus to Pilate. And finally Luke says that Pilate and Herod, formerly bitter enemies, became friends that day.

Herod Antipas feared that John could successfully lead rebellion in his territory, so he imprisoned John and finally executed him. That is is why John died, according to Josephus. Matthew's account of John's death also assigns blame primarily to Herod, although for more religious reasons. Matthew is interested in the leaders. He assigns to leaders blame for the Jews' rejection of Jesus. And Matthew challenges Church leaders to set a good example, to devote themselves to the "little ones."

The evangelists often draw on the Old Testament Scriptures not only for inspiration but to help fill in the gaps of their sometimes scanty sources. Mark's presentation attributes John's execution to the hatred of Herodias, whose evil cunning to rid herself of a prophet who crossed her evokes the Old Testament image of Jezebel, who was married to Ahab, king of Israel (1 Kings 19, 21). Jezebel imported pagan idols and pagan prophets, and Elijah spoke out against her. Out of jealousy, Jezebel hounded Elijah for years. Matthew's presentation of this story, while following Mark, attributes blame for John's death to a weak and vacillating King Herod. Matthew obscures the role of Herodias and her daughter; the result is that Matthew gives a confusing account as to why and how they are involved. The Baptist more directly confronts the king himself in Matthew's account, while the women provide only a subplot.

In order to personalize the conflict between John and Herod and to give it a religious context showing John as a prophet, Mark and Matthew give the motive of John's protest that Herod is living in incest, with his "brother's wife."[2] This is forbidden in Leviticus 18:14: "You shall not disgrace your father's brother by being intimate with his wife"; and 20:21: "If a man marries his brother's wife and thus disgraces his brother, they shall be childless because of this incest." As the Gospels tell the story of John, the prophet confronts the king and challenges him for not leading the people in the way of the Law. Certainly that charge fits Herod Antipas, as his behavior in our story clearly shows.

---

[2] One exception is the so-called levirate marriage that allowed a woman to have a child by her husband's brother if he had been the eldest and had left her childless. This privilege is dramatized in the wonderful story of Tamar in Genesis 38.

Mark identifies the real villain as Herodias, whose power with her husband is undermined by John and also by Herod's mixed feelings about John. Mark says, "Herodias harbored a grudge against [John] and wanted to kill him but he was unable to do so. Herod feared John, knowing him to be a righteous and holy man, and kept him in custody" (Mark 6:19-20). Mark had just described the rejection of Jesus by the townspeople of Nazareth (6:1-6). Now Mark shows how their weak and jealous king thinks that Jesus is John come back to haunt him. Herod is pictured as restless and fearful for having put John, a just and good man, to death. Almost as if recounting his nightmare, Mark and Matthew give us a flashback to fill in the details of John's demise.

The images of Herodias and Salome fit a stereotype of woman as seductress and temptress. For example, Old Testament Wisdom literature contains many warnings against giving too much influence to women.[3] The vacillating king is pushed over the edge of decency by a young girl and a conniving woman whose own power is threatened. First Herodias enlists her daughter to seduce her husband. Then Herodias counsels her daughter to make a gruesome request for John's head.

In Mark, Herod is portrayed as a drunk, a braggart, fearful of reneging on a promise to a little girl in front of guests. His reputation outweighs any sense of justice, his fears outweigh the value of human life. He appears not at all kingly but subject

---

[3] For example, Sirach 9:2 says, "Give no woman power over you / to trample on your dignity," and in 9:8, Sirach continues, "Through women's beauty many perish, / for lust for it burns like fire." A pervasive view is the androcentric interpretation of Genesis 3 expressed in Sirach 25:23: "In woman was sin's beginning / and because of her we all die." This is a view carried over into the New Testament with insinuations that women are more gullible and susceptible to temptation than men: for example, in 2 Corinthians 11:3, Paul says, "But I am afraid that, as the serpent deceived Eve by his cunning, your thoughts may be corrupted from a sincere [and pure] commitment to Christ." Such a view seems to overlook the inevitable conclusion that men are thereby portrayed as even more weak and gullible, since they apparently "fall" so readily, and without moral resistance of their own.

to one of the weakest members of society—a young girl. The death of John will be all the more tragic because Herod does not really want to order it. If he could have postponed it just one day, he might have sobered up and changed his mind. He might have had the courage to confront his wife. But in Mark, John dies at the will of this young girl who is a patsy for her mother.

Matthew attributes more blame to the king (tetrarch) and thus lifts some of it from Herodias. Throughout his Gospel, Matthew is interested in leadership. He has the king confront the prophet. He may be closer to the historical reasons Josephus also mentions. But the outcome is the same. The king abuses his power. Even Josephus agrees that the death of John was wrong and that Herod was punished for it.

"[Pilate's] wife sent him a message,
'Have nothing to do with that righteous man.
I suffered much in a dream today because of him'" (Matt 27:19).

PILATE'S WIFE

Suggested Reading: Matthew 27:15-23

[15]Now on the occasion of the feast the governor was accustomed to release to the crowd one prisoner whom they wished. [16]And at that time they had a notorious prisoner called [Jesus] Barabbas. [17]So when they had assembled, Pilate said to them, "Which one do you want me to release to you, [Jesus] Barabbas, or Jesus called Messiah?" [18]For he knew that it was out of envy that they had handed him over. [19]While he was still seated on the bench, his wife sent him a message, "Have nothing to do with that righteous man. I suffered much in a dream today because of him." [20]The chief priests and the elders persuaded the crowds to ask for Barabbas but to destroy Jesus. [21]The governor said to them in reply, "Which of the two do you want me to release to you?" They answered, "Barabbas!" [22]Pilate said to them, "Then what shall I do with Jesus called Messiah?" They all said, "Let him be crucified!" [23]But he said, "Why? What evil has

he done?" They only shouted the louder, "Let him be crucified!" (Matt 27:15-23).

The "story" of Pilate's wife is actually told in a single verse,
and only by Matthew. Whereas Herodias escalated the crisis to
bring about the death of the Baptist, this unnamed woman of
Matthew's passion narrative intervenes with her powerful husband to try to stop the condemnation of the "just man" Jesus.
Matthew manages to say quite a lot with this one sentence.

The scene shows Pilate sitting on the judgment seat. He is reluctant to follow the prompting of the Jewish leaders because he
can find no cause to have Jesus executed. Pilate sought a way
out in a traditional "gift" he as governor gave to the Jews on the
important feast of Passover. It was his custom to release to them
one prisoner that they asked for. He hoped, Matthew says, that
they would have a change of heart about Jesus, whom he knew
they "handed over" out of envy. So, in his official capacity, Pilate wonders whether he and they can avoid a dilemma in re-
leasing Jesus now. But suddenly, out of nowhere, comes word
from his wife, who admonishes him, "Have nothing to do with
[the murder of] that righteous man. I suffered much in a dream
today because of him." Pilate's fears about Jesus' innocence are
confirmed from this off-stage voice, and now he is all the more
eager to be rid of his role as judge of Jesus.

Readers will be reminded of other dreams in Matthew's
Gospel and what they symbolize. Especially in the infancy
narrative, dreams played the role familiar to them from the
Old Testament. Dreams are a divine medium, warning people
to take or to avoid a certain action. Thus, for example, Joseph
is warned in a dream to take Mary and their baby to Egypt to
flee the atrocities of Herod. Similarly, the Magi are warned not
to return to Herod but to go home by another route. This dream
of Pilate's wife functions as a warning that Pilate should have
"nothing to do" with Jesus. This is not just a woman's fantasy,
it is a divine message.

Further, the dream revealed Jesus' identity to this woman.
Jesus is indeed "righteous," an honored and completely desirable description of the person truly seeking God. Matthew is
steeped in the Old Testament, which often repeats the mantra
that justice is found in God alone. But God revealed justice

through the Torah, through the prophets. And God finally promised to send a Messiah who would teach us the way of justice (see 3:15). Jesus is this person. In the Sermon on the Mount, Jesus says, "Seek first the kingdom [of God] and his righteousness (justice) . . ." (Matt 6:33). Matthew has Pilate's wife correctly identify Jesus as "just," even though the religious leaders fail to do so. While they lobby and conspire for the release of the unjust Barabbas and the execution of Jesus, this female outsider is divinely inspired to plead on behalf of Jesus the just one.

Pilate's wife's advice is very appropriate for Matthew's context. The notion of innocence (see 27:19, 23, 24) and the unjust shedding of blood (27:24-25) are important parts of the entire passion narrative.[4] Matthew is the only Gospel writer to record the suicide of Judas, an act committed because he realized he had shed "innocent blood" (Matt 27:3-10). Matthew often employs the so-called prophecy-fulfillment schema. That is to say, he usually shows how a prophecy, such as might be represented in the medium of the dream in which God speaks, is somehow fulfilled. The passage about Judas's suicide, while part of the Christian tradition (note that it is found also in Acts 1:15-20), might serve as a warning to others who refuse to accept Jesus. This is one of the functions of such a prophecy as this being fulfilled. That prophecy-fulfillment relationship is often signaled by a use of the same terminology in the two passages. Here the similar terminology has to do with the shedding of innocent blood.

Pilate's wife says that she has "suffered much" on account of Jesus. This is a phrase more typical of Mark than of Matthew. Mark attributes it to Jesus twice in the midst of his passion predictions: "The Son of Man must suffer greatly . . . and be killed" (see Mark 8:31; 9:12). The only other time the phrase "suffer much" occurs in Mark is in reference to another woman, the one who suffered from a hemorrhage for twelve years (5:26). "Suffering much" is a mark of a disciple according to

---

[4] See Donald P. Senior, *The Passion Narrative According to Matthew*, Bibliotheca ephemeridum theologicarum Lovaniensium (Leuven: Leuven University Press, 1975) 242–248, at 245.

the Gospels; Mark especially suggests that this is in imitation of Jesus. But the Gospels would also emphasize that this is not suffering for suffering's sake. Pilate's wife appears to want her suffering to be meaningful, to at least ensure that she and her husband do what they can to avoid complicity in the death of Jesus. Her suffering was a result of not knowing what action to take. She clarified for Pilate what God's inspiration told her. She tried to influence her husband to judge on the side of justice rather than injustice.

Since his "parable chapter" (Matthew 13), Matthew has been distinguishing between the real Israel and the pseudo-Israel. He has shown that oftentimes the outsider is more receptive to Jesus' message than the Jewish leaders. This verse about Pilate's wife (27:19) creates a dramatic parallel between two sets of intercessors: Pilate's wife pleads for Jesus, and the Jewish hierarchy, the "high priests and elders," plead for Barabbas. The dream is the key. Jesus' innocence is attested by God, while the choice for Barabbas is prompted by blindness and envy on the part of those who could not get truthful witnesses (see Matt 26:60). As the figures in the scene wring their hands and shrug their shoulders in nightmarish discomfort, Jesus alone remains serene and unmoved. While the governor appears as powerless in seeking truth or doing the right thing, his divested wife uses all the power she can muster to avoid her husband's complicity with injustice. The majesty of Jesus and God's control of events are emphasized at the expense of the leaders.

Note that Matthew omits Mark's comments on the significant role of women in the death of John the Baptist. Mark attributed his death to the conniving and collusion of Herodias and her daughter. Matthew lays the blame for John's death on Herod. But in the instance of the condemnation of Jesus, it is the wife of another powerful ruler, Pilate, who intercedes for Jesus. So not only does Matthew exonerate women in the case of John the Baptist, but he alone asserts the positive role of a woman in trying to secure Jesus' release. And it is only Matthew who claims the role of intercessor of yet another woman, the mother of Zebedee's sons, in a pericope that has its roots in all three Synoptics.

> *"There were many women there, looking on from a distance,*
> *who had followed Jesus from Galilee, ministering to him.*
> *Among them were . . . the mother of the sons of Zebedee"*
> (Matt 27:55-56).

THE MOTHER OF ZEBEDEE'S SONS

Suggested Reading: Matthew 20:20-28 (see Mark 10:35-45) and
Matthew 27:55-56 (see Appendix, pages 266–267)

Matthew follows Mark for the context of this story, but it is only in Matthew that we hear about this woman's request for preferential treatment for her sons; in Mark the sons of Zebedee ask for privileges for themselves. But we need to go to yet another passage found only in Matthew to get the rest of the story. The mother of the sons of Zebedee is specifically identified by Matthew as one of the women who followed Jesus from Galilee and was at the foot of the cross when he died (see Matt 27:55-56). Here's how Matthew introduces the "mother of the sons of Zebedee."

20Then the mother of the sons of Zebedee approached him with her sons and did him homage, wishing to ask him for something. 21He said to her, "What do you wish?" She answered him, "Command that these two sons of mine sit, one at your right and the other at your left, in your kingdom." 22Jesus said in reply, "You do not know what you are asking. Can you drink the cup that I am going to drink?" They said to him, "We can." 23He replied, "My cup you will indeed drink, but to sit at my right and at my left, [this] is not mine to give but is for those for whom it has been prepared by my Father." 24When the ten heard this, they became indignant at the two brothers. 25But Jesus summoned them and said, "You know that the rulers of the Gentiles lord it over them, and the great ones make their authority over them felt. 26But it shall not be so among you. Rather, whoever wishes to be great among you shall be your servant; 27whoever wishes to be first among you shall be your slave. 28Just so, the Son of Man did not come to be served but to serve and to give his life as a ransom for many" (Matt 20:20-28).

And here is how Matthew illustrates how well this woman learned the lessons of discipleship. She mastered them at the foot of the cross.

> [55]There were many women there, looking on from a distance, who had followed Jesus from Galilee, ministering to him. [56]Among them were Mary Magdalene and Mary the mother of James and Joseph, and the mother of the sons of Zebedee (Matt 27:55-56).

Again we have a woman identified by the men in her life. She is at an age when she is entitled more by her sons than by her husband. Usually James is named first,[5] so it can be presumed that he is the eldest. Her husband, Zebedee, is not mentioned in his own right, but, like her, in relation to his sons. Yet at least he, unlike her, has a name. Since nothing is said about his being a disciple of Jesus, perhaps he is deceased and this woman is a widow. That situation would help explain why she is free to accompany her sons and Jesus on their journey from Galilee to Jerusalem. Matthew follows Mark in noting that three times in the course of his journey, Jesus predicts his passion.[6] There is a pattern to this part of Mark's story. The three passion predictions are each followed by misunderstanding on the part of one or more disciples; this misunderstanding becomes the occasion for Jesus' further instruction on the meaning of the journey and its implication for those who accompany him. The whole journey, then, becomes a kind of instruction on the high cost of discipleship.

In order to understand what Mark is saying and the changes Matthew makes to this story, we have to digress to consider the synoptic Gospels' portrayal of the followers of Jesus. First, note that several terms are used to describe the makeup of Jesus' entourage. There are the "Twelve," who are named and listed in the three Synoptics and in Acts,[7] although they are not

---

[5] Except in Acts 1:13, where John appears before James.

[6] See Mark 8:31-33; 9:30-32; 10:32-34; Matt 16:21-27; 17:22-23; 20:17-19.

[7] See their names in Mark 3:16-19; Matt 10:2-4; Luke 6:14-16; Acts 1:13-14. These are referred to simply as the Twelve in other places: for example, Mark 6:7; Luke 9:1.

named in John. These Twelve compose an identifiable group of men; the number "twelve" represents the fulfillment of God's promises to the twelve tribes of Israel.

Among these Twelve is the triumvirate of Peter, James, and John, who appear to be especially favored by Jesus. They were among the first called to follow Jesus (see Mark 1:16-20). Jesus began his ministry with the call of two sets of two brothers (Andrew, Peter's brother, was also called at the very beginning). Peter, James, and John are invited by Jesus to accompany him to the Mount of the Transfiguration and also to the Garden of Gethsemane (see Mark 9:2; 14:33 and par.).

In addition to this group of identifiable men, the Synoptics contend that there was a wider circle of followers known as "disciples" and some known as "apostles." The term "disciples" means "learners," whereas the term "apostles" means "sent." There is some overlap in these designations, for, at a certain moment of the journey, Jesus sends out his disciples to do the work he has done himself and taught them to do. Luke, for example, says that Jesus sent out the Twelve first, then another seventy (see Luke 9:1-6; 10:1-12). In Acts, Luke implies that out of the pool of apostles and disciples, the leaders of the early Church chose one to fill the place vacated by the traitor Judas Iscariot. Candidates had to be someone who has been "among us, beginning from the baptism of John" (see Acts 1:21-22). Paul makes it clear that although he did not know Jesus during his earthly ministry, he, Paul, was truly an apostle; in fact, he insisted on this title. Paul also refers to others as apostles, including in one instance, at least, a couple named Andronicus and Junia (see Rom 16:7).

There are other indications that women as well as men were disciples and apostles. Women accompanied Jesus on his journey from Galilee to Jerusalem, and that is one of the ways disciples and apostles are described in the Gospels. Women were at Jesus' death, and they were there at the empty tomb to witness to the resurrection. Women heard the word and "embraced it" (see Luke 8:15). They attached themselves to Jesus unconditionally and for life. They are the first witnesses to their male counterparts of the resurrection.

One of the major areas of discussion about the Gospel of Mark has to do with the fairly negative if not downright pejorative portrait he paints of the Twelve, including even the three who appear to be so close to Jesus. For Mark, all of them fail, despite the instructions and the fellowship extended to them by Jesus. Mark tells us that in the Garden, all his followers abandoned him and ran away. None were at the cross except for a few women who had followed him from Galilee and who looked on at a distance. And even they seem to be a disappointment when they run away in fear from the empty tomb (see Mark 16:8). Mark portrays an unrelieved failure of discipleship that seems to involve everyone, but certainly indicts the Twelve and even Peter, James, and John.

Returning to our pericope, it is clear from his treatment of the Twelve that Mark's Church was struggling with problems of leadership. Mark is writing at a time when Christians faced persecution and martyrdom from Rome and rejection by Jews. It may be that Mark is not really trying to malign the reputations of Peter and the other leaders so much as to show the Christians he was addressing that the Twelve were not without their own fear and misgivings, sufferings and need for correction, encouragement and perseverance. Some Christians may have been scandalized by the fact that their hopes and faith in Jesus did not preserve them from intense suffering and even death. Mark may have been trying to get such believers to identify with Peter, who had, as a matter of fact, been just as reluctant to accept suffering but who had faced martyrdom and death under Nero only a few years before Mark wrote.[8]

While scholars debate why Mark portrayed them as he did, no one can deny that the Twelve and even the triumvirate of Jesus' favorite companions are not spared disgraceful failings in Mark. The scene in the Garden of Gethsemane is a good example. Although Jesus selects Peter and James and John to

---

[8] Peter was killed under Nero around 64 C.E. Mark was writing somewhere between 65–70 C.E. The Roman-Jewish wars were in 66–72 C.E. Mark was writing when his world and the world of his Church was disintegrating. It may be hard to believe that he is intentionally undermining the authority of the early leaders. It may be easier to understand that he is trying to relate the experience of his Church to the feelings and fears of these leaders, thereby actually reinforcing the faith of his audience.

accompany him, to watch and pray with him the night before he died, they appear weak and listless, falling asleep and unable to respond to Jesus' request for support. Peter's denial of Jesus is a chilling example of discipleship failure. Mark spares no one when he describes the dullness and ineptitude even of Jesus' closest associates.

After the first prediction of the passion, Peter shows his misunderstanding by "rebuking" Jesus when he speaks about suffering (Mark 8:31-33). Jesus responds by "rebuking" Peter, saying, "Get behind me, Satan. You are thinking not as God does, but as human beings do" (8:33). After the second prediction of the passion, Mark shows that all the disciples misunderstand Jesus, since they immediately start bickering about which of them is the greatest (9:30-32). Jesus teaches them that such concerns are not to be theirs. Jesus sets a child before them and says, "If anyone wishes to be first, he shall be the last of all and the servant of all" (9:35). After the third prediction of the passion (10:33-34), James and John approach Jesus and request special honors when he comes into "his glory" (10:37). Jesus replies that they do not know what they are asking, saying that indeed they will share in the "cup" of suffering that he drinks (10:38).

And this is the real point. Peter and James, we know, did suffer martyrdom.[9] Mark does portray the failings of Jesus' followers, but the Church is built on faith in Jesus, not on the courage or strength of any human leaders. Thus, Mark has Peter and James and John make stupid statements and ask silly questions. These become the occasion for Jesus' instruction about how different it all is in the kingdom of God.

When Matthew first introduces the mother of Zebedee's sons, Jesus and his entourage are near Jerusalem, toward the end of his journey. Matthew is following his source Mark here but makes some changes that might now be more understandable in the light of the way Mark treats Jesus' disciples. Matthew often attempts to protect or improve the image of the

---

[9] Acts says that Herod Antipas had James, the brother of John, killed and found that it pleased the Jews. So Herod attempted to have other believers killed, including Peter. See Acts 12:1-3.

disciples that Mark projects. For example, in Matthew, when Peter says that Jesus is the Messiah, Jesus blesses Peter; there is no rebuke of Peter as there is in Mark (compare Mark 8:33 with Matthew 16:16-19). And where Mark says that James and John ask for special privileges for themselves, Matthew puts this request on the lips of their mother. In Matthew, even she can be excused for making such a request because Matthew noted that Jesus took the Twelve aside to explain to them once again his purpose in going to Jerusalem (Matt 20:17). It is as if she makes a request that is legitimate albeit self-serving, since she was not privy to the discussion Jesus just had that included her sons. Yet it is interesting that even Matthew's defense of the Twelve is not complete. The mother's role disappears as Jesus directly addresses her sons in 20:22. There Jesus speaks directly to James and John and promises them that they shall indeed drink of the cup of his suffering.

Matthew shows that the lesson about the necessity of suffering was not lost on this mother either. Only Matthew says that the mother of the sons of Zebedee was at the cross. Mark had identified the women who were at the cross as "Mary Magdalene, Mary the mother of the younger James and of Joses, and Salome. These women had followed him when he was in Galilee and ministered to him. There were also many other women who had come up with him to Jerusalem" (15:40-41). The third named woman in Mark is Salome, a person who is not mentioned further in the New Testament but whom we can assume was known to the early Christians, or at least to the community Mark addressed. Matthew substitutes "the mother of the sons of Zebedee" for this third woman. Perhaps Matthew's community did not know Salome; but they did know or they had heard of the mother of Zebedee's sons previously in Matthew. The first evangelist likes to tidy up loose ends. When he introduces a topic, he tends to go back and tell the rest of the story. Only Matthew had inserted this woman into the course on discipleship Jesus gave to his followers on the way to the cross. Like her male counterparts, she misunderstands the purpose of this journey. Her previously skewed view of Jesus' messiahship had prompted her to request an inappropriate favor for her sons. But unlike her male counterparts, she needs only a mid-course correction to adjust her perspective. Matthew hastens to add her to the disciples at the foot of the cross to show that she learned the most important lesson of discipleship. She is willing to follow Jesus unconditionally and without limit to the self-sacrifice involved.[10] She goes the distance, even to the cross and beyond.

"Why did you agree to test the Spirit of the Lord?" (Acts 5:9).

SAPPHIRA

Suggested Reading: Acts 5:1-11

The story of Sapphira and her husband Ananias is enough to shock us and send a shudder of fear through us. They appear to be a well-meaning couple who conspire to withhold only a portion of the proceeds from a sale of property for themselves rather than putting the whole purchase price at the service of the community. So they lie about the profit they received, setting aside some for themselves. As John Gillman puts it, they keep back some of the money for security, as if God's providence were not enough.[11]

> [1]A man named Ananias, however, with his wife Sapphira, sold a piece of property. [2]He retained for himself, with his wife's knowledge, some of the purchase price, took the remainder, and put it at the feet of the apostles. [3]But Peter said, "Ananias, why has Satan filled your heart so that you lied to the holy Spirit and retained part of the price of the land? [4]While it remained unsold, did it not remain yours? And when it was sold, was it not still under your control? Why did you contrive this deed? You have lied not to human beings, but to God." [5]When Ananias heard these words, he fell down and breathed his last, and great fear came upon all who heard of it. [6]The

---

[10] In keeping with his tendency to search the Old Testament Scriptures for profiles of some of his characters, Matthew might have modeled this woman on the mother of the sons of Zebedee, who strongly and gently showed her sons the way to martyrdom (see 2 Macc 7).

[11] See John Gillman, *Possessions and the Life of Faith: A Reading of Luke-Acts* (Collegeville: The Liturgical Press, 1991) 98.

young men came and wrapped him up, then carried him out and buried him.

⁷After an interval of about three hours, his wife came in, unaware of what had happened. ⁸Peter said to her, "Tell me, did you sell the land for this amount?" She answered, "Yes, for that amount." ⁹Then Peter said to her, "Why did you agree to test the Spirit of the Lord? Listen, the footsteps of those who have buried your husband are at the door, and they will carry you out." ¹⁰At once, she fell down at his feet and breathed her last. When the young men entered they found her dead, so they carried her out and buried her beside her husband. ¹¹And great fear came upon the whole church and upon all who heard of these things (Acts 5:1-11).

We are probably shocked at the severity of the punishment of these people, for it seems reasonable to take care of one's own. Isn't that better than ourselves becoming dependent on the community? The offering these people do make seems generous and praiseworthy, and the ingratitude of the community and of leaders like Peter seems outrageous and extreme. What is going on here?

The problem is dishonesty and hypocrisy, both disallowed in a true community of faith that practices a witness of total unity of mind and heart. Perhaps the context of Acts can shed some light on Luke's purpose in telling this story and the possibilities of its meaning for us. Even the first-time reader of Acts has to be struck by the dynamic operating there. In one passage after another Luke will eloquently describe the unity and harmony of the early Christian community, as he does in the summary of 2:42-47.

⁴²They devoted themselves to the teaching of the apostles and to the communal life, to the breaking of the bread and to the prayers. ⁴³Awe came over everyone . . . . ⁴⁴All who believed were together and had all things in common; ⁴⁵they would sell their property and possessions and divide them among all according to each one's need. ⁴⁶Every day they devoted themselves to meeting together in the temple area and to breaking bread in their homes. They ate their meals with exultation and sincerity of heart, ⁴⁷praising God and enjoying favor with all the people. And every day the Lord added to their number those who were being saved.

Or again, in 4:32-37:

> [32]The community of believers was of one heart and mind, and no one claimed that any of his possessions was his own, but they had everything in common. . . . [[33]] [34]There was no needy person among them, for those who owned property or houses would sell them, bring the proceeds of the sale, [35]and put them at the feet of the apostles, and they were distributed to each according to need.
>
> [36]Thus Joseph, also named by the apostles Barnabas (which is translated "son of encouragement"), a Levite, a Cypriot by birth, [37]sold a piece of property that he owned, then brought the money and put it at the feet of the apostles.

The reader could easily become nostalgic and long for a revival of these early honeymoon days of the Church. Not only was everyone joined in prayer and mind and thoughts but the total equanimity was expressed in an open and generous sharing of all material goods, so that there was no need, no inequality. It all sounds so ideal. But this same Luke is also quick to add that it was not all that easy. Participation in the community of faith will not only involve generosity and self-sacrifice, but unless we are vigilant in prayer and constantly on guard, Satan will find an opportunity even in the most reasonable of impulses.

Thus Luke, with his penchant for dramatization, balances the idyllic summary of life in the early Christian community with a story that illustrates that there is never room for complacency or half-measures. He may be depending on the Old Testament as inspiration for this story. In Joshua 7:1-26, we are told of Achan, who also withholds a portion for himself of what belongs to God. As punishment, he is stoned to death by the community, according to the order of God. Luke could also be thinking of the rejection of Saul, the first king of Israel, who, against God's wishes, held back a part of the booty both for himself and his friends (1 Sam 15). Luke's story about the not-so-generous couple follows upon, and is in contrast to, the exuberance of Joseph Barnabas, "who placed everything" he received at the feet of the apostles.

Luke emphasizes the importance of witness. He portrays the spread of the Gospel as extending outward, in ever-widening circles, to reach the "ends of the earth." While Christians are required to testify to the Good News of what they have seen and heard, it is also absolutely crucial that this testimony be true, consistent with their own experience. There is a warning implicit in even the most eloquent of Luke's summaries of the unity of the Christian community. The warning says that if we are not fully alive to faith and its demands, we are in danger of dying to the community.

The stark account of the death of Judas is another example of this same dynamic. At the beginning of Acts, Luke tells us that before he ascended into heaven, Jesus gave his disciples a promise and a command. The promise was that they would be baptized with the Holy Spirit (Acts 1:5) and that they would "receive power when the holy Spirit comes upon" them (1:8). The command is linked to this promise: "You will be my witnesses in Jerusalem, throughout Judea and Samaria, and to the ends of the earth" (1:8).

Luke proceeds to describe how the disciples remained together, devoting themselves to prayer. They also undertook the election of one to replace Judas Iscariot. Luke then reminds his readers, in the form of a flashback that was part of Peter's speech, of what happened to Judas. His betrayal was a form of suicide, whether literally or symbolically or both.[12] In any case, Judas cut himself off from the community and from its life. He chose to affirm his betrayal of Jesus in rejecting reconciliation with the community. It was the kind of reconciliation Peter himself must have accepted after his triple denial of Jesus (see Matt 26:69-75; Luke 22:54-62; John 18:15-18, 25-27; Acts 1:13-14). Judas's sin was not merely a fleeting weakness or human inadequacy but a failure to accept grace. His sin is presented as a fatal, mortal act by which he became "dead" to the Church. The startling definitiveness of his fate, like that of Ananias and Sapphira, Achan, and Saul, is meant to shock and to awaken to the seriousness of the choice. For Luke, the choice for or against the Church is for or against the Holy Spirit. But it is not necessarily a single act; it is part of a pattern.

---

[12] Note certain discrepancies in the manner of Judas's death in the accounts of Matthew 27:3-10 and Luke (Acts 1:15-20). Matthew, drawing on Old Testament sources, says that Judas hanged himself. Luke says that he fell headfirst and burst open. Both link his death to the purchase of a field.

In our story, besides the abrupt death of Ananias and Sapphira, Luke uses other terminology that is reminiscent of the Judas story. The crisis involves the purchase of a field. Peter asks Ananias why Satan has filled his heart. Background for the figure of Satan is in the later period of the Old Testament, after the Exile (sixth century B.C.E.); the Hebrew term refers to an adversary of God who belongs to the heavenly realm. Sometimes Satan's activities actually have a positive outcome, as, for example, in the story of Job. In the course of his being tempted by Satan, Job shows himself faithful to God even when he loses everything, including his health, his understanding. God is on Job's side, wagering that Job will remain faithful even when his own interests in piety and faith have been taken away. In the New Testament as a whole, Satan, a term that appears thirty-six times, refers to an intelligent being who tests Jesus. Satan is the adversary against whom Jesus directs his ministry.[13]

In the Synoptics, Jesus' ministry is described as a life-and-death contest with Satan. Satan, also called the "devil," appears on-stage at the beginning of Jesus' ministry and tempts him, as Luke especially shows, to deny the terms of his baptism (Luke 4:13). At his baptism Jesus is declared Son of God. Once he rejects Satan after the temptation, Jesus accepts his sonship by proclaiming his message of freedom for the poor, the outcast, the ill, the handicapped, the disenfranchised. Satan however returns at the passion, entering Judas's heart (Luke 22:3; John 13:27). Jesus is tempted to not accept suffering. It is Luke who relates Satan to Peter also; he pictures Jesus warning Simon Peter at the Last Supper, "Simon, Simon, behold Satan has demanded to sift all of you like wheat, but I have prayed that your own faith may not fail; and once you have turned again, you must strengthen your brothers [and sisters]" (Luke 22:31-32). This is perhaps the one time in Luke's Gospel that Satan's temptation may have had a positive effect, not because of Satan but because of Jesus' prayer for Peter. It appears that after his denial, the climactic moment of his temptation, Peter is stronger and better able to lead others as a witness and as an example.

<hr/>

[13] See R. Schreiter, "Satan," in *The Collegeville Pastoral Dictionary of Biblical Theology*, ed. Carroll Stuhlmueller (Collegeville: The Liturgical Press, 1996) 875–876.

For Luke, temptation is almost always bad.[14] The one positive outcome of temptation may be strengthening one's character. Christian faith sets people on a very difficult road, a road that leads to the cross. The problem for Luke is that people might lack perseverance. Persecution and suffering are temptations in that they can lead to apostasy. Faith is the thin thread that binds us to a faithful God. Temptation threatens faith. Believers might be enthusiastic at first but then give up and give in to temptation, which comes in many forms. Only the fellowship of the community sustained by persistent prayer will empower believers to be faithful despite their "trials," another word for temptation. Luke's version of the Lord's prayer stresses this concern of the evangelist: "do not subject us to the final test" (Luke 11:4).

In Luke, disciples learn to pray as Jesus prayed. They pray that the loving God of Jesus will preserve them from apostasy and despair and guide them along the "way," Luke's name for following the Gospel. Christians need true and worthy models who will exemplify the required perseverance. Joseph Barnabas, of whom we hear much as Acts outlines the growth of the Church, is one such model. Ananias and Sapphira, who live no longer in the Church, are not.

The contemporary reader will appreciate the "feminist consciousness" that seems to have prompted Luke to twice insist that Sapphira was in on Ananias's decision to withhold from the Church (Acts 5:1-2). She seems to participate equally with her husband, or at least he does not make this decision alone but with Sapphira's "knowledge" (Acts 5:2) and consent (Acts 5:1). Peter's question to Sapphira is, "Why did you agree to test the Spirit of the Lord?" (Acts 5:9). This question intimates that she could have made a difference in Ananias's behavior. She and her husband are both liable for deception, and both suffer the same consequences. She becomes as "dead" to the community as he is. Again, in Luke there are no half measures. One cannot

---

[14] J. Fitzmyer says that for Luke it is always bad: "The Gospel of Luke," in the *New Jerome Biblical Commentary,* ed. Raymond E. Brown, Joseph A. Fitzmyer, Roland E. Murphy (Englewood Cliffs, N.J.: Prentice Hall, 1990) 703. However, I believe that what Luke says about Peter's temptation in 22:31-32 may be one exception.

fully participate in the life of the Spirit unless one receives grace "with a generous and good heart, and bear[s] fruit through perseverance" (Luke 8:15). The holding back by Ananias and Sapphira is a "testing" and limiting of the Holy Spirit.

Another word for temptation is trial. Luke sees the world as the forum where witnesses outwardly testify for Jesus and for the kingdom of God or for Satan and the kingdom of Satan. The deadly sin of Ananias and Sapphira is that their testimony is false and misleading. Their own testimony judges them. The question of whether they were historical people who actually died suddenly or whether they are a symbol of death is not really relevant. For Luke the truth is that, regardless of the many pitfalls and threats, persecutions, trials, and failures, the Gospel is spread through the power of the Holy Spirit residing in the Church. People may either participate and cooperate with grace or lose their life in the spirit.

Possessions and money seem to be almost a preoccupation of Luke-Acts. Luke, like Paul, develops a theology about material goods that would be understandable, though an imposing challenge to the Gentiles they addressed. In arguing for the Gentile mission, Paul puts this theology into words, saying,

> For Macedonia and Achaia [i.e., Greek communities] have decided to make some contribution for the poor among the holy ones in Jerusalem [i.e., Jews]; they decided to do it, and in fact they are indebted to them, for if the Gentiles have come to share in their spiritual blessings, they [the Gentiles] ought also to serve them [the Jews] in material blessings" (Rom 15:26-27).

Spiritual goods, the Greeks would agree, are far superior to material goods. If, then, the Jews shared their spiritual blessings with the Gentiles, the Gentiles owe the much less significant material goods to the Jews.

Generalizing this principle, the story of Sapphira and Ananias shows that failure to support the community in material things is evidence that they have not really received and shared to the fullest the spiritual blessings of the early Church. Luke (and Paul) were addressing primarily Gentiles, who in many ways were better off financially than most of the Jews, and certainly, it seems, than the Jewish Christians. These writers had to develop a collective social conscience for the Gentiles that would illustrate their debt to the Jews for their sharing in Israel's spiritual legacy. Luke and Paul indicate that the new family of Jews and Gentiles represented by the Church had priority over all other previous and future commitments. From that full participation in spiritual blessings flows a responsibility to share material blessings.

Sapphira needed to use her status as a Christian and generously support the community without reserve, for that is what she professed to do. Note that she is not condemned with her husband, nor is she condemned because he is. In fact, he does not answer, but she does respond after she is given an opportunity to tell the truth. Women as well as men, by virtue of their common baptism, are full participants in the Church. It should also be noted that although the early Christians argued about whether and under what conditions Gentiles could be baptized, there never seems to have been an analogous argument about whether women could be baptized. And once baptized, they enter into a new community, based on a new definition of the human person and of relationships with one another, the same as men do.

Sapphira's sin makes her an example of one who dared to face temptation without adequate and persistent prayer. She stands as an everlasting negative example designed to warn against hypocrisy and complacency. Sapphira may be part of Luke's shock technique. But if her image causes us to reexamine our own integrity and commitment to the Church as well as our dependence on material goods, we are in her debt.

Finally it must be said that although the specific cause of these deaths has to do with the sharing of possessions, the warning represented by this story is more general. It is about sins against the spirit. The response Luke hopes to elicit is the "great fear" (awe) which seized not only other members of the Church but which spread with this story throughout the whole world. God is Lord of the universe, and people take note of God's power at work in this fledgling group of not-so-powerful people.

Immediately following our story about this man and woman, Luke tells us that both men and women kept joining the Church in great numbers (Acts 5:14). This is a clue that

Luke was not trying to discourage with this story. Sapphira is the first individual woman named in Acts after Mary, the mother of Jesus, was named along with the Twelve in the initial chapter (Acts 1:14). Sapphira who died will find her counterpart in the next named woman, Tabitha, whose life is restored. She is remembered because in contrast to Sapphira, Tabitha "was completely occupied with good deeds and almsgiving" (Acts 9:36).

"I recall your sincere faith that first lived in your grandmother Lois and your mother Eunice and that I am confident lives also in you" (2 Tim 1:5).

LOIS AND EUNICE

Suggested Reading: 2 Timothy 1:5; 3:14-15; see Acts 16:1-3

It is commonplace to note that women are often held responsible for the religious education of children. The same may be said of the women in the biblical tradition. In the Old Testament we can find references warning against the sabotage foreign women might bring to home and hearth, not to mention nation. They will import their own gods, as Jezebel did, influencing people with strange religious ideas. By the same token, marrying within the religious community will contribute to harmony, to the proper education of the children. The goal, of course, is to develop a strong tradition that is passed unbroken through generations, developing good religious thinking and loyalty and behavior based on strong faith.

Among the letters ascribed to Paul, there are three known as the Pastoral Letters. Two of these are addressed to Timothy.[15] In these letters a strong mentor (father)-protégé (son)

---

[15] The three are 1 and 2 Timothy and Titus. Interpreters disagree whether these were actually written by Paul or by one of his disciples. Most tend to think that they reflect circumstances of churches which developed later than around 64, when Paul was martyred under Nero. In

relationship is implied, as between the older Paul and a much younger Timothy. In 2 Timothy we have two short but intriguing passages about Timothy's religious formation. Referring to Timothy's grandmother and mother, 2 Timothy 1:5 says, "I recall your sincere faith that first lived in your grandmother Lois and in your mother Eunice and that I am confident lives also in you." Later this same letter says, "But you, remain faithful to what you have learned and believed, because you know from whom you learned it, and that from infancy you have known [the] sacred scriptures, which are capable of giving you wisdom for salvation through faith in Christ Jesus" (2 Tim 3:14-15).

The second letter to Timothy presents an idealized picture of the perfect religious formation as passing on traditions through generations. As the Torah often instructed, "Teach this to your children"; believe and act in accordance with our beliefs so that others may see faith at work. Integrity is the basis of religious education.

Acts, however, presents a rather different picture of Timothy's religious pedigree than does 2 Timothy. After his disagreement and separation from Barnabas, Paul chooses Timothy as his traveling companion according to Acts 16:1-3, saying:

> [Paul] reached [also] Derbe and Lystra where there was a disciple named Timothy, the son of a Jewish woman who was a believer, but his father was a Greek. The brothers in Lystra and Iconium spoke highly of him, and Paul wanted him to come along with him. On account of the Jews of that region, Paul had him circumcised, for they all knew that his father was a Greek.

Here is an allusion to Timothy's mixed parentage: his mother was Jewish and his father Greek. Not only that, but his Jewish mother had a Greek name (Eunice), as did her mother (Lois). Timothy had not been circumcised. Before setting out with

---

any case, we will refer to the author, as he himself does, as "Paul," without getting into the issue of the authenticity of this claim. These letters are certainly within the Pauline tradition expressed by the Apostle himself in his own authenticated letters.

him, Paul had him circumcised so that he would be more acceptable to "Jews of that region." Timothy had probably been considered Jewish by Gentiles, and a Gentile by the Jews. Luke implies that Paul stabilized and "normalized" Timothy's identity by having him circumcised.

We can assume from other things that Acts and Paul himself say that Paul might have also been concerned about the acceptability of his mission with the Jewish Christians, especially those in Jerusalem, and maybe also in Antioch, where there was a strong sentiment among Christians that Jewish practices ought to be retained. But if Acts is to be believed, it seems that Timothy's mother, Eunice, had not raised Timothy according to her own Jewish tradition in not having him circumcised. Here is an example, as happens often when we compare material from Acts with Paul's letters (or letters ascribed to him), that there are certain discrepancies in the information we have.

Like Paul himself, Timothy is a child of the Diaspora, that is, of a Judaism "dispersed" from the time of the exile in Babylon in the sixth century B.C.E. Timothy's family was from Lystra in Lycaonia. Many scholars trace the practice of matrilinear (that is, children were considered Jewish if their mother was Jewish) Judaism back to the Exile. Yet it is unclear whether this was the custom practiced not only in Palestine but in the Diaspora in the first century. Then as now, we have to speak not of Judaism but of Judaisms. Customs varied widely. And although religious education was often the province of the women, circumcision, for example, would not have been. Circumcision was the responsibility of the father and later of the rabbis. In addition, there might have been reasons why Diaspora Jews would hide their circumcision. In some Greek cities and especially in sports circles, for example, anti-Jewish sentiment sometimes prompted Jewish men to make an effort to cover up or obliterate circumcision in order to be better accepted. Paul could be alluding to something similar to this in 1 Corinthians 7:18-20 where he says, "Was someone called after he had been circumcised? He should not try to undo his circumcision. Was an uncircumcised person called? He should not be circumcised. Circumcision means nothing, and uncircumcision means nothing; . . . Everyone should remain in the state in which he was called."

Whatever the exact historical situation, Acts not only says that Timothy was uncircumcised but that Paul had him circumcised, a decision that sometimes mystifies interpreters in the light of what Paul himself says here in 1 Corinthians and elsewhere. We may not be able to satisfactorily explain the discrepancy between Acts and 2 Timothy or other Pauline passages as they might have some bearing on the circumcision of Timothy. Fortunately that task is not required here.

One further intriguing aside is the conspicuous absence of further mention of Timothy's father, except for the note that he was a Greek. It appears that he was not a Christian. The lack of his influence or further mention suggests that Eunice was a widow.[16] This conjecture may be supported by the lack of reference to any interference from Timothy's father when Paul decided to take him on his second missionary journey.[17]

We can dwell for a moment on the two short passages of 2 Timothy quoted above. This is a letter that appears to be very interested in developing Christian religious tradition through religious education. Timothy is described as a model pastor. He is not to be despised for his youth[18] or for any other superficial shortcoming. Paul wants to underscore the consistency of the religious education he has received from earliest childhood at the hands of his grandmother and mother. That Eunice was a Jew suggests that her mother Lois was Jewish also. Apparently, they, along with Timothy, had been converted and baptized on the first missionary journey of Paul and Barnabas. Paul says that Lois was first and then Eunice and then Timothy. It may be that Lois and Eunice themselves "converted" the child or young man. This is consistent also with the already established tradition in the early Church that whole households converted along with the heads of households, another indication that there was no *paterfamilias* in this particular

---

[16] Luke might not have known or accepted the so-called "Pauline privilege" as stated in 1 Corinthians 7:15, which decreed that if an unbelieving spouse would not allow the believer to practice her or his belief, they could separate.

[17] See Florence Gillman, *Women Who Knew Paul* (Collegeville: The Liturgical Press, 1992) 23, n. 2.

[18] See 1 Tim 4:12.

household. If one were present, he almost surely would have been mentioned.

Often whole households, including wives, children, slaves, clients, and everyone dependent on the household followed the religion of the *paterfamilias*. Yet from the earliest times of the Church, baptism entitled women as well as men to full status within the new community in which they had a new identity as equals. Women as well as men were admitted into the Church on the same basis, whether married or unmarried. If their husbands chose not to follow Christ, that could precipitate a crisis and could possibly lead to divorce, Paul says (see 1 Cor 7:15). The instance of a "mixed marriage" between a believer in Christ and a nonbeliever became especially problematic when the nonbeliever was the husband. Rather than simply submitting to the husband's religion, a Christian wife was entitled to follow her own faith. This no doubt led to charges that the Christians were anti-family, and that they supported sabotage of the husband/father's authority. This is part of the background for some of Paul's material on marriage, family, and divorce.

Lois and Eunice are cited for having educated Timothy in the faith "from early childhood." They taught him about "salvation in Jesus Christ." It is significant that Paul attributes Timothy's education to his grandmother and mother. Apparently they sustained Paul's and Barnabas's initial instruction by a study of the Scriptures and faith in the salvation that comes in Jesus Christ. There are several implications in the statement that these women were responsible for passing on the legacy of reading and teaching the Scriptures to the young Timothy. They must have been fairly well educated themselves, able to read, to interpret, and to teach. They must have believed that the Gospel they received from Paul and Barnabas was consistent and continuous with the Old Testament, for that was their Scripture.

Typically in the Greco-Roman as well as the Jewish household, the mother-son relationship was probably the strongest of an already strong family culture. The role of the eldest son, for example, was to learn and pass on, as well as to defend fiercely, the traditions and the honor of the family. If these were in any way challenged or threatened, it was up to the sons to do all in their power to reestablish respect and honor. Thus a mother doted on her sons because her own future and welfare were tied up in theirs.

Young children, both boys and girls, were raised mostly by women.[19] Men had little to do with childrearing. But at or near puberty, girls went off to join their husbands or the families of their husbands-to-be. And boys were suddenly taken from their mothers and thrown into the all-male culture that would be their proving ground.

The portrait of the young Timothy gleaned from the combined short passages suggests that he was strongly influenced first in his Jewish faith and then in his Christian faith by his grandmother and mother, and then turned over to his mentor-father-teacher, Paul. The Apostle refers to Timothy as "child" and "son."[20] Paul was eager to underscore the continuity of these familial ties, not only to strengthen Timothy's self-confidence and personal family history but to use Timothy's experience as a kind of example to others. That is exactly what Paul does with his own experience.

The New Testament world is androcentric.[21] And it is unfortunate that even in the New Testament the memory of women is "accidental,"[22] that is to say, they are remembered primarily in function of their relationships to men. Yet probably not too many parents and grandparents would mind terribly if what they are "accidentally" remembered for is their exemplary education and upbringing of their children, who go on to be themselves models for future generations. Lois and Eunice are mentioned by Paul because he wanted to invoke the tradition begun by them and continued in the leadership of Timothy. Paul says Timothy's religious formation was steeped in the Scriptures and leading to salvation in Jesus Christ. The continuity of the Scriptures and the promise of salvation,

[19] Osiek and Balch, *Families in the New Testament World*, 42, 67.

[20] See 2 Tim 1:2; 2:1.

[21] That is, male-oriented, with a bias toward men; women belong to the males and relate tangentially to their world.

[22] This term is used and well explained by Florence Gillman: *Women Who Knew Paul*, 21.

exemplified in the nurturing education that Lois and Eunice gave Timothy, provide for Paul and for us the criteria for a model Christian education.

"But when Priscilla and Aquila heard [Apollos], they took him aside and explained to him the Way [of God] more accurately" (Acts 18:26).

PRISCA (PRISCILLA)

Suggested Reading: Acts 18:2, 18, 26; Romans 16:3; 1 Corinthians 16:19; 2 Timothy 4:19

Unfortunately we have very little information on Prisca and her husband Aquila, although what we do have is tantalizing. The couple is mentioned by name six times in the New Testament; in four of these occurrences, Prisca is named first. As Elizabeth Castelli points out, this is hardly due to social etiquette, a kind of literary "ladies first."[23] Rather, her mention before her husband is more likely because of her greater prominence in the Christian community. She was better known than her husband. We will glean what we can from the snippets of information we have in Acts and in the Pauline Letters.

Prisca and her husband are mentioned three times in chapter 18 of Acts. Here is what Luke tells us:

> There [in Corinth] he [Paul] met a Jew named Aquila, a native of Pontus, who had recently come from Italy with his wife Priscilla because Claudius had ordered all the Jews to leave Rome. [Paul] went to visit them and, because he practiced the same trade, stayed with them and worked, for they were tentmakers by trade (Acts 18:2-3).

A few verses later, Luke notes,

> Paul remained for quite some time, and after saying farewell to the brothers [in Corinth] he sailed for Syria, together with

---

[23] Elizabeth Castelli, "Romans," in Elisabeth Schüssler Fiorenza, *Searching the Scriptures* (New York: Crossroad, 1994) 2:272–300, at 279.

Priscilla and Aquila. . . . When they reached Ephesus, he
left them there, while he entered the synagogue and held
discussions with the Jews (Acts 18:18-19).

Summing up what we have from Acts, we can say that
Priscilla (as she is called by Luke) and her husband are co-
workers and missionaries, practiced and knowledgeable about
the "Way," an exemplary couple who host the Church, including itinerant preachers such as Paul as well as the locals, in
their home. Prisca and her husband are influential Christians in
Corinth and in Ephesus; they came to Greece from Rome.

Aquila was a Jew who had been born in Pontus and somehow had migrated to Rome. He married Priscilla, which is the
diminutive form of the name Prisca, a more familial nick-
name. Paul met this couple in Corinth, where they had gone
when Jews were expelled from Rome because of an edict of
Claudius. It appears that disturbances in the Jewish community of Rome had come to the attention of the emperor sometime in the late forties, and he had reacted with an edict
around 49 C.E. by which he expelled all Jews from Rome. Sue-
tonius says that these disturbances erupted "at the instigation
of a certain Chrestus," a likely misspelling of the Greek term
Christus, the equivalent of the Hebrew title Messiah.[24] This
could have meant, not that Christ was causing the disturbances, but that Jewish and Christian arguments over the
identity of Jesus as the Christ could have reached as far as
Rome and as far up as the emperor. For the sake of peace,
Claudius expelled Jews and Christians alike, not differentiat-
ing between them.

When Paul first came to Corinth around 50, it appears that
Prisca and Aquila were already there and that they were already believers in Christ. It does not seem that Paul converted
them. In fact, to the contrary. Acts says that Paul stayed with
them, as if to insinuate that they had already established a

[24] Claudius was emperor from 41-54 C.E. The Roman historian Sueto-
nius confirms Luke's notation about there being an edict from Claudius
that expelled Jews from Rome, including Christians who were Jewish. For
a good explanation of this, see J. A. Fitzmyer, *The Acts of the Apostles*, Anchor Bible 31 (New York: Doubleday, 1998).

household and a trade there, which Paul joined. After a year and a half, Paul, Prisca, and Aquila left Corinth for Ephesus, where again they seem to have lived and worked together until Paul left them there and traveled on to Antioch, Galatia, and Phrygia (Acts 18:22-23).

After Paul's departure, Priscilla and Aquila met the eloquent and learned Apollos, from Alexandria. Of that encounter, Luke says:

> A Jew named Apollos, a native of Alexandria, an eloquent speaker, arrived in Ephesus. He was an authority on the scriptures. He had been instructed in the Way of the Lord and, with ardent spirit, spoke and taught accurately about Jesus, although he knew only the baptism of John. He began to speak boldly in the synagogue; but when Priscilla and Aquila heard him, they took him aside and explained to him the Way [of God] more accurately (Acts 18:24-26).

Here Luke tells us that Priscilla and Aquila met up with Apollos, an Alexandrian Jew and a fairly new convert to Christ. Prisca and Aquila "took him aside" and instructed him further in the faith. In this endeavor Priscilla is named first by the author of Acts, a suggestion that she was the main tutor of Apollos. Based on Luke's introduction of Apollos as well versed in the Scriptures and well educated in Alexandrian circles, we can surmise that Prisca was also very well educated. This supposition is reinforced by the consequent success her student Apollos would have later in her old Corinthian neighborhood. For Luke adds that after some time, under the tutelage of this couple in Ephesus, Apollos wanted to go to Corinth. Luke tells us that Priscilla and Aquila and the others encouraged him and wrote to the disciples to receive him. When Apollos arrived in Corinth, "he vigorously refuted the Jews in public, establishing from the scriptures that the Messiah is Jesus" (Acts 18:28).

With Apollos in Corinth, Paul returned from the missions to Ephesus and was reunited with Priscilla and her husband (Acts 19:1). In addition to Acts, the couple is named three other times: two times in Paul's own letters (1 Cor 16:19 and in Rom 16:3) and once in a deutero-Pauline letter (2 Tim 4:19). These notations, while too brief to satisfy us, attest to the singular and special relationship that Paul enjoyed with this couple.

It was from Ephesus that Paul wrote 1 Corinthians; in the closing chapter of that letter, Paul says, "The churches of Asia send you greetings. Aquila and Prisca together with the church at their house send you many greetings in the Lord" (1 Cor 16:19). The implication here is not only that Prisca and Aquila join Paul in sending greetings to the Corinthians but that, once again, in Ephesus as in Corinth, the church meets at their house. Prisca and Aquila seem to have established another household and tentmaking business in Ephesus. Paul does not like to write letters in his own name only, but he joins other names to his for added authority. If he mentions this couple to the Corinthians, he hopes that the warm memory of them will help deepen the impression made by his own words.

After remaining in Ephesus for a time, perhaps as long as two years, Paul left after a riot over what he was teaching. Apparently Prisca and Aquila stayed on in Ephesus at least for awhile. When Paul sends greetings to them in the closing chapter of Romans, he adds that they risked their necks for him. Perhaps he is referring to his escape from the rioters in Ephesus and some intervention they made on his behalf in that city. We cannot know for sure what he is referring to, but he insinuates that they did have some clout that they used to get him out of trouble. Specifically, what Paul says regarding Prisca and Aquila in Romans 16 is this: "Greet Prisca and Aquila, my co-workers in Christ Jesus, who risked their necks for my life, to whom not only I am grateful but also all the churches of the Gentiles; greet also the church at their house"(Rom 16:3-5).

Romans was written by Paul near the end of his missionary career, around 58 C.E. Chapter 16 is unusual for two main reasons: Paul greets a number of people there, although earlier he had indicated that he had not yet visited that community. Whereas chapters 1–15 are impersonal and some interpreters understand them to be a kind of self-introduction to Paul and his message in anticipation of the trip Paul hopes to make to Rome, chapter 16 greets some twenty-eight people, not counting Phoebe, who seems to be the bearer of the letter.

The second unusual aspect of this chapter is the number of women mentioned—ten in all, counting Phoebe. Because of the relatively personal characteristics of this chapter in contrast to the tone of the rest of the letter, some have suggested that chapter 16 is a "cover letter" Paul sent not to Rome but to Ephesus, which is near Cenchrae, where Phoebe was from. Whether sent to Ephesus or to Rome, Paul greets Prisca and Aquila with the church that meets at their house. If this chapter is in fact an original part of the letter to the Romans, this means that by the time Paul wrote it, Prisca and Aquila had gone back to Rome, where they had been before they met Paul in Corinth about eight years previously. Apparently when Nero came to power[25] after the death of Claudius around 53 C.E., Jews were allowed to return to Rome. It also means that Prisca and Aquila hosted a house church in Rome as they had in Corinth and in Ephesus.

The sixth and final reference to Prisca and Aquila is in the deutero-Pauline letter of 2 Timothy; there the author says: "Greet Prisca and Aquila and the family of Onesiphorus" (2 Tim 4:19). We have a hint in 1:18, though hardly more than that, that Timothy may be in Ephesus when this letter is sent to him. The "family of Onesiphorus" that is linked with Prisca and Aquila in 4:19 is contrasted with Paul's opponents who abandoned him. But Onesiphorus "often gave me new heart and was not ashamed of my chains . . . he promptly searched for me and found me" (2 Tim 1:16-17).

Interpreters do not agree whether 1 and 2 Timothy were written at the same time, by Paul, to the Timothy we know from Paul's own letters and from Acts 16. It is not even certain whether 1 and 2 Timothy ought to be closely linked; 1 Timothy and Titus have more in common than do the two letters of Timothy. But since they are all pastoral letters written around the same time generally, we can draw some conclusions from the two letters that bear Timothy's name.

In 2 Timothy, Paul and Timothy (and maybe the other named people, such as Prisca and Aquila) are idealized, as if their

---

[25] Nero ruled from 54 to 68 C.E. His early years were relatively benign. By the sixties his reputation was as a cruel and capricious emperor who created gladiator sports and had Christians killed as a diversion for those who suspected him of burning down a large section of the city of Rome. Although Tacitus indicates that not many believed this charge against them, the use of the Christians as scapegoats was acceptable, since outsiders were wary of this secretive new sect.

memory by the Church was as models. The images of "Paul" as an old man who had suffered and had kept the faith through all kinds of trials, and of "Timothy," the pastor who is inspired by the memory and the example of his teacher, may be devices used by the author to encourage a certain kind of behavior in the Church. Timothy is young but wise beyond his years, and able to discern the difference between good and bad examples of Christian living (1 Tim 4:11-16) and the importance of models for believers to follow. Timothy is advised to hold true to the tradition and the examples he has had in a number of people: Paul himself, the perfect martyr, is portrayed as an example for Timothy, his "child," to follow (see 1 Tim 1:2, 18; 2 Tim 1:6–2:7; 3:10-17). Timothy is also reminded once again of positive examples such as Onesiphorus and his family (2 Tim 1:16-18; 4:19). Timothy is also reminded of the positive examples of Christian women, in his grandmother and mother, Lois and Eunice (2 Tim 1:5), and in Prisca and her husband Aquila (2 Tim 4:19).

By way of contrast, Timothy is given negative examples in the traitors Phygelus and Hermogenes (2 Tim 1:15), and Hymenaeus and Philetus (2:17), who did not preserve the traditions of Paul but rather deserted him and his teaching. Some, like Hymenaeus and Alexander, "have made a shipwreck of their faith" (1 Tim 1:19). Timothy is also given a negative example in "women weighed down by sins, led by various desires, always trying to learn but never able to reach a knowledge of the truth" (2 Tim 3:6-7).

The fact that Prisca was a married woman could have enhanced her "use" and value as a role model in the changing Church reflected in the Pastoral Letters. The deutero-Pauline author makes it clear that problems were arising in the Church with regard to false teachings; women were seen as particularly susceptible and gullible, probably all the more vulnerable because of their lack of education. This general concern is reflected, for example, in the author's instruction about women in 1 Timothy 2:12-15. There, "Paul" says:

> I do not permit a woman to teach or to have authority over a man. She must be quiet. For Adam was formed first, then Eve. Further, Adam was not deceived, but the woman was deceived and transgressed. But she will be saved through

motherhood, provided women persevere in faith and love and holiness, with self-control (1 Tim 2:12-15).[26]

A concern in this church is false teaching on the one hand and susceptible women on the other. Apparently one of the areas in which false teaching was having some success, especially among women, affected marriage. A little later in the same letter, the author writes:

> Now the Spirit explicitly says that in the last times some will turn away from the faith by paying attention to deceitful spirits and demonic instructions through the hypocrisy of liars with branded consciences. They forbid marriage . . . . (1 Tim 4:1-3).

These "liars" taught a false asceticism, including a Christian requirement for celibacy, and they were attracting women who are described as being more gullible, following the example of Eve. To counteract this, Paul says, women are to be "saved through motherhood" (1 Tim 2:15). In other words, the salvation of women is within the family, in their roles as wives and mothers. This, by the way, is the only place in the New Testament where the salvation of women is alleged to be on a difference basis than man's!

It is possible that the claim that celibacy is superior to married life was based in Paul's own teaching as stated in 1 Corinthians, where Paul answered the Corinthians, saying,

> Now in regard to the matters about which you wrote: "It is a good thing for a man not to touch a woman," but because of cases of immorality every man should have his own wife, and every woman her own husband. . . . Do not deprive each other, except perhaps by mutual consent for a time, to be free for prayer, but then return to one another. . . . Now to the unmarried and to widows, I say: It is a good thing for them to remain as they are, as I do (1 Cor 7:1-2, 5, 8).

---

[26] With the majority of commentators, I do not accept 1 Timothy as an authentic letter from Paul; it reflects situations that arose in churches in the latter decades of the first century.

Paul clearly states his own preference for celibacy, based on his own experience. And since everything else he says to the Corinthians appears to have been misunderstood, apparently this bias for celibacy could easily have been too. The Corinthians were Greeks, who showed a decided interest in the spiritual realities. More easily than Jews who honored their long history of family traditions and who held marriage in high esteem, Gentiles might have been predisposed to reject sexuality as inferior and latch on to a teaching that exalted a celibate lifestyle.

It is even possible that eventually those who were teaching a Christian preference for celibacy were women. Perhaps this is one reason that the author of 1 Timothy restricts women from teaching men. It may also be why we can discern in 1 Timothy 5:3-16 and perhaps Titus 2:3-5 an "order of widows," that is, older, pious, and reverent women whose charge it was to "train younger women to love their husbands and children, to be self-controlled, chaste, good homemakers, under the control of their husbands, that the word of God may not be discredited" (Titus 2:4-5).

Such advice might have been necessary in a later Church that was given to following heretical advice erroneously based on a Christian requirement for celibacy. Prisca and Aquila represent a Christian couple modeling equality and partnership in marriage, business, education, and the Church. They also serve as a corrective example to those too eager to champion celibacy as a superior lifestyle advocated for Christians.

But before the Pastoral Letters, in Paul's own time, there is every indication that he depended on couples such as Prisca and Aquila, not only to be his "co-workers," as he describes them in Romans 16:3, but to receive him and the believing community in their "house," to encourage and sustain him, to supplement his work as residents and patrons of local churches, and to offer him safety, hospitality, and resources to send him to the next mission. If the later restriction against women's "teaching" had applied to Prisca, then Apollos and Paul, as well as the "rest of the Gentile churches" would have been missing a vital, well-educated, and apparently very well-loved Christian model.

5. Women and Discipleship

There is no single text or New Testament book that gives us a clear definition of discipleship. Our understanding of what marks or qualifies someone as a disciple of Jesus comes from the many sayings and stories we have that depict the relationships Jesus formed with his companions. We read how Jesus called people early in his ministry with the simple instruction "Follow me." It is an open-ended demand requiring courage, self-sacrifice, and perseverance. For the Synoptics, it involves following Jesus on a journey that leads to his death. The disciples (=learners) are instructed along the way. Miracles and parables have a single purpose: to challenge disciples to see and accept, to hear and understand. Luke does give us a summary of discipleship in his chapter 8, in the course of Jesus' explanation of a parable: "But as for the seed that fell on rich soil, they are the ones who, when they have heard the word, embrace it with a generous and good heart, and bear fruit through perseverance" (Luke 8:15).

At times Jesus' directions are very explicit. Disciples must be ready to sacrifice everything for the sake of following him without condition or limit. A number of descriptive terms are used for the attitudes and actions of the disciples. They are to "proclaim the kingdom of God and to heal," taking nothing for the journey, "neither walking stick, nor sack, nor food, nor money. . . ." They may accept hospitality; but whether or not they receive it, they are to press on (see Mark 6:7-13; Matt 10:5-15; Luke 9:2-5; 10:1-12). They must persevere despite difficulties and deprivations, which will be numerous. They must testify to what they have seen and heard.

Jesus' disciples experience mercy and healing, enabling them to become instruments of that same mercy and healing. They are not to judge others. They are required to love God, themselves, their neighbors, their enemies, and one another. They are to prepare themselves to give witness when they are "dragged" before courts and kings, even if they "lose" their lives in the process.

Men and women follow Jesus. They are with Jesus in and around Galilee and then on to Jerusalem. The manner and degree to which women in particular are faithful from Jesus' cradle to tomb to Church are remarkable. Even more so is that in the telling, the evangelists often contrast the women's behavior with that of the men disciples, to the dishonor of the latter. Traits of true discipleship are noted in the majority of the women the New Testament tells us about. In this and the following chapter we shall reflect on some of these women.

WOMEN COMPANIONS OF JESUS (SEE LUKE 8:1-3)

The synoptic Gospels of Matthew, Mark, and Luke present Jesus' life as a single journey that begins in Galilee and proceeds to Jerusalem, where Jesus is executed. Women who followed Jesus from Galilee are referred to as a discernible group only in Luke.[1] And only Luke names some of these women in the course of Jesus' journey.[2] Luke probably takes his list of the names of the

---

[1] Luke has been called "extremely dangerous" in that, while appearing to favor women, to give women more attention in his narrative than the other evangelists do, what Luke says about women, upon reflection and scrutiny, is less than flattering. See Jane Schaberg, "Luke," in *Women's Bible Commentary*, 275–292, at 275. Luke appears seductive in using the authority of Jesus to reinforce models of subordinate service for women. In this way it is possible to read this addition of Luke as emphasizing the role of women merely as one of support of the mission of Jesus and the Twelve.

[2] But while Luke seems to presuppose the presence of women with Jesus, they are a silent presence, until finally, at Pentecost, it is simply noted that "some women" were present including "Mary, the Mother of Jesus" (Acts 1:14). This is another example of a discernible Lukan ambivalence about women. For instance, the few times that women are given speaking roles, they are corrected by Jesus. Typically Luke qualifies women

women who followed Jesus from Mark 15:40. To these names Luke adds his own notations. He inserts these names and descriptions into the course of Jesus' journey in this manner:[3]

> [1]Afterward he journeyed from one town and village to another, preaching and proclaiming the good news of the kingdom of God. Accompanying him were the Twelve [2]and some women who had been cured of evil spirits and infirmities, Mary, called Magdalene, from whom seven demons had gone out, [3]Joanna, the wife of Herod's steward Chuza, Susanna, and many others who provided from them out of their resources (Luke 8:1-3).

From the beginning of his ministry Jesus calls people to "follow" him. The "call stories," properly speaking, tell of some of the men he called: for example, Peter and Andrew, James and John (Mark 1:16-20), and Levi (Mark 2:13-17, or Matthew in Matthew 9:9). The annunciation stories of Luke's infancy narrative could also be considered "call stories." If so, the call or annunciation to Mary constitutes one of the few calls of a woman in the New Testament; perhaps Simon's mother-in-law is another.[4] Yet, even though we do not learn when or how these women were "called," the Synoptics and John all agree

---

with pejorative attributes; for example, the unnamed woman who anoints Jesus according to Matthew and Mark becomes the "woman known to be a sinner" in Luke (Mark 14:3; Matt 26:7; Luke 7:37). For him, the women who follow Jesus are finally merged into the crowd by the time of the passion and not believed at the resurrection. In Acts, Luke presents women as inappropriate witnesses, not as leaders in the early Church. Acts assigns women only diminishing roles outside of the domestic, traditional ones.

[3] Luke 8:1-3 is the final episode in the so-called little interpolation that Luke inserts into his source, Mark. Luke begins this insertion with the Sermon on the Plain (6:20-29) and ends with this list of Jesus' companions from Galilee (8:1-3). These followers are composed of the Twelve and some women, three of whom are named (Mary Magdalene, Joanna, and Susanna) and many more who are unnamed. Luke added that the women "provided for them out of their resources" (8:3).

[4] As we have seen in our chapter 2, Matthew seems to consider the story of Simon's mother-in-law as a "call" story; and this is supported by Luke's account, which has her cured before Peter ever came to know Jesus.

that women were with Jesus throughout the course of his ministry. It is as if no one could remember when they weren't there, as if they had always been there. Their following of Jesus appears natural and is taken for granted, at least by the Christian communities.[5]

Women followed Jesus in and around Galilee and then on to Jerusalem. They were at the cross and at the empty tomb. In fact, women present a clear contrast to their male counterparts in that the women persevered on the journey despite all the opposition to Jesus and, most certainly, to them. We might be surprised to realize how few references we have to these women and how little information these references contain. That there are women with Jesus at the end, at the cross and the resurrection, who had apparently followed Jesus all along is attested by all the Gospels.

THE GALILEAN WOMEN AT THE CROSS AND AT THE TOMB

Suggested Reading: Mark 15:40-41, 47; 16:1-8; Matthew 27:55-61; 28:1-10; Luke 23:49-56; 24:1-12; John 19:25-27; 20:1-3, 10-18

Women from Galilee provide the link between the ministry of Jesus and his passion; their presence at the cross, the burial, and the resurrection of Jesus is significant. These women have been with him from the beginning of his ministry; they have heard his words and seen his actions. They are witnesses not only to the earthly ministry of Jesus but to its meaning as

---

[5] We should note in this regard that it never seems to have been an issue whether women should be baptized, in contrast, for example, to the lively debate over the baptism of Gentiles. The baptism, and therefore the implied equality of discipleship of women and men, appears to have always been accepted practice. Yet historically, the association of women, some married (e.g., Joanna, the wife of Herod's steward, Chuza; see Luke 8:3) and some without family identification (e.g., Mary Magdalene), with Jesus and the freedom they enjoyed in "following him" must have raised more than a few eyebrows.

understood in the light of the resurrection. In simple terms the story of their fidelity cuts across all four Gospel accounts. Their story is inextricably bound up with Jesus' own. This is how it is told. Since all four Gospels attest to the presence at the cross of women who had followed Jesus from Galilee, we start there.

Mark 15:40-41, 47

[40]There were also women looking on from a distance. Among them were Mary Magdalene, Mary the mother of the younger James and of Joses, and Salome. [41]These women had followed him when he was in Galilee and ministered to him. There were also many other women who had come up with him to Jerusalem. . . . [47]Mary Magdalene and Mary the mother of Joses watched where he was laid.

Matthew 27:55-61

[55]There were many women there, looking on from a distance, who had followed Jesus from Galilee, ministering to him. [56]Among them were Mary Magdalene and Mary the mother of James and Joseph, and the mother of the sons of Zebedee.

[57]When it was evening, there came a rich man from Arimathea named Joseph, who was himself a disciple of Jesus. [58]He went to Pilate and asked for the body of Jesus; then Pilate ordered it to be handed over. [59]Taking the body, Joseph wrapped it [in] clean linen [60]and laid it in his new tomb that he had hewn in the rock. Then he rolled a huge stone across the entrance to the tomb and departed. [61]But Mary Magdalene and the other Mary remained sitting there, facing the tomb.

Luke 23:49-56

[49][B]ut all his acquaintances stood at a distance, including the women who had followed him from Galilee and saw these events.

[50]Now there was a virtuous and righteous man named Joseph who, though he was a member of the council, [51]had not consented to their plan of action. He came from the Jewish town of Arimathea and was awaiting the kingdom of God. [52]He went to Pilate and asked for the body of Jesus. [53]After he had taken the body down, he wrapped it in a linen cloth and laid him in a rock-hewn tomb in which no one had yet been buried. [54]It was the day of preparation, and the sabbath was about to begin. [55]The women who had come from Galilee with him followed behind, and when they had seen the tomb and the way in which his body was laid in it, [56]they

returned and prepared spices and perfumed oils. Then they rested on the sabbath according to the commandment.

John 19:25-27

²⁵Standing by the cross of Jesus were his mother and his mother's sister, Mary the wife of Clopas, and Mary of Magdala. ²⁶When Jesus saw his mother and the disciple there whom he loved, he said to his mother, "Woman, behold, your son." ²⁷Then he said to the disciple, "Behold, your mother." And from that hour the disciple took her into his home.

All four Gospels place women at the tomb to become the first witnesses to the resurrection. The evangelists tell that part of the story like this.

Mark 16:1-8

¹When the sabbath was over, Mary Magdalene, Mary, the mother of James, and Salome bought spices so that they might go and anoint him. ²Very early when the sun had risen, on the first day of the week, they came to the tomb. ³They were saying to one another, "Who will roll back the stone for us from the entrance to the tomb?" ⁴When they looked up, they saw that the stone had been rolled back; it was very large. ⁵On entering the tomb they saw a young man sitting on the right side, clothed in a white robe, and they were utterly amazed. ⁶He said to them, "Do not be amazed! You seek Jesus of Nazareth, the crucified. He has been raised; he is not here. Behold the place where they laid him. ⁷But go and tell his disciples and Peter, 'He is going before you to Galilee; there you will see him, as he told you.'" ⁸Then they went out and fled from the tomb, seized with trembling and bewilderment. They said nothing to anyone, for they were afraid.

Matthew 28:1-10

¹After the sabbath, as the first day of the week was dawning, Mary Magdalene and the other Mary came to see the tomb. ²And behold, there was a great earthquake; for an angel of the Lord descended from heaven, approached, rolled back the stone, and sat upon it. ³His appearance was like lightning and his clothing was white as snow. ⁴The guards were shaken with fear of him and became like dead men. ⁵Then the angel said to the women in reply, "Do not be afraid! I know that you are seeking Jesus the crucified. ⁶He is not

here, for he has been raised just as he said. Come and see the place where he lay. ⁷Then go quickly and tell his disciples, 'He has been raised from the dead, and he is going before you to Galilee; there you will see him.' Behold, I have told you." ⁸Then they went away quickly from the tomb, fearful yet overjoyed, and ran to announce this to his disciples. ⁹And behold, Jesus met them on their way and greeted them. They approached, embraced his feet, and did him homage. ¹⁰Then Jesus said to them, "Do not be afraid. Go tell my brothers to go to Galilee, and there they will see me."

Luke 24:1-12

¹But at daybreak on the first day of the week they took the spices they had prepared and went to the tomb. ²They found the stone rolled away from the tomb; ³but when they entered, they did not find the body of the Lord Jesus. ⁴While they were puzzling over this, behold, two men in dazzling garments appeared to them. ⁵They were terrified and bowed their faces to the ground. They said to them, "Why do you seek the living one among the dead? ⁶He is not here, but he has been raised. Remember what he said to you while he was still in Galilee, ⁷that the Son of Man must be handed over to sinners and be crucified, and rise on the third day." ⁸And they remembered his words. ⁹Then they returned from the tomb and announced all these things to the eleven and to all the others. ¹⁰The women were Mary Magdalene, Joanna, and Mary the mother of James; the others who accompanied them also told this to the apostles, ¹¹but their story seemed like nonsense and they did not believe them. ¹²But Peter got up and ran to the tomb, bent down, and saw the burial cloths alone; then he went home amazed at what had happened.

John 20:1-3, 10-18

¹On the first day of the week, Mary of Magdala came to the tomb early in the morning, while it was still dark, and saw the stone removed from the tomb. ²So she ran and went to Simon Peter and to the other disciple whom Jesus loved, and told them, "They have taken the Lord from the tomb, and we don't know where they put him." ³So Peter and the other disciple went out and came to the tomb. . . . ¹⁰Then the disciples returned home.

¹¹But Mary stayed outside the tomb weeping. And as she wept, she bent over into the tomb ¹²and saw two angels in white sitting there, one at the head and one at the feet where

> the body of Jesus had been. [13]And they said to her, "Woman,
> why are you weeping?" She said to them, "They have taken
> my Lord, and I don't know where they laid him." [14]When she
> had said this, she turned around and saw Jesus there, but did
> not know it was Jesus. [15]Jesus said to her, "Woman, why are
> you weeping? Whom are you looking for?" She thought it
> was the gardener and said to him, "Sir, if you carried him
> away, tell me where you laid him, and I will take him."
> [16]Jesus said to her, "Mary!" She turned and said to him in He-
> brew, "Rabbouni," which means Teacher. [17]Jesus said to her,
> "Stop holding on to me, for I have not yet ascended to the
> Father. But go to my brothers and tell them, 'I am going to
> my Father and your Father, to my God and your God.'"
> [18]Mary of Magdala went and announced to the disciples, "I
> have seen the Lord," and what he told her.

On the third day after his crucifixion, the women who had
followed him all along are commanded to tell the other disciples
that he is not in the tomb; rather, Jesus is risen and would appear
to them in Galilee: "there you will see him, as he told you" (Mark
16:7). The course of the Gospel leads readers full circle, following
Jesus from Galilee to Jerusalem, from miracles to the cross, from
power to powerlessness; and then, after the resurrection, to return to the beginning and finally to "see" Jesus as he is, for who
he is. He had told them all this previously, although they had not
understood. But the resurrection changed all that.

While all four Gospels are unanimous in saying that women
were at the cross and also that they also bore witness about the
resurrection to the male disciples, the evangelists are not
unanimous in their identification of the women. Nor do they
all agree in telling us how many women were present. Mark,
the first Gospel to be written, names three women at the cross:
Mary Magdalene; Mary, the mother of the younger James and
Joses; and Salome (see Mark 14:40 and 16:1). Matthew tells us
that at the cross were "Mary Magdalene and Mary the mother
of James and Joseph, and the mother of the sons of Zebedee"
(Matt 27:56). A few verses later (v. 61), Matthew says that two
of these, "Mary Magdalene and the other Mary remained sitting there, facing the tomb." These are the same two who came
to "see the tomb" as the first day of the week was dawning; they
discovered that it was empty and they heard the announcement that Jesus had been raised (Matt 28:1).

Luke describes the women as those who "had followed him from Galilee" (Luke 23:49; see also 23:53-55) and names them in 24:10 as "Mary Magdalene, Joanna, and Mary the mother of James." In Luke 8:1-3, Luke also named women as prominent among those who followed Jesus in his journey throughout Galilee and then to Jerusalem. Luke further refers to "others who accompanied them," all of whom were supported by the women. John tells us that "standing by the cross of Jesus were his mother and his mother's sister, Mary the wife of Clopas, and Mary of Magdala" (John 19:25). John also records a resurrection appearance only to Mary of Magdala (John 20:1-2, 11-18).[6]

In Mark's account these women link the cross and the empty tomb. Although the women appear to have obeyed the command to inform the other disciples of what they had seen, Mark utilizes his "secrecy" motif, with its Christological implications, to the end.[7] Thus the original ending of Mark says that

---

[6] In all the lists of the women from Galilee except in John 19:25, Mary Magdalene is named first, an indication of her leadership role in the early Church, at least among the women. See Mark 15:41, 47; 16:1; Matt 27:56, 61; 28:1; Luke 8:3; and John 19:25. Some authors suggest that women are referred to separately for a dual purpose: to show inclusiveness and also the segregation of groups of women from groups of men. See, for example, Turid Karlsen Seim, "The Gospel of Luke," in Elisabeth Schüssler Fiorenza, *Searching the Scriptures* (New York: Crossroad, 1994) 2:728–762, at 730–731. Yet one interesting point that could be made to support this segregation is that stories might have originated and circulated among women's groups that are hard to explain as circulating among the men; among these would be the "womb stories," such as we find in Luke's infancy narrative. The stories of the annunciation to Mary, the visitation, the conversation between Mary and Elizabeth are examples. It is hard to imagine that birthing stories or stories about women's duties such as taking oils and spices to anoint Jesus' body were popular among men, especially when these stories suggested the women's commitment and dedication to him, to the detriment of the men's. It is possible that the men did not even know these stories about the women's concerns and activities until they needed to provide a link between the cross and the crucifixion, a link the women inevitably provided.

[7] The "secrecy motif," as it is sometimes called, is a literary device allowing Mark to assert that Jesus is truly the Messiah, the Son of God (see Mark 1:1), while insisting that this truth can only be known through faith. So, for example, no human being can recognize who Jesus truly is until the

the women all ran away from the tomb, telling no one any-thing, "for they were afraid" (Mark 16:8).[8] In Mark, Jesus' dis-ciples, including the women, do not yet understand, even after the resurrection. They must return to Galilee, to the beginning, before they will grasp the mystery of it all. Then, with the ex-perience of both the cross and the resurrection informing their vision and their hearing, they will at last be disciples of faith.

In contrast to Mark, the other Gospels tell us that the women did as they were told, adding that the male disciples heard the news from the women. Thus historical and theological necessity appear to finally prevail over literary license; alternative endings were added to make Mark conform to the consensus that Peter and the others heard the report of Jesus' rising from the women.

Mark and Luke link the crucifixion with the resurrection by having the women note the place of Jesus' burial so that they could go, prepare the spices, and, after the Sabbath, return to anoint the body. But Matthew took literally Jesus' prophecy that the unnamed woman had anointed him "for burial" (Matt 26:12), so that no further anointing was necessary. Thus in Matthew the women go to the tomb to "watch"—the action of the disciple, the same action the women performed at the foot of the cross (see Matt 27:55, 61; 28:1).[9] Jesus' last words before the passion were a

---

centurion confesses, at Jesus death, "Truly this man was the Son of God!" (15:39). Mark challenges his readers to realize that even Peter stumbled when he acknowledges Jesus as the Messiah but balks at Jesus' prediction of his passion (8:29-33). At the very end of his Gospel, Mark includes even the faithful women among those who falter until they return again to Galilee, to the beginning, to see and to interpret the whole of Jesus' life and ministry in the context of his resurrection.

[8] As the note in the New American Bible tells us, Mark's composition ends with this verse 8; the other endings of Mark (the so called Longer Ending of 16:9-20 as well as the Shorter Ending that follows verse 20, a kind of summary conclusion) seem to be later additions. Mark 16:9-20 presents a summary of material found in Mark 24 and John 20, and may have been added to present a more appropriate ending to the Gospel, with the disciples of Jesus carrying on his preaching mandate.

[9] In Matthew, "seeing" verbs link the women with the cross and the resurrection. Matthew 26:55 says, "There were many women there, look-ing on from a distance." Matthew 27:61 says, "Mary Magdalene and the

command to "watch" and be prepared for the terrible events that would accompany the destruction of the Temple as well as the end of time (see Mark 13:37). The disciple is to be on guard, on the alert, to watch! This is the posture of the women from Galilee.

Aside from the above, we have disappointingly little information about any of these Galilean women. While the mother of Jesus and Mary Magdalene will be treated elsewhere at greater length,[10] we can say a few words about the other named women who are further described as "following Jesus from Galilee, and ministering to him," present at the cross, and entrusted to bring to the others the resurrection message. To the women of the crucifixion, Easter will be first disclosed.[11] And they will be the first witnesses to it. Let us examine what we can know about each of the women named as present at the cross and at the tomb.

MARY, THE MOTHER OF JAMES AND JOSES
(SEE MARK 6:3; 15:40; ALSO MATTHEW 27:56)

We have heard these names earlier in Mark 6:3, where the evangelist describes the rejection of Jesus by the people of his hometown of Nazareth (see 6:1-6). They reason that he is too well known to them. They "took offense" at what Jesus was saying and doing. They asked one another, "Where did this man get all this? . . . Is he not the carpenter, the son of Mary, and the brother of James and Joses and Judas and Simon? And are not his sisters here with us?" This is one of a few passages that seems to imply that Jesus had brothers and sisters.[12] In

---

other Mary remained sitting there, facing the tomb." Finally, 28:1 omits any reference to spices or the women preparing to anoint Jesus' body but says simply, "Mary Magdalene and the other Mary came to see the tomb."

[10] For the mother of Jesus, see chapters 1 and 6; for Mary Magdalene, see this chapter, below, pp. 182–191.

[11] Donald Senior, *The Passion of Jesus in the Gospel of Mark* (Collegeville: The Liturgical Press, 1984) 131–132.

[12] Ambiguity about the family of Jesus seems to have bothered interpreters for a long time. One issue is that the "brothers and sisters" are associated only with Mary in Mark. Since nothing is said about Joseph, some have presumed that he is dead. If we only had the New Testament, one could assume that these are children born to Mary and Joseph after Jesus. This was the opinion of Tertullian and most Protestants today. Yet already

chapter 3 Mark told us that Jesus' family wanted to take him away because of the reports they were hearing about him. John mentions that Jesus' mother and brothers were invited to the wedding at Cana (John 2:12), and Paul refers to "James, the brother of the Lord" (Gal 1:19).

Mark's readers are suddenly caught unawares. Is Mark saying that this "Mary, the mother of James and Joses" who was present at the foot of the cross, is Jesus' own mother? The evidence is unclear and the answer at best ambiguous. Mark makes a point of showing that Jesus had been rejected from the beginning of his ministry, even when he was performing miracles, even by his own. The shadow of the cross reaches back to the beginning of the Gospel. Already in chapter 3 Mark reported that there was a conspiracy to put Jesus to death (Mark 3:6). His mother and his "brothers," thinking him to be "out of his mind," sought to take him away (Mark 3:21, 31-33). Their opinion is almost the same as that of his staunchest opponents, the scribes and Pharisees, who consider him possessed (Mark 3:21-22). His family remains "outside" the circle, while the insider disciples inform Jesus that his mother and brothers want to see him. Mark suggests that Jesus refuses to go to them, perhaps an implication that Jesus is estranged from his family. Jesus responds, "Who are my mother and [my] brothers? . . . Here are my mother and my brothers. [For] whoever does the will of God is my brother and sister and mother" (Mark 3:33-35).

What Mark could be doing is redefining "family" to include members of the common faith that Jesus is the Messiah. Even Mary, Jesus' mother, appears to have had her own questions about his identity and mission. She, like the rest of us, seems to have needed to come to know who Jesus is by faith. So, some would say, Mary is not identified as the "mother of

---

in the second century these "brothers and sisters" were identified as children of Joseph from a former marriage (see the *Protoevangelium of James* 9:2). This is generally held today by Eastern Churches. In the fourth century Jerome explained that James and Joses were cousins of Jesus, an opinion that became common in the Western Church, where belief in the virginity of Mary even after Jesus' birth is considered part of the Church's teaching.

Jesus" at the cross, but described as the disciple she is, as one who followed Jesus from Galilee and ministered to him.

If this is truly Jesus' own mother, Mark might also be hinting that he is still alienated from his brothers in 15:40; they are not present but, with the other males, have fled from him. Yet Mary is included among those who followed him and ministered to him. These same women raise the question on their way to the tomb, "Who will roll back the stone for us?" (Mark 16:3). His blood brothers, his relatives, his apostles, and male followers are not forthcoming. Mark portrays Jesus as practically abandoned. It is only the defenseless, powerless women who attend to his burial.

But Mark may not be focusing on family discord at all. He could be suggesting that family ties are not as important as becoming "kin" by following Jesus and persevering in faith. True, many of his own, including his family and his own disciples, abandon him. But some of them, like his mother, may have become joined to his fellowship not through blood but through faith. In the glaring absence of Jesus' elect disciples, Mark highlights the women's faithfulness. Mark is probably less interested in showing the superiority of women over men than the superiority of a faith community over blood relationships.

The idea that Mary is best described not as Jesus' biological mother but as his disciple is reinforced by John's account of the crucifixion and of the disciples present there. Only John explicitly and clearly identifies one of the women standing by the cross as Jesus' mother (see John 19:25-27). Yet this identification is not without theological reflection on discipleship. When he sees his mother and the Beloved Disciple standing there, Jesus says, "Woman, behold, your son," and to the disciple, "Behold, your mother." John, like the other evangelists, affirms the priority of the community of faith. Mary's sorrow at the cross is not only for her personal loss. Mary's fidelity at the cross is not merely blind, ferocious mother love. Mary is distinguished primarily as a disciple who came to accept Jesus' messiahship, including the necessity of the cross, through faith. Just as we do.

It is impossible to say with certainty whether this woman identified by Mark as "Mary the mother of the younger James and of Joses" (Mark 15:40; and by Matthew as "Mary, the mother of James and of Joseph") can really be identified as Jesus' own mother. We can note that the reference to her sons may mean that they were also among Jesus' followers, since they were remembered by name in the community. By thus naming her, the evangelists are saying that her relationship to James and Joses (or Joseph) is more than a biological one. She is a mother in the spiritual sense, bringing forth and nurturing the faith of her children.

SALOME (SEE MARK 14:40)

Mark names the third woman at the cross as Salome (14:40). Unfortunately, there is no further information about this woman. A popular legend identifies her with the daughter of Herodias, whose dance for Herod the tetrarch prompted him to make the ill-advised promise that ended with the death of John the Baptist. Although Herodias had a daughter named Salome, there is nothing to support the idea that either mother or daughter came to believe in Jesus.

For this third woman in Mark, Matthew substitutes the "mother of the sons of Zebedee" (Matt 27:56). But we ought not to be too quick to assume that Matthew means to identify Salome as the name of this woman. Matthew's substitution can probably be better explained by his usual interest in showing how the words of Jesus find their fulfillment. Matthew prefers to tie up loose ends using a "prophecy-fulfillment schema." Only Matthew had inserted this woman into the story of the sons' request for preferential treatment when Jesus comes into his kingdom (Matt 20:20-28).[13] Once mentioned there, some resolution of Jesus' dialogue with this woman will concern Matthew. He indicates that she did indeed listen to Jesus and learn the harsh lesson of the high cost of discipleship. According to Matthew, it appears as if Jesus asks *her* if she is able to "drink the cup [of suffering] which I am going to drink"(20:22). She appears willing and able to do so as she stands by the cross. Like the mother of the Maccabees (2 Macc 7),

---

[13] See pp. 134–140 above.

it may well be that this woman prepares her sons to also be able to share in this cup. Acts 12:2 tells us that Herod did in fact put James to death. If this woman, the mother of the sons of Zebedee, is not the same as Salome, it is possible that she is rather the one called the "other Mary," in Matthew 27:61. If so, this is first time she is named.

JOANNA (SEE LUKE 8:3 AND 24:10)

Joanna is mentioned only in Luke's Gospel, identified in 8:3 as the wife of Chuza, who was Herod's steward. Mention of Herod foreshadows Luke's description a chapter later:

> Herod the tetrarch heard about all that was happening, and he was greatly perplexed because some were saying, "John has been raised from the dead"; others were saying, "Elijah has appeared"; still others, "One of the ancient prophets has arisen." But Herod said, "John I beheaded. Who then is this about whom I hear such things?" And he kept trying to see him (Luke 9:7-9).

We should recall that Luke does not have a detailed account of the role of some women in Herod's court in the death of John. The association of Joanna with Herod's court is validated somewhat by Mark's and Matthew's reflections on the cause and manner of John's death. What is asserted by all three of these evangelists is that word of Jesus' preaching and actions had reached high places, even Herod's court. Luke tends to pair and balance characters. Luke knew of Mark's account of John's death and of the role of Herodias and her daughter in bringing that about. Luke also knew of Herod's paranoid fear that Jesus was John resuscitated, an absurd judgment. Luke refers to Herod's desire to see Jesus because of what everyone was saying; only Luke tells us that Herod would in fact have this desire fulfilled when Pilate sent Jesus to him (see Luke 23:6-12). We could conjecture that Herod and members of his court heard about and formed opinions about both John the Baptist and Jesus.

For Luke, witness is very important. Thus Luke notes that some drew incorrect conclusions from Jesus' actions; others, often women, were drawn to Jesus, followed him, and dedicated their resources and their very lives to him. One such woman was Joanna, who heard the same things as Herod but came to a better conclusion.

SUSANNA (SEE LUKE 8:3)

This woman is not mentioned elsewhere. Her association with Mary Magdalene and Joanna in Luke 8:3 suggests that, like them, she followed Jesus and provided for him out of her own resources.

Acts reinforces this impression that women, especially those with means, were vital to the success of the early Church. Mary of Jerusalem, mother of John Mark, for example, provided the house where "many people gathered in prayer" (Acts 12:12) and to which Peter came after escaping from prison. Lydia's house was the gathering place of the church at Philippi (16:13-14, 40). The conversion of prominent women such as Demaris of Athens (17:34) helped offset the mockery to which Paul and his message of the resurrection were subjected. It is as if Luke notes the support of influential women (as well as men) to authenticate the credibility of the Gospel (see also Acts 17:4, 12). Luke leads us to believe that not only the community of Acts but Jesus himself depended on the generosity and courage of women such as these. Yet, despite his unique signaling of the contribution of women in the course of Jesus' ministry by the time of the passion, Luke seems to downplay their significance by glossing over the failure of the male disciples, thus avoiding too stark a contrast.

SUMMARY OF LUKE'S PRESENTATION OF THE WOMEN FROM GALILEE

Luke notes that there were more witnesses to the crucifixion than a lone centurion. His testimony is added to that of "all the people" who "saw what happened; they returned home beating their breasts" (Luke 23:47-48). There were also all Jesus' acquaintances, "including the women who had followed him from Galilee and saw these events" (Luke 23:49). Thus immediately before and immediately after Jesus' death, Luke consistently underscores the presence of at least three groups of witnesses: the crowds, the women who followed him (the daughters of Jerusalem and the women from Galilee), and a "foreign" male, who represents the faithful (Simon of Cyrene and the Roman centurion).

Luke does not name the women present at the cross, as the other evangelists do. Further, he omits reference to the flight of the disciples. Rather, Luke says that "all of Jesus' acquaintances" (Luke 23:49), as well as "the women who had come with him from Galilee," stood at a distance looking on.[14] Luke gives the impression that these women, outstanding and memorable for their faithfulness, merged with the crowds and stood apart, in the company of the male companions.

Luke omits any reference to women at the Last Supper, where Jesus describes his followers, saying, "It is you who have stood by me in my trials" (Luke 22:28). Yet Luke knows that Peter and all the others will not be up to the challenge of standing by Jesus. Luke transposes to the Last Supper setting the inelegant argument among Jesus' disciples about which of them is the greatest (Luke 22:24-30), an argument found in Mark during the course of the journey to Jerusalem (Mark 9:33-37). Likewise in the setting of the Last Supper Luke rehabilitates Peter even before his denial three times when accused by a peasant girl who recognized from his Galilean accent that Peter had been "with Jesus." In contrast, the women who were consistently "with Jesus," actually standing by him during his trials, even to the cross, do not imprint their name in Luke's memory. These women are simply not given due credit by Luke.

We ought not give a negative connotation to the Synoptics' note that the women were looking on "from a distance." Mark and Matthew especially relied on the Old Testament to fill in spaces in their story. The "distance" from which the women observed these events could be an example. Psalm 38:12, the prayer of the afflicted one, for example, says, "Friends and companions shun my pain; my neighbors stand far off." And the lament of Psalm 88:9 complains, "Because of you my friends

---

[14] This is another indication that some interpreters may be correct in contending that men and women are segregated in the Christian community.

shun me; / you make me loathsome to them." The women are placed sufficiently far away so as not to participate or give active assent to what was happening. Yet they are still close enough to be witnesses of these events. These women persevere and are still there at the end, not only at the cross but at the burial. Luke says in 23:55-56: "The women who had come from Galilee with him followed behind, and when they had seen the tomb and the way in which his body was laid in it, they returned and prepared spices and perfumed oils. Then they rested on the sabbath according to the commandment."

Luke makes a point of showing that after Jesus' death the women returned to their homes and prepared the spices and oils needed to anoint Jesus. And then, after the Sabbath, they returned to the tomb prepared to anoint him (see 24:1). For Luke, the women are Sabbath observants. This note reminds readers of the birth of Jesus, when everything was done according to the Law. As Raymond Brown observes, "From beginning to end, Jesus lived within the confines of the law," according to Luke.[15]

Galilee is also a link between the resurrection and the instructions Jesus had given to his followers during his ministry. The "two men in dazzling garments" reminded the women of what Jesus had said:

> "Why do you seek the living one among the dead? He is not here, but he has been raised. Remember what he said to you while he was still in Galilee, that the Son of Man must be handed over to sinners and be crucified, and rise on the third day." And they remembered his words. Then they returned from the tomb and announced all these things to the eleven and to all the others. The women were Mary Magdalene, Joanna, and Mary the mother of James; the others who accompanied them also told this to the apostles, but their story seemed like nonsense and they did not believe them. But Peter got up and ran to the tomb, bent down, and saw the burial cloths alone; then he went home amazed at what had happened (Luke 24:5-12).

---

[15] Brown, "Luke," in *An Introduction to the New Testament*, 260.

Luke follows this account with the story of the disciples' encounter with Jesus on the road to Emmaus. As they proceed to explain to the stranger whom they did not recognize as Jesus what had happened, they said, "Some women from our group . . . were at the tomb early in the morning and did not find his body; they came back and reported that they had indeed seen a vision of angels who announced that he was alive. Then some of those with us went to the tomb and found things just as the women had described" (Luke 24:22-24). Despite the credibility they should have earned for their unwavering attendance to these events, the women's report had to be verified, apparently by the men, before it was believed. The cruelest blow of all, however, comes a little later in the story when the Emmaus disciples return to Jerusalem, where they found "the eleven and those with them," saying, "The Lord has truly been raised and has appeared to Simon!" (Luke 24:34). In Simon Luke finds at last a credible witness!

The ending of Luke's story might be more acceptable and understandable if we read it together with the beginning, the infancy narrative.[16] Luke forms an "inclusion," relating themes here at the end that he had introduced at the beginning. This technique forces the reader's memory to pick up on what Luke had said before. There are several examples of such recurrent themes and ideas. For example, the story begins and ends with people described in similar terms. In the beginning and near the end there is someone named Simon. Joseph of Arimathea, like Anna and Simeon, lived in expectation of the kingdom of God (Luke 2:25 and 23:51). Some representatives from Judea and from Galilee witness the birth as well as the death and burial. And both at his birth and at his death, everything was done in accordance with the law.

---

[16] Luke's ending ought to be evaluated as his source Mark's is in relation to the purposes of the rest of the Gospel. Mark, for example, ends with the women running away and telling no one, for "they were afraid" (Mark 16:8). That ending serves Mark's secrecy motif, but clearly this is not history as it happened. Although Luke may be qualifying or limiting the leadership roles of women in the Church as he minimizes them increasingly in the Gospel and in Acts, Luke can't take away history. He is forced to reckon with the women who were the only witnesses at the cross and then at the tomb to hear the resurrection message.

Women are described by Luke as following Jesus and ministering to him. These are metaphors of authentic discipleship rooted in the narrative of the Synoptics. Women from Galilee who had provided for him all along the course of his journey (Luke 8:3) provide also for Jesus' burial. They act as witnesses when they follow after Joseph and the body of Jesus. The role of witness is important in Lukan theology, and in a sense, it begins here in a special way.[17] Luke's resurrection account in chapter 24 will make much of it.

The women notice the tomb and see "how the body was laid." They knew how to care for a corpse and realized that in the haste necessitated by the Sabbath, there was insufficient washing and anointing of Jesus. These women were resourceful. They were used to providing for Jesus' needs, and they weren't about to stop now. They went and bought spices to anoint him, and then they observed the Sabbath.[18] From Luke we learned that Jesus defended a woman's Sabbath observance (Luke 13:10-17) and the action of a woman who anointed him (Luke 7:36-50). Luke could be hinting here that these women observe the Sabbath most appropriately when they use it to prepare for Jesus' anointing. He is "the Lord of the Sabbath" (Luke 6:5). The women's anointing of him is a prophetic gesture.

"I have seen the Lord!" (John 20:18).

MARY MAGDALENE

Suggested Reading: Luke 8:3; (see Mark 16:9); John 20:1-2, 11-18; see also Mark 15:40, 47; 16:1; Matthew 27:56, 61; 28:1; John 19:25.

Although identification of the other women accompanying Jesus differs somewhat in the various Gospels, all four

---

[17] This comment is made by J. Fitzmyer, *The Gospel of Luke,* 1515.

[18] It is interesting in this regard that Luke has three episodes of controversy between Jesus and his opponents on how to observe the Sabbath (see Luke 6:1-11; 14:1-6 and 13:10-17, which is unique to Luke, the only evangelist to include a Sabbath healing of a woman).

Gospels are unanimous in placing Mary Magdalene at the cross and also as a witness to the resurrection. Indeed, she is the only woman who is described as being there in all four Gospels.[19] Mary Magdalene is one of the most popular characters of the New Testament. Yet it is surprising how little we are actually told about her. And some of what we think we know might be a result of confusing her with other women in the New Testament.[20] Mary Magdalene is sometimes erroneously identified as the "sinner" who anointed Jesus according to Luke's description in 7:36-50. She is at times also confused with Mary of Bethany, sister of Martha and Lazarus (John 12:1-8). Mary Magdalene is also sometimes mistaken for the unnamed woman caught in adultery (see John 7:53-8:11). Nowhere in the New Testament is Mary Magdalene referred to as a sinner, still less a prostitute.

Actually very little is said of her. She is associated with a town in Galilee, Magdala, which is otherwise not known to us. Luke unwittingly may be the culprit responsible for so many misconceptions because he qualifies her as one who had been healed; Luke says of this Mary, "from whom seven demons had gone out" (Luke 8:2; see also Mark 16:9). When she is associated with other named women, Mary Magdalene is almost always listed first (except in John 19:25), an indication of her position of leadership with regard to women, at least.

---

[19] Only John (see John 19:25) places Jesus' mother at the cross: John says, "Standing by the cross of Jesus were his mother and his mother's sister, Mary the wife of Clopas, and Mary of Magdala." The Synoptics say nothing about the presence of Jesus' mother there. John's list here is the only time that Mary Magdalene's name does not appear first among the women named (see Mark 15:40, 47; 16:1; Matt 27:56, 61; 28:1; Luke 8:2; 24:10; and John 19:25). Mary Magdalene appears by herself, without other women, in John 20:1, 11-18; Mark 16:9, see 9-11.

[20] This confusion is more typical of Western traditions, which, influenced by Augustine's thinking on "original sin," sometimes exaggerate sexual sins such as adultery and prostitution. Interestingly, in the Eastern Churches, which emphasize less the "sins of the flesh," these women are not confused, and Mary Magdalene is not known as a "sinner," and certainly not a prostitute.

With its primitive knowledge of the origins of mental and physical illnesses, the New Testament would appear to exaggerate the prevalence of "possession" by demons. Yet the miracle of exorcism aptly represents Jesus' struggle against evils that afflict people in many forms: demons, Satan, chaos, temptation, erratic behavior, fearsome, unexplainable symptoms, etc. The Gerasene demoniac, for example, was so afflicted by a "legion" of demons that he eventually was chained, nude, to tombs outside the city (see Luke 8:26-36). Similarly, Mary Magdalene was beset by not one but seven demons who controlled her life. The number seven signifies completeness and illustrates the degree of her malady. It is interesting that in a saying from Q (meaning "source," material that is common to Matthew and Luke but absent in Mark) Jesus links "seven demons" with a warning to those who demand a sign but refuse to accept him. Jesus says,

> "When an unclean spirit goes out of a person it roams through arid regions, searching for rest but finds none. Then it says, 'I will return to my home from which I came.' But upon returning, it finds it empty, swept clean, and put in order. Then it goes and brings back with itself seven other spirits more evil than itself, and they move in and dwell there; and the last condition of that person is worse than the first. Thus it will be with this evil generation" (Matt 12:43-45; see also Luke 11:24-26).

Jesus' listeners were to understand that without faith and perseverance even one who has been cured is in danger. Evil is self-perpetuating. If one demon is expelled, it will look for seven others and return to make the condition of its victim much worse. The story of Mary Magdalene provides a contrast to this scenario. She remains close to Jesus, ministering to him and serving as an example to the other disciples, and thereby remaining healthy, free from the demons that had so plagued her in the past. But there is nothing, even in Luke's description of her, to suggest that Mary Magdalene was possessed because she was sinful.

Luke implies that seven demons had "gone out" of Mary Magdalene by some intervention of Jesus. The telling result was that now Mary dedicates her life to following Jesus and ministering to him. Luke favors this same dynamic of chaotic illness (accompanied by some social insecurity, impurity, or isolation) being met with healing by Jesus and resulting in faithful ministry as well as social reintegration, leadership, and recognition. It is a recurring pattern. And although we ought not to be overly simplistic about Luke's presentation of women, clearly his reference is less to Mary's former state of possession and more to her liberated state of leadership in the believing community. Mary Magdalene is one of Jesus' success stories. People move from the marginalized fringes to prominence as examples worthy of praise and emulation because of their encounters and their response to Jesus.

In the Gospels a number of miracles relate to how women are the representatives of the wondrous healing of Jesus. About half of Luke's miracles worked on behalf of women are taken from Mark, and the other half are unique to Luke. For both Mark and Luke, exorcisms are liberating acts and part of an eschatological event proclaiming that the kingdom of God is "within you." For Mary Magdalene, like most of the women of the Gospels, healing means being "resocialized into the community."[21] Formerly an outcast beset by many demons, she is now an exemplary leader with some measure of authority. It is significant that Luke makes a connection between the experience of a wondrous act of Jesus and the calling to follow him and remain with him.

Although all four Gospels picture women from Galilee at the foot of the cross and at the empty tomb, only Luke inserts into Jesus' Galilean ministry this summary of the women following Jesus from Galilee and ministering to him. And only John narrates a story that Mary Magdalene is our single, consistent link between Jesus' Galilean ministry and the cross and the resurrection. That "story" is presented in John's account of the first resurrection appearances in chapter 20 (see John 20:1-2, 11-18).

The original conclusion to John's Gospel is chapter 20; chapter 21 is often seen as an epilogue, added especially to explain the relationship between the Beloved Disciple and Peter, and between the Church of the Beloved Disciple and the greater

[21] Seim, "The Gospel of Luke," 736.

Church Peter represents, which looked to John's community with a certain suspicion and uncertainty. In any case, John depicts in chapter 20 three foundational appearances of Jesus in which his disciples are retooled and refitted to continue the ministry Jesus had started. The early Churches are represented in this chapter by the Beloved Disciple, Peter, and Mary Magdalene. We shall concentrate on the portrayal of the latter.

John introduces Mary Magdalene in 20:1-2, then has her leave, only to reappear in verses 11-18. In his own words John tells us what happened that first Easter Sunday:

> [1]On the first day of the week, Mary of Magdala came to the tomb early in the morning, while it was still dark, and saw the stone removed from the tomb. [2]So she ran and went to Simon Peter and to the other disciple whom Jesus loved, and told them, "They have taken the Lord from the tomb, and we don't know where they put him. . . ."
>
> [11]But Mary stayed outside the tomb weeping. And as she wept, she bent over into the tomb [12]and saw two angels in white sitting there, one at the head and one at the feet where the body of Jesus had been. [13]And they said to her, "Woman, why are you weeping?" She said to them, "They have taken my Lord, and I don't know where they laid him." [14]When she had said this, she turned around and saw Jesus there, but did not know it was Jesus. [15]Jesus said to her, "Woman, why are you weeping? Whom are you looking for?" She thought it was the gardener and said to him, "Sir, if you carried him away, tell me where you laid him, and I will take him." [16]Jesus said to her, "Mary!" She turned and said to him in Hebrew, "Rabbouni," which means Teacher. [17]Jesus said to her, "Stop holding on to me, for I have not yet ascended to the Father. But go to my brothers and tell them, 'I am going to my Father and your Father, to my God and your God.'" [18]Mary of Magdala went and announced to the disciples, "I have seen the Lord," and what he told her (John 20:1-2, 11-18).

John says in 20:1 that Mary Magdalene came to the tomb while it was still dark. She searches the darkness for the answer to her unvoiced question, "Where is the Lord?" She seems to feel as Jesus felt on the cross, wondering why God had abandoned him at this darkest moment. Although interpreters rightly point out that darkness and sleepiness are linked to disbelief in John,[22] in the case of Mary this is not so. All four Gospels testify that women came to the tomb early on Sunday morning, before light. In John, of course, darkness is often symbolic of disbelief, pain, sin, even rejection of Jesus.

But as the story of Mary Magdalene will make clear, she searches for Jesus as if unable to sleep, to give up, despite the seeming finality of Jesus' death and of seeing with her own eyes where he was laid. Although the darkness may convey her hopelessness and confusion, it does not convey disbelief. As Gail O'Day says so well, "Mary's confusion reflects the world-shattering dimension of the empty tomb. The pre-resurrection world cannot make sense of an empty tomb with any theory except grave robbing."[23] Mary saw that the stone was taken away and took that to mean that Jesus was taken away, too. She immediately thought of the community and ran to tell the others. She reported her news to Peter and the other disciple, saying in verse 2, "They have taken the Lord from the tomb, and we don't know where they put him."[24] Then she returns to the tomb herself. Meanwhile, the others rush to see for themselves. The Beloved Disciple stoops to look but does not enter; rather he waits for Peter to come. Peter arrives and they enter only to see that everything is as Mary told them. Then Peter and the Beloved Disciple, John tells us, "returned home"

---

[22] E.g., Moloney, *The Gospel of John*, 524–525. But Moloney appears to overstress Mary's alleged disbelief, while exaggerating the male disciples' immediate belief. Mary, Peter, and the other disciple are linked in the collective, "We do not know where he is." But it is characteristic of John to portray someone as having initial belief that progresses to fuller faith (see, for example, Nicodemus, the Samaritan woman, the man born blind). This is how Mary is presented, whereas Peter especially is not rehabilitated until after his thrice-repeated insistence that he "loves" Jesus in chapter 21.

[23] Gail R. O'Day, "John," in *Women's Bible Commentary*, ed. Carol A. Newsom and Sharon H. Ringe (Louisville: Westminster/John Knox, 1992) 293–304, at 300–301.

[24] John first introduces the Beloved Disciple in the Book of Signs: see John 13:23-26; 19:25-27; referred to in 18:15-16 as the "other disciple." The two are linked for the first time in 20:2. Up until this point, there has been tension between Peter and this "other disciple"; here and finally in chapter 21, after the resurrection, that tension is resolved.

(v. 10), while Mary remained there. O'Day's comment on this is pertinent: "The male disciples, like Mary, could find no words out of their prior experience to describe the empty tomb. Yet Mary bore witness to the tomb even in her confusion. Peter and the Beloved Disciple kept silent."[25]

In John's Gospel there is no question about Mary's credibility. Peter and the Beloved Disciple do not know what to make of these events and seek instead the comfort of what they know. But Mary remained at the tomb, vigilant. In John it is the male disciples who are dismissed. With Mary's scene in 20:1-18, John reintroduces the mourning theme, depicting Mary as weeping *(klaiein)*, the same verb used of Mary and the Jews at the tomb of Lazarus (see John 11:32-33). This is not, as Francis Moloney claims, a "faithless wailing."[26] Such weeping is the reaction of Rachael for her children (Matt 2:18), of the wailer and the household of Jairus (Mark 5:38-39), and of the daughters of Jerusalem (Luke 23:28), and of several others in the Gospels.

In her search for Jesus in the dark and cold of early morning on the first day of the week soon after the crucifixion, Mary combines the actions of the Beloved Disciple, who stoops down (20:5, 11), and Peter, who peers into the site (20:6, 12). Two angels have taken the positions of the cherubim who occupy the mercy seat on the ark of the covenant (Exod 37:7-8). They inquire, "Woman, why are you weeping?" (20:13), a question Jesus will repeat in 20:15. John's readers are reminded of Jesus' address to his mother as "Woman" at Cana (2:4) and at the cross (19:26-27) in John. Mary Magdalene's own presence at the cross and this address as "Woman" link her to his mother, and both as exemplary disciples. Mary's response repeats her

---

[25] O'Day, "John," 301. It is hard to understand how, based on this text, another commentator can say, "The two disciples, and especially the Beloved Disciple, have gone beyond the experience of Mary, moving toward (vv. 3-4) and away from (v. 10) the empty tomb," while Mary remains "stationary." See Moloney, *John,* pp. 524–525.

[26] Ibid., p. 525. He contrasts this with the "deep frustration and weeping" of Jesus expressed in a different verb, *dakruein*, at Lazarus's grave (John 11:35). But then what of Luke's use of *klaiein* in the Beatitudes: "Blessed are you who are now weeping, for you shall laugh. . . . but woe to you who laugh now, you shall grieve and weep" (Luke 6:21, 25).

words to the Beloved Disciple and Peter, but in more personal terms this time: "They have taken *my* Lord, and *I* do not know where they laid him" (20:13). She still does not understand[27] because of her grief.

Jesus repeats the angel's question to Mary Magdalene, "Woman, why are you weeping?" He adds a second question that goes back to his first words to the emissaries of John in chapter 1: "Whom are you looking for?" (see 1:38; 20:15). Recognizing Jesus' voice because she "belongs" to him, Mary then turns to behold Jesus, who now calls her by name—"Mary!"[28] The mutual recognition is instantaneous. Mary is living evidence of Jesus' prophecy, "I am the good shepherd, and I know mine and mine know me" (John 10:14). As he did the first time he used the term (see 1:38), John explains that her response means "Teacher." She pledges her faith in Jesus.

Mary moves to be closer to him, but Jesus says, "Stop holding on to me . . . . Go to my brothers and tell them." This is not a harsh or cruel rebuke. Rather, Jesus teaches Mary that he cannot be limited or "held" in certain preconceived expectations. As Gail O'Day puts it, "If Mary had stopped Jesus from ascending to God, holding him with her in the garden, the Easter story would be incomplete."[29] Indeed, it would never be told or spread. This prohibition is linked with a command "Go to my brothers and tell them, 'I am going to my Father and your Father, to my God and your God'"(20:17). The message she is to tell the others is that with the resurrection and ascension, Jesus' disciples are now part of the family of God.

John simply concludes Mary's story, saying, "Mary of Magdala went and announced (*angelousa*) to the disciples, 'I have seen the Lord,' and what he told her" (Luke 20:18). With an

---

[27] "Knowing" or understanding is another Johannine theme related to faith.

[28] See John 10:4: "When he has driven out all his own, he walks ahead of them, and the sheep follow him, because they recognize his voice." Referring to the image of the shepherd, John adds, "Although Jesus used this figure of speech, they did not realize what he was trying to tell them" (10:6). But Mary finally does realize, when she lets go of her fears and accepts the reality of the resurrection.

[29] O'Day, "John," 301.

unusual change of speaker in mid-sentence, John verifies Mary's credibility. She receives the first resurrection announcement and mission mandate. And her announcement is received and believed in the beloved community. When Jesus appears again that evening (John 20:19-29), he does not repeat what Mary had told them. He presumes they know it.[30] Indeed, Mary's testimony was received as true and preserved not only in John's Church but in the universal Church, as witnessed by the fact that all four Gospels agree that Mary was the premier witness to the resurrection, which she announced as a result of Jesus' appearance to her. But in John she is the first witness, and the only one, to receive an individual appearance and a commission to preach to the others.[31]

When Mary announces, "I have seen the Lord," she uses a formula of authority, one that confirms her credentials as an apostle. This is the same one that Paul employs to adamantly insist on his own apostolic authority (see 1 Cor 9:1). It is also implied in Paul's list of the foundational resurrection appearances in 1 Corinthians 15:3-8 as evidence of Peter's and James's and Paul's own authority as well as to verify the resurrection itself. The disciples returning from Emmaus report, "We have seen the Lord," and then to Thomas, who was absent that first night, the others said, "We have seen the Lord." The Beloved Disciple bears witness to what he has seen (19:35). In John, bearing witness is always based on what is seen and heard.[32]

In John's passion narrative, there was a certain amount of tension between Peter and the Beloved Disciple. When Jesus spoke of his betrayer, for example, Peter beckons to the Beloved Disciple to inquire about the traitor's identity (John 13:23-26). When Jesus is arrested, Peter and the "other disciple" follow at a distance and later warm themselves by the fire while Jesus is being interrogated (John 18:15-16). Whereas Peter then denies that he "knows" Jesus, the Beloved Disciple is at the cross with Jesus' mother and Mary Magdalene and

[30] Sandra M. Schneiders, "Encountering and Proclaiming the Risen Jesus," in *Written That You May Believe: Encountering Jesus in the Fourth Gospel* (New York: Crossroad, 1999) 189–201, at 200.

[31] Ibid.

[32] Ibid.

some other women (John 19:25-27). These three—Peter, the Beloved Disciple, and Mary Magdalene—are foundational figures whose relationship is reconciled as part of John's resurrection agenda.

Peter and the Beloved Disciple are reconciled in chapter 21, after Peter's rehabilitation in the eyes of the Johannine Church. John makes it clear in 20:1-18 that both Peter and the Beloved Disciple receive the resurrection message and mandate from Mary Magdalene. John will not compromise the privileged position Mary Magdalene enjoys in his beloved community. Her faith is vindicated and celebrated there. The community's knowledge and belief in the resurrection are based on the witness of this woman who has been rightly called the "Apostle to the Apostles."

"Now Jesus loved Martha and her sister [Mary] and Lazarus"
(John 11:5).

MARTHA AND MARY

The sisters Martha and Mary remain a source of perennial interest, debate, and sometimes frustration, especially for women. Luke's anecdote, apparently about sibling rivalry among them, somehow eclipses the much more theologically significant story featuring these women as told by John. A comparison of these stories illustrates once again why some authors consider Luke to be "dangerous." First we will look at Luke's version of the story.

Suggested Reading: Luke 10:38-42

> As they continued their journey he entered a village where a woman whose name was Martha welcomed him. She had a sister named Mary [who] sat beside the Lord at his feet listening to him speak. Martha, burdened with much serving, came to him and said, "Lord, do you not care that my sister has left me by myself to do the serving? Tell her to help me." The Lord said to her in reply, "Martha, Martha, you are

anxious and worried about many things. There is need of
only one thing. Mary has chosen the better part and it will
not be taken from her."

This is apparently such a simple, commonplace exchange
that one would wonder why Luke would even observe, much
less preserve it. Jesus is a guest in their house, and the two sisters
vie with each other for his attention. One serves him and the
other sits "at his feet." One man, two women, palpable tension.
One of the oldest scenes in the world. Why is it in the Gospel?

Martha becomes impatient and harried with the stress of
her hospitable efforts. She asks Jesus to side with her by telling
Mary to help her. Implicitly Martha complains also about Jesus:
"Do you not care that my sister has left me by myself to do the
serving?" Jesus' answer seems to be a mixture of indulgence
and impatience. Depending on his tone, the repetition of her
name, "Martha, Martha," could seem off-putting and even
condescending. Jesus knows that she is burdened with "many
things." But he refuses to rebuke Mary. A lot of women who
feel sympathy with Martha might even ask why Jesus himself
does not lend a hand with the various chores. It might seem to
be a disrespectful suggestion. But didn't Jesus take a towel
and wash the feet of his disciples? Didn't he say that he came
to serve? Wouldn't his example move Mary to be more considerate of her sister? We have to look further into why this small
exchange was included in the Gospel of Luke.

The context in Luke's Gospel is not very helpful here. Luke
has just recounted the parable of the good Samaritan (see Luke
10:29-37), which shows the importance of hospitality in this
Gospel. Service is one of the marks of a disciple. So it would be
self-defeating for Luke to claim that Martha was doing something wrong in "welcoming" Jesus, attending to his needs and
serving him.

Some traditional interpretations have tried to show that
what Martha is doing isn't wrong, but it is second best. Martha
is the busy one, while Mary represents the contemplative side
of Christian life. Given a choice, Mary has the "better part."
Related to this is the reminder that there can be no fruitful
ministry without first hearing the word. Mary's part has priority not only in importance but in time.

Some interpreters rather see a tension between the "many things" and "one thing." From this perspective, Jesus chides Martha because she does not have her priorities in order. She has welcomed Jesus, but not wholeheartedly. She remains resentful that Jesus and her sister benefit from her ministrations but do not assist her. She ought not be concerned with what they are doing but should be more generous and loving.

But these efforts to understand the place of this story in Luke fail to satisfy. The reader still feels sympathy with Martha and frustration that some "sharing" of the workload is not encouraged. The satisfaction we seek might not be found if we only consider the immediate context of Luke and take this as a story that actually occurred, as told, in the lifetime of Jesus. Rather, this scene reflects more the situation in Luke's community than a situation in the life of Jesus. In the eighth decade, when Luke was writing, the respective role(s) of women was much debated. At least one of Luke's concerns is showing that being a Christian did not conflict with the Greco-Roman ideals for men and women living in the empire. Luke is at pains to be "politically correct" for his own times. He shows that Christian men and women were pious and observant of religious tradition, that they adhered to accepted standards for behavior as members of society, that their family life, including the women, was exemplary.

In this context Martha represents the women who had taken on "many concerns" in an earlier church, which had been living more on an apocalyptic edge. The Pauline churches of the fifties, for example, might well have been able to "afford" women prophets, teachers, apostles, deacons, that is, women who took on untraditional roles, or roles that the society of the day restricted to males. In the early aftermath of Jesus' resurrection, Christians like Paul assumed the near-end of this world. The Pauline churches, like their leader Paul, saw this world coming to an end, and soon; the "new age" had already dawned. Caution may be thrown to the wind in such a situation. There is no "tomorrow," no future, no lasting home here on earth. The Church was not yet in the survival mode it would later assume. But in Luke we see a more domesticated Church.

As the Messiah, Jesus was thought to be one who would bring on the end of time. Paul repeatedly tells Christians at

Corinth, for example, "The time is near." But three decades later the end had not come. Rather, Christianity had endured at least one persecution under Nero in the sixties, when Peter and Paul had been executed. The Twelve and the other original apostles and disciples of Jesus had died, many a martyr's death. The Romans had destroyed the Temple and decimated Palestinian Judaism in the Jewish-Roman wars of 66–72. The Church faced an indefinite future as a minority within a minority. It was trying to survive despite odds against it.

Luke tries to show that Christian life is compatible with the social patterns of Roman-administered Judea and Galilee.[33] Jesus praises certain behavior in women, as if suggesting that they could serve as models to others. For example, the widow of Luke 21:1-4, who gives even out of her own need, would appear to be a model of generosity and virtue.[34] So also, the woman of Jesus' parable who lost a coin shows good household management by giving every priority to finding it again (Luke 15:8-10). In the same vein, Martha is chided, however kindly by Jesus, for her ambition about "many things." She ought to be more like Mary, who embodies the virtues Rome also found praiseworthy.

Many interpreters point out that Luke is concerned with the image of the Church in the mind of Rome. He offers a defense of Christianity, a way of showing how the Church "fit in" with the goals and priorities of the Roman Empire. Luke's Church had lost its apocalyptic edge and was more domesticated than Paul's churches had been. For Luke, what was important was maintaining allegiance to Jesus the universal Lord, spreading the Gospel and the Church to "the ends of the earth" and persevering over the long haul. Within this context, Luke appears to be willing to qualify or mitigate as needed some of the freedom Paul described as characteristic of life in the spirit. This would have influenced the way Luke treats women in his Gospel and in Acts.

---

[33] For a clear and interesting discussion of this, see Richard Cassidy, *Society and Politics in Acts* (Maryknoll: Orbis, 1987) 22–23; 57–59; and *passim*.

[34] Although I think she serves the opposite purpose in the Gospels; see below, pp. 205–212.

In the Pauline churches, women had served the community in a variety of roles: as heads of house churches, as preachers, as itinerant missionaries, as leaders with authority. For example, Lydia was the head of the original house church established in Philippi, one of Paul's favorite and strongest communities (see Acts 16:11-15, 40). Euodia and Syntyche, of the same community, were two women who developed a rivalry that was important enough to be reported to Paul (Phil 4:2-3). His anxiety that they be reconciled is one indication of the prestige and influence of these women. Although he does not dictate how (or who was in the right), Paul implores them to resolve their differences and return to the "one mind" that was characteristic of Jesus and of the Philippian community from the start. It would seem that when Luke was confronted with a similar situation, he advocated the position of one of the women (those represented by Mary) and "corrected" those who would have sided with Martha, invoking the authority of Jesus to bolster such a resolution.

Within the context of Luke's Church, taking a public stand on the roles of women seems to have been a concern. While Luke and the other evangelists did not write the stories of women *into* their Gospels, neither could they write such stories *out*. The story of Jesus apparently couldn't be told without also telling about the Gospel women who interacted with him, believed in him, brought him out, served and supported him, and bore witness to him. Yet Luke appears unwilling to sacrifice for women the reputation and perhaps the future of the Church he was trying so hard to defend. Thus Luke can be expected to do what he does, namely, to side with the standards that will be more culturally acceptable in the Roman milieu in which he was making every effort to ensure the Church's survival. This would have included certain expectations about the behavior of pious and good women.

Within this perspective, Martha must relinquish her ambitious concern about "many things" and adopt the more passive role such as Mary exemplifies. When Martha turns to Jesus to resolve her dispute, she refers to Mary as "my sister." This reflects the way Christians in the early Church referred to one another as "brothers and sisters." Martha's complaint that "my sister" does not help suggests a rift in the "sisterhood" of the early Christians. What probably made this rift the more painful was that it pitted sister against sister; women were taking sides over the issue of the proper role(s) for women in the Church. Mary appears satisfied with the traditional female roles. Luke draws on the authority of Jesus to sustain preference for Mary's take on this.

There is an alternative interpretation of this story in Luke that presents some possible food for thought. It results in a very different perspective on the images of these two women and what they meant for the early Church as well as what they could mean for us. Within the Church of the first couple centuries modes of discipleship developed along at least two interdependent lines.

On the one hand, there were some, like Paul, who were charismatic, itinerant preachers. Jesus seems to be describing their radical mandate in the "missionary discourse" (see Mark 6:6-13; Matt 10; Luke 9, 10). Jesus sends them out two by two into the world to preach the Gospel and to heal the sick and needy. They must demonstrate a remarkable courage and trust, as well as detachment and poverty. Jesus told them to

> "Take nothing for the journey, neither walking stick, nor sack, nor food, nor money, and let no one take a second tunic. Whatever house you enter, stay there and leave from there. And as for those who do not welcome you, when you leave that town, shake the dust from your feet in testimony against them" (Luke 9:3-5).

There was a radical poverty and a complete dependence on the communities that would support them. Like Jesus, these itinerants would have "nowhere to rest his head" (Matt 8:20).

On the other hand, there must have been communities and hosts of such communities who would have provided for the needs of these itinerant preachers. Essential to the success of the Church's preaching mission would be resident hosts who would receive these missionaries and preachers, show them hospitality, take care of them, feed and clothe them, and send them on their way to their next destination. Residents of a locale where the Church was established would also receive the community and provide a place and often meals for the regular liturgical celebrations of Christian life. There would be risk and a certain danger in doing this as well as a certain amount of expense, not to mention the inconvenience of consistently offering generous and continuous hospitality.

It is possible that Martha represents the local hosts who provided the place and the support required by the traveling missionaries. Martha is a symbol of those who were expected to give cheerfully without counting the cost, without expecting any recognition in return. Jesus also describes their mandate in rather inglorious and more laborious terms: "When you hold a lunch or a dinner, do not invite your friends or your brothers or your relatives or your wealthy neighbors, in case they may invite you back and you have repayment. Rather, when you hold a banquet, invite the poor, the crippled, the lame, the blind; blessed indeed will you be because of their inability to repay you" (Luke 14:12-14).

Mary could represent the itinerant preacher who moved from place to place, preaching the word, dependent on the reception she (or he) met wherever she went. Usually these preachers did not support themselves but were supported by the community they served.

There certainly could have been tension between these groups.[35] If such tension could have arisen among the men who were disciples of Jesus, a comparable tension might have arisen also among the women. And among the women it might have been even more problematic if one or other of these stances

---

[35] In fact, we can discern tension that may be related to this issue in Paul's letters, between the itinerant Paul and the freedom he exercises, and the more traditional views espoused by apostles who stay put in Jerusalem, like James for instance (see Gal 1:18-19; 2:1-4). Paul suggests the acceptable practice of the local resident church hosting the itinerants and even their dependents (see 1 Cor 9:4-5), referring to the example of Peter, whose wife accompanied him; both are apparently supported by the churches. Paul even invokes a teaching of Jesus on the subject: "The Lord ordered that those who preach the gospel should live by the gospel" (1 Cor 9:14; see Matt 10:10; Luke 10:7-8). Paul's allusion to this practice suggests that various aspects of it had come under fire. If male missionaries such as James and Peter and Paul differed in their interpretation of this issue, we can assume it may have also been problematic and debated among women, or at least we can wonder to what extent different roles for women could have been practiced without being questioned.

represented a freedom and actions that would have seemed contrary to accepted norms of the wider society.

What Luke is doing with the Mary-Martha story could be defending both forms of discipleship also for women. As the representative of the itinerant preacher who heard the word of God and preached it to others, Mary's chosen "part" ought not to be taken from her by resentful hosts who thought she should be doing something else, like staying within the more traditional roles women held. The role of resident host could belong to women as well as to men, as Martha, Mary of Jerusalem, and Lydia demonstrate. The role of host was difficult and demanding. Martha was busy about many things, and this was the way she was answering her call and her faith-commitment. The role of itinerant preacher was also demanding and wrought with difficulties. It is not that Martha is choosing a wrong way to follow Jesus, but that she ought not dispute the right of other women, like her sister Mary, to pursue a less traditional form of service to the Church.

Suggested Reading: John 11:1-44

John first introduces his readers to Martha, Mary, and their brother Lazarus near the end of Jesus' earthly ministry, as Jesus approaches Jerusalem to face death. John's Gospel is often divided into two main parts: the so-called Book of Signs in John 1–12 and the Book of Glory in 13–21. John refers to Jesus' wondrous acts as "signs," meaning that they reveal a reality beyond the acts themselves. For John, Jesus' miraculous works point to who Jesus himself is. His healings or his feeding of the multitudes, for example, serve as the occasion for the "I Am" discourses, in which Jesus reveals that he is the Light of the World, the Bread of Life, the Way, the Truth. Thus, the multiplication of the loaves in John 6:1-5 prompts Jesus' Bread of Life discourse (6:22-65). The death of Lazarus and Jesus' visit to his tomb (John 11:1-44) occasion Jesus' declaration, "I am the resurrection and the life" (11:25). The greatest sign of all is the resurrection from the dead, a sign that Jesus is Life. This is the sign that occasions John's account of Jesus' visit with the sisters Martha and Mary and their brother Lazarus, who was raised from the dead.

¹Now a man was ill, Lazarus from Bethany, the village of Mary and her sister Martha. ²Mary was the one who had anointed the Lord with perfumed oil and dried his feet with her hair; it was her brother Lazarus who was ill. ³So the sisters sent word to him, saying, "Master, the one you love is ill." ⁴When Jesus heard this he said, "This illness is not to end in death, but is for the glory of God, that the Son of God may be glorified through it." ⁵Now Jesus loved Martha and her sister and Lazarus. ⁶So when he heard that he was ill, he remained for two days in the place where he was. ⁷Then after this he said to his disciples, "Let us go back to Judea." ⁸The disciples said to him, "Rabbi, the Jews were just trying to stone you, and you want to go back there?" ⁹Jesus answered, "Are there not twelve hours in a day? If one walks during the day, he does not stumble, because he sees the light of this world. ¹⁰But if one walks at night, he stumbles, because the light is not in him." ¹¹He said this, and then told them, "Our friend Lazarus is asleep, but I am going to awaken him." ¹²So the disciples said to him, "Master, if he is asleep, he will be saved." ¹³But Jesus was talking about his death, while they thought that he meant ordinary sleep. ¹⁴So then Jesus said to them clearly, "Lazarus has died. ¹⁵And I am glad for you that I was not there, that you may believe. Let us go to him." ¹⁶So Thomas, called Didymus, said to his fellow disciples, "Let us also go to die with him."

¹⁷When Jesus arrived, he found that Lazarus had already been in the tomb for four days. ¹⁸Now Bethany was near Jerusalem, only about two miles away. ¹⁹And many of the Jews had come to Martha and Mary to comfort them about their brother. ²⁰When Martha heard that Jesus was coming, she went to meet him; but Mary sat at home. ²¹Martha said to Jesus, "Lord, if you had been here, my brother would not have died. ²²[But] even now I know that whatever you ask of God, God will give you." ²³Jesus said to her, "Your brother will rise." ²⁴Martha said to him, "I know he will rise, in the resurrection on the last day." ²⁵Jesus told her, "I am the resurrection and the life; whoever believes in me, even if he dies, will live, ²⁶and everyone who lives and believes in me will never die. Do you believe this?" ²⁷She said to him, "Yes, Lord. I have come to believe that you are the Messiah, the Son of God, the one who is coming into the world."

²⁸When she had said this, she went and called her sister Mary secretly, saying, "The teacher is here and is asking for you." ²⁹As soon as she heard this, she rose quickly and went

to him. [30]For Jesus had not yet come into the village, but was still where Martha had met him. [31]So when the Jews who were with her in the house comforting her saw Mary get up quickly and go out, they followed her, presuming that she was going to the tomb to weep there. [32]When Mary came to where Jesus was and saw him, she fell at his feet and said to him, "Lord, if you had been here, my brother would not have died." [33]When Jesus saw her weeping and the Jews who had come with her weeping, he became perturbed and deeply troubled, [34]and said, "Where have you laid him?" They said to him, "Sir, come and see." [35]And Jesus wept. [36]So the Jews said, "See how he loved him." [37]But some of them said, "Could not the one who opened the eyes of the blind man have done something so that this man would not have died?"

[38]So Jesus, perturbed again, came to the tomb. It was a cave, and a stone lay across it. [39]Jesus said, "Take away the stone." Martha, the dead man's sister, said to him, "Lord, by now there will be a stench; he has been dead for four days." [40]Jesus said to her, "Did I not tell you that if you believe you will see the glory of God?" [41]So they took away the stone. And Jesus raised his eyes and said, "Father, I thank you for hearing me. [42]I know that you always hear me; but because of the crowd here I have said this, that they may believe that you sent me." [43]And when he had said this, he cried out in a loud voice, "Lazarus, come out!" [44]The dead man came out, tied hand and foot with burial bands, and his face was wrapped in a cloth. So Jesus said to them, "Untie him and let him go" (John 11:1-44).

A number of characteristics of John's description are reminiscent of what Luke said about these women. It seems that Jesus is a good friend and perhaps a frequent guest of these sisters. Martha appears to be the head of a household, perhaps widowed. (If she had shared the same household with her brother, he would probably have been the host; but Luke agrees that Martha plays the role of host. No husband of Martha is noted.) Martha is the one who welcomes Jesus; in John she goes out to meet him on his way to her house. Martha has a greater speaking part in the stories, whereas Mary is more "quiet." John notes that Mary stays at home; Luke had pictured Mary wordlessly sitting at Jesus' feet.

But there are also a number of significant differences noted in a comparison of these stories. In John there is no trace of tension between the two women as there is in Luke.[36] John does not pit the sisters against one another as Luke does with his story. Both send Jesus word of their brother's death (John 11:3), and both greet him with the same belief: "Lord, if you had been here, my brother would not have died" (John 11:21 and 32). They are united in their grief and mourning, and in their courage in receiving Jesus when his enemies had already decided to put him to death. Both sisters in John profess their belief in Jesus, and both act as messengers to others after their encounter with Jesus (John 11:28, 31). Both address Jesus with various Christological titles that express their faith.

Luke has the setting for this encounter with the sisters in the course of Jesus' journey from Galilee in the north to Jerusalem in the south. John locates it in Bethany, not far from Jerusalem. The Synoptics refer to Bethany as the place where Jesus stayed the week before his death. John's story is significant as foreshadowing Jesus' own death and resurrection; it immediately precedes Mary's anointing of Jesus (John 12:1-8), apparently motivated by love and her gratitude for this sign Jesus does on behalf of her brother and family. From the beginning of this story, Jesus clearly reveals the ultimate value of this sign: it will lead to his glory (that is, in John, Jesus' death and its glorious implications).[37]

The introduction to this story is pure John. The evangelist almost takes for granted our acquaintance with Mary, Martha, and Lazarus, as if assuming that we already know circulating traditions about Jesus and his friends. As William Countryman says, "This [John's Gospel] is not a work of reportage so much as of interpretation."[38] In introducing Mary of Bethany

[36] Interestingly, some commentators seem to inject some tension even into John's story. Francis J. Moloney asserts that Jesus shows a preference for Mary, whose expression of faith exceeds that of Martha: *The Gospel of John,* 328–329. Other commentators tend to read the relationship between Martha and Mary (and Martha and Jesus) very differently in John than in Luke. See, for example, Reid, *Women in the Gospel of Luke,* 144–162.

[37] See Raymond E. Brown, *The Gospel and Epistles of John: A Concise Commentary* (Collegeville: The Liturgical Press, 1988) 62.

[38] L. William Countryman, *The Mystical Way in the Fourth Gospel: Crossing Over into God,* rev. ed., 1994 (Valley Forge, Pa.: Trinity Press International, 1941) 82.

in 11:2, John anticipates her anointing of Jesus, which will only come in the next chapter. John presumes we have heard about this. Thus John ties these two stories of the women's faith and their witness of the resurrection of their brother with Jesus' anointing for his own burial. Both sisters send word to Jesus that Lazarus is very ill. Their message refers to Lazarus as the "one you love." John tells us that Jesus loved Martha and her sister Mary and Lazarus. In his last discourse Jesus tells his disciples to "love one another as I have loved you." When Jesus weeps for Lazarus, the Jews say, "See how he loved him" (11:36). "Beloved" was a term used by early Christians for one another. Lazarus may represent the Christian to whom Jesus gives life. Through Lazarus's experiences, even of illness and death, the glory of God would shine forth.

Martha's profession of faith is remarkable, even in a Gospel like John's that consistently depicts women favorably.[39] Martha progresses through stages of faith in her dialogue with Jesus, first calling him *"Kyrie"* and complaining that if he had come sooner, her brother would not have died. She adds that she knows that even now whatever he asked of God could be done, making us think of Mary's prodding of her son at the Cana wedding. Jesus' saying that he is the Resurrection and the Life provokes an expression of partial faith from Martha. She "knows" that her brother will rise on the last day.

Although Martha was not in on the conversation Jesus had with his disciples in verses 11:8-16, she says that all along she has believed in the resurrection from the dead. Finally she adds an extraordinarily mature Christological profession of faith, saying, "I have come to believe [past perfect tense] that you are the Messiah [i.e., the Christ], the Son of God, the one who is coming into the world" (John 11:27). Martha is the one

---

[39] For example, Jesus' mother elicits the first sign at the wedding feast; Jesus has a very developed theological conversation with the Samaritan woman; Mary Magdalene is the first woman witness to a resurrection appearance. Commentators have debated a possible Gnostic influence here. Gnostic groups, which later would be considered heretical, advocated, among other things, the equality and leadership of women. It seems that the greater Church, as represented by the synoptic Gospels, did not share John's apparent views on women as equals.

to express the faith that won Peter Jesus' blessing and the "keys to the kingdom," according to Matthew 16:16.

In her own faith statement, Martha combines lines right out of John's prologue, poetry of the highest Christology of the New Testament. Jesus is the Christ, the Son of God, who comes into the world from God (see John 1:3, 10-11, 17-18). Jesus is Life and, as William Countryman so beautifully put it, ". . . no one associated with him can possibly be deprived of what he is. Death may seem to intervene, but it is not the ultimate reality."[40] When Martha had thus made clear her unshakable faith, but before she saw any sign of Lazarus's life restored, she ran to tell her sister that Jesus was with them. Such witness is the stuff of the resurrection.

John tells us then that Mary arose quickly and, followed by other mourners, went to Jesus, greeting him with the same words that her sister had used moments before: "*Kyrie*, if you had been here, my brother would not have died." Some interpreters claim that Mary has the greater faith according to this story, whereas Martha's faith is conditional that "even now Jesus would ask God" for a favor and God would do it.[41] But Sandra Schneiders appears to be more on target when she says: "Mary's part in the scene (11:28-32) serves merely to introduce her in preparation for her leading role in the anointing scene in 12:1-8, and to introduce the Jews who witness the sign that will divide them into those who believe in Jesus (see 11:45) and those who report him to the authorities (see 11:46)."[42]

Then Mary wept, and seeing her weep, Jesus also wept. Jesus' tears are mixed with anger, which John emphasizes by saying it twice (John 11:33 and 38). John's view of the incarnation implies that when Jesus took on our humanity, he took it on completely. His anger is that death is still wreaking havoc on the world. Jesus' victory over death will come with the resurrection and ascension. But they are not yet.

---

[40] Countryman, *The Mystical Way,* 83.

[41] Moloney, *The Gospel of John,* 328–329.

[42] Sandra M. Schneiders, "Women in the Fourth Gospel," in *Written That You May Believe: Encountering Jesus in the Fourth Gospel* (New York: Crossroad, 1999) 93–114, at 105.

Jesus asks, "Where have you laid him?" (11:34). Lazarus is wrapped in death and entombed, just as Jesus will be. The time lapse since his death, the bandages and the cloths, and the rock, all show the reality of death. As in the case of Jesus himself, the constraints of death did all in its power to limit life's possibilities for Lazarus.

Despite her immense faith, Martha's objection shows that she still lacks understanding, a spiritual virtue in John. Her imperfect faith is pre-resurrection faith, like Mary's at Jesus' tomb. She has no paradigm for speaking of resurrection yet. Again Martha can be forgiven her misgivings because they are an occasion for Jesus to state again (for our benefit as well as hers) his purpose. He had told his disciples before his arrival there that "this illness is not to end in death, but is for the glory of God, that the Son of God may be glorified through it." Now Jesus testifies before Martha that he is to manifest his glory in this last and greatest sign. John's readers are reminded of John's reflection on the first sign in Cana (see 2:11).

John has an "onion" style of writing, adding layer upon layer of meaning. Earlier, in John 5:28-29, Jesus said, "The hour is coming in which all who are in the tombs shall hear his voice and will come out." According to John 10, Jesus is the Good Shepherd who calls and the sheep answer; he calls his own by name, and "they recognize his voice." So Jesus called, "Lazarus, come out!" The one Jesus loved comes forth. And when the dead man appears now living, Jesus says, presumably to Martha and Mary, "Untie him and let him go."

There is great irony in the observation of John that, based on this miracle, the efforts to have Jesus put to death are increased. Jesus departs soon after and retreats to a town in Ephraim with his disciples. And John notes that the Passover was very near. This will be the Passover in which the forces of darkness and death, the same forces that resulted in the death of Lazarus, will converge to silence and to kill once and for all Jesus, the Light and Life of the world. But the story of the raising of Lazarus will inspire Christians to believe and to know that such darkness will not prevail. Jesus will not be held by death.

By the end of the week Jesus will have returned to Bethany. His hour was fast approaching. He will be present again at the house of Martha, Mary, and Lazarus, when Mary will anoint him for his burial.

"She, from her poverty, has contributed all she had, her whole livelihood" (Mark 12:44).

THE POOR WIDOW

Suggested Reading: Mark 12:41-44; Luke 21:1-4

Mark and Luke both have this short story about the widow whose "two small coins" offered out of her poverty represent a greater gift than the large sums the wealthy contribute to the Temple treasury. Luke's readers will be reminded of the widow Anna, who dedicated her life to God at the Temple. The devotion of these women is admirable. The meaning of this particular anecdote appears to be quite clear. Here's how the Gospels tell it.

Mark 12:41-44

[41]He sat down opposite the treasury and observed how the crowd put money into the treasury. Many rich people put in large sums. [42]A poor widow also came and put in two small coins worth a few cents. [43]Calling his disciples to himself, he said to them, "Amen, I say to you, this poor widow put in more than all the other contributors to the treasury. [44]For they have all contributed from their surplus wealth, but she, from her poverty, has contributed all she had, her whole livelihood."

Luke 21:1-4

[1]When he looked up he saw some wealthy people putting their offerings into the treasury [2]and he noticed a poor widow putting in two small coins. [3]He said, "I tell you truly, this poor widow put in more than all the rest; [4]for those others have all made offerings from their surplus wealth, but she, from her poverty, has offered her whole livelihood."

Mark notes that Jesus "sat down," the posture of a teacher. Jesus observes what is going on in the Temple, just as he had the first day of his arrival in Jerusalem (Mark 11:1-11). Then, Mark says, Jesus "looked around at everything and, since it was already late, went out to Bethany with the Twelve" (Mark 11:11). On this third and last day in the Temple, Jesus saw how the people were contributing to the Temple treasury. He noted that rich people were putting in large sums; in contrast, a widow contributed a few pennies. He then "called his disciples to himself" and pointed out this discrepancy. The rich contributed out of their "surplus," while the widow, out of her poverty, contributed her "whole livelihood." Commentators note that in this last line, the Greek term *bios*, translated "livelihood," more concretely means "life" itself.[43]

Thus the offering of the woman might be seen as anticipating Jesus' own offering of his life for the salvation of humankind. Mark and Luke deliberately use vocabulary that link the example of this woman with the sacrifice of Jesus himself. The power of this observation is all the more real when one considers that it is placed near the end of the Gospel, and as one of the last episodes before the passion.

This little story is consistent with others we find in the Gospel and seems to be an authentic part of the teaching of Jesus for a number of reasons. The offering of this woman is contrasted with that of the rich, and Jesus makes sure that the disciples take notice of that contrast. The "wealthy" and the "religious" people are implicitly warned that outward appearances are not equivalent with justice. There are many instances in the Gospels, especially in Luke, where the exemplary way of acting as a believer has to do with money and generosity with regard to sharing one's possessions.

Many interpreters believe that Luke is writing for a mixed community of predominantly Gentiles who were probably better off financially than their Jewish counterparts. The Jews had a long tradition of social justice that required them to take care of their poor. The Law called for tithing. The poor represent a scandal to the Jews, a clear demand on the community to take care of its own. The poor are appropriately represented by widows and orphans, who, as persons without proper legal

---

[43] For example, Reid, *Women in the Gospel of Luke*, 195.

protection, are dependent on the good will of the community to provide for them. The Gentile readers of Luke had no such tradition. Luke had to create one for them and base it on the authority and priorities of Jesus.

Often the mention of a word will trigger memory of another episode or saying. This term is then called a "catchword." The mention of widows in the warning against the scribes acts as such a catchword for Mark (followed closely by Luke, but not by Matthew in this instance). In his contrast of the rich people and the poor widow, Jesus seems to be praising the extent of her offering, which is greater than that of the wealthy.

Some interpreters offer a number of nuances that would explain what Jesus is praising. For example, it is not only the amount of money offered but the proportion of the sacrifice it represents for ourselves. For the rich, a large amount is still a surplus; for the poor, a small amount is more meritorious, because it involves a greater sacrifice for themselves.

Some interpretations note that this story illustrates the adage that it is not the gift but the thought that counts. More important than the amount is the spirit behind the giving. These positive interpretations focus on this episode itself and the contrast drawn between the rich and the poor in this story.

But broadening the context to a contrast between the scribes and the widow seems to create a problem for positive interpretations of this story. Why would Jesus praise the actions of the widow who gives all that she has, when he has just condemned the scribes for demanding that kind of sacrifice from people like her? (See Mark 12:38-40). Once we include his warning against the scribes in the preceding saying in our consideration of the meaning of this story, Jesus seems not to be praising her so much as lamenting her actions.[44] And he may also be preparing his disciples for his comments on the Temple that will follow as they leave its precincts. Let us consider this larger context of the warning against the scribes that precedes this episode, and the discourse linking the demise of the Temple and the end of the world that follows it.

[44] See Elizabeth Struthers Malbon, "The Poor Widow in Mark and Her Poor Rich Readers," *Catholic Biblical Quarterly* 53 (1991) 589–604.

Mark and Luke place this incident toward the end of their Gospels, just before the so-called eschatological discourse that is followed by the passion narrative. Jesus has arrived in Jerusalem, having instructed his disciples on the high cost of discipleship all along the way from Galilee. Jesus has predicted his own passion and death. His followers have had a hard time hearing; they barely seem to listen. Jesus warned them that following him will involve huge sacrifices on their part as well. They are expected to be ready to take up their own cross. They may have to "leave everything" behind (e.g., Luke 14:25-33). They must be prepared to give up their very lives.

Already in Galilee, while he worked many miracles, his enemies began the conspiracy to put Jesus to death (see Mark 3:6). By the time Jesus reached Jerusalem, the plot was well developed. The synoptic writers describe Jesus' journey to Jerusalem as an inexorable journey to his death. When he first arrived there, people went out to see him. But his few days there were fraught with controversy.

On the first day, Luke tells us, the Pharisees complained that Jesus ought to curb his disciples, preventing them from saying, "Blessed is the king who comes / in the name of the Lord." But Jesus replies, "I tell you, if they kept silent, the stones would cry out" (Luke 19:39-40). Mark says that on each of the three days he spent in Jerusalem, Jesus visited the Temple. On the first day he simply looked around at everything and then left for Bethany, a few miles away, where he was staying.

On the second day in Jerusalem, Jesus "drove out those selling and buying there" (Mark 11:15). Jesus spent the third and last day at an exhausting teaching session, where he was confronted with a barrage of controversies. His authority to "do these things" was questioned by the "chief priests, the scribes, and the elders" (Mark 11:27). His answers caused the leaders to intensify their efforts and resolve to arrest him.

The confrontational tone mounts with each day. The tone becomes more urgent. Finally, Jesus pronounces a warning against the religious leaders of the people:

> In the course of his teaching he said, "Beware of the scribes, who like to go around in long robes and accept greetings in the marketplaces, seats of honor in synagogues, and places of

> honor at banquets. They devour the houses of widows and, as
> a pretext, recite lengthy prayers. They will receive a very se-
> vere condemnation" (Mark 12:38-40; see also Luke 20:45-47).

This warning directly precedes our story of the widow's offering in both Mark and Luke. In trying to understand what Jesus
is teaching his disciples by calling attention to the widow, we
need to take into consideration why the evangelists juxtapose
this story of the widow with a warning against the scribes.

The designations "scribes" and "widows" seem to be natural opposites according to the sayings of Jesus. Scribes are usually associated with other Jewish groups in the New Testament,
such as Pharisees, Sadducees, or chief priests. Probably the
term "scribes" as used by the evangelists could include members of any of these groups or a combination of people from
these groups. Especially from the sixth century B.C.E., the time
of the Exile, scribes were recognized as religious leaders. Their
skills as writers and interpreters made them indispensable for
the preservation of Judaism and valuable for handing on these
traditions as teachers. As with the other groups of Jews mentioned in the New Testament, we must be careful to separate
"images shaped by late first century C.E. Jewish and Christian
polemics from other historical concerns."[45]

The overwhelming impression of scribes as used in the
New Testament is pejorative because of the Christian bias of
the New Testament, which was written by believers for believers. Tensions existed between Jews and Christians for a number of reasons. Roman pressure, for example, became outright
hostility and persecution of both Jews and Christians by the
time of the unsuccessful Jewish revolt against Rome in 66–72.
The scribes were spurred on by the absence of the Temple as
well as by Christian animosity in the form of a critique of accepted interpretations of the Law, the claim that the Messiah
could be one who was crucified, and the entrance of many
Gentiles into fellowship with believers.

The scribes, especially the Pharisees, pressed for greater
stringency in a more narrow interpretation of the Law, which

---

[45] See Ronald D. Witherup, "Scribe," in *The Collegeville Pastoral Dictionary of Biblical Theology*, 883.

they perceived was threatened by developing Christian ideas. Their fears were legitimate. The Gospels indicate that real tensions existed between Jesus and Jewish teachers, who believed that their claim to authority was essential to Jewish survival. There were many honest differences of opinion competing with one another. The New Testament does not give an objective, balanced, unbiased presentation of conflicting Jewish ideas current in Jesus' own time; rather, the New Testament writers were writing for people of their own time. They were influenced by the many forces against Christian faith, including the leadership of the Jews.

Scribes probably included the Pharisees, who tended to be more powerful in the synagogues, and the Sadducees, who appear to have been more influential in and around Jerusalem, and the priests. The Sadducees and the priests, however, diminish in influence after the destruction of the temple in 70 C.E.

In the New Testament, "priests" (including chief priests and high priests) are often associated with the scribes. On the one hand, Jesus is pictured as sometimes recognizing the legitimacy of the priests' power. For example, he sends the healed leper to the priests and tells him to offer the required sacrifice so that he can be pronounced ritually clean (Mark 1:44; Matt 8:4; Luke 5:14; see Lev 14:1-4). But historically, the priests, with their concerns for rituals, for purity and contamination, and for the administrative affairs of the Temple and of Jerusalem, are prime targets for the prophets, with their social concerns and their lack of sympathy for externals such as legalism or hypocrisy. Now Jesus is presented in the synoptic Gospels as a prophetic figure, often opposed to the leadership represented by the Pharisees, the Sadducees, and the priests.

Jesus is presented as a teacher, but not like the Pharisees. Nor is Jesus a priest. He was anointed by God for his ministry to the poor, the sick, the forgotten. Jesus challenges many accepted interpretations of the Law. He repudiates even the Temple. He laments the future of Jerusalem, whose destruction he predicts. Jesus attaches a warning reminiscent of the prophets to his confrontations with all these leaders.

Jesus acknowledges that the scribes and Pharisees "have taken their seat on the chair of Moses. Therefore, do and observe all things whatsoever they tell you" (Matt 23:2-3). But, he continues,

> . . . do not follow their example. For they preach but they do not practice. They tie up heavy burdens [hard to carry] and lay them on people's shoulders, but they will not lift a finger to move them. . . . Woe to you, scribes and Pharisees, you hypocrites. You traverse sea and land to make one convert, and when that happens you make him a child of Gehenna twice as much as yourselves (Matt 23: 3-4, 15; see all of Matt 23).

To the Sadducees, who did not believe in the resurrection and who tried to entrap Jesus with an absurd story about a woman married seven times, Jesus replied to their question about whose wife she would be in heaven, "Are you not misled because you do not know the scriptures or the power of God?" (see Mark 12:18-27; Luke 20:27-39). When the priests challenge his authority to "cleanse" the temple, Jesus says, "My house shall be called a house of prayer for all peoples . . . But you have made it a den of thieves" (see Mark 11:15-19: Matt 21:12-17; Luke 19:45-48).

The "thievery" of the leaders may be demonstrated also in our story about the poor widow, which is connected with Jesus' indictment against the scribes who "devour" widow's houses. Malachi says, for example, "I will draw near to you for judgment . . . Against those who defraud widows and orphans" (Mal 3:5). Joseph Fitzmyer, summarizes a number of ways interpreters have understood this accusation of Jesus against the scribes.[46] Some of the ways in which they "devoured" the widows' houses could include that they accepted payment for legal aid to widows, even though they were forbidden to do so, they cheated widows when they acted as lawyer-guardians to take care of widows' estates, or they sponged off of the hospitality of widows, taking advantage of them. Some interpreters link this accusation to Jesus' allusion to prayer and claim that they might have taken money for the promise of praying for the widows. Any of these meanings could have been possible then and now. The contemporary "scribe," whether evangelist,

---

[46] J. Fitzmyer, *The Gospel of Luke*, 1318.

pastor, theologian or scholar, business person or caretaker, ought to be open to honesty and true justice to which this story calls us. This warning may be much more important than whether the story itself has a positive or negative connotation with regard to the woman's offering.

The episode that follows pictures the disciples of Jesus overly enthusiastic about the luxuries of the Temple which was being built. As they were leaving on the last day of Jesus' life, the disciples turn back to see the sun setting and the Temple gleaming in its reflection (Mark 13:1-2; Matt 24:1-2; Luke 21:5-6). They comment on the Temple's beauty. They seem justifiably proud. The Temple had been under construction since some twenty or so years before Jesus was born. Its expansion and reconstruction had been started by Herod in hopes of winning approval from the Jewish people he so badly abused. Jesus' answer to his disciples that "there will not be one stone left upon another" could be read in the context of our story and the disciples' misguided pride. The woman's offering to the Temple treasury was a waste. It would be better to construct a temple not made of human hands. Jesus' approval of the woman who anoints him for his burial is expressed with a lot less ambiguity.

"Let her alone . . . She has done a good thing to me" (Mark 14:6).

THE WOMAN OF BETHANY WHO ANOINTED JESUS

Suggested Reading: Mark 14:3-9; Matthew 26:6-13; John 12:1-12

In chapter 2 we considered Luke's version of the story of an unnamed woman who anointed Jesus in the course of his journey from Galilee to Jerusalem (Luke 7:36-50). The other Gospels connect an anointing of Jesus by a woman to his passion, death, and burial. In Matthew, Mark, and John, the woman acts as a prophet; her anointing is a prophetic recognition of Jesus as Messiah. It ought to be noted that an anointing of Jesus by a woman is one of the few stories that is recorded in all four Gospels. That is one indication of how significant this event was for the evangelists and therefore also for us.

It is impossible to know whether this is the same story or accounts of two different events. What we can observe is that Luke uses the anointing story for a different purpose in his Gospel that the other Gospels do. Therefore, we have separated our treatment of them. In this chapter we will focus on the stories as told by Mark, Matthew, and John, and compare their accounts.

Mark 14:3-9

[3]When he was in Bethany reclining at table in the house of Simon the leper, a woman came with an alabaster jar of perfumed oil, costly genuine spikenard. She broke the alabaster jar and poured it on his head. [4]There were some who were indignant. "Why has there been this waste of perfumed oil? [5]It could have been sold for more than three hundred days' wages and the money given to the poor." They were infuriated with her. [6]Jesus said, "Let her alone. Why do you make trouble for her? She has done a good thing for me. [7]The poor you will always have with you, and whenever you wish you can do good to them, but you will not always have me. [8]She has done what she could. She has anticipated anointing my body for burial. [9]Amen, I say to you, wherever the gospel is proclaimed to the whole world, what she has done will be told in memory of her."

Matthew 26:6-13

[6]Now when Jesus was in Bethany in the house of Simon the leper, [7]a woman came up to him with an alabaster jar of costly perfumed oil, and poured it on his head while he was reclining at table. [8]When the disciples saw this, they were indignant and said, "Why this waste? [9]It could have been sold for much, and the money given to the poor." [10]Since Jesus knew this, he said to them, "Why do you make trouble for the woman? She has done a good thing for me. [11]The poor you will always have with you; but you will not always have me. [12]In pouring this perfumed oil upon my body, she did it to prepare me for burial. [13]Amen, I say to you, wherever this gospel is proclaimed in the whole world, what she has done will be spoken of, in memory of her."

John 12:1-8

[1]Six days before Passover Jesus came to Bethany, where Lazarus was, whom Jesus had raised from the dead. [2]They

gave a dinner for him there, and Martha served, while Lazarus was one of those reclining at table with him. ³Mary took a liter of costly perfumed oil made from genuine aromatic nard and anointed the feet of Jesus and dried them with her hair; the house was filled with the fragrance of the oil. ⁴Then Judas the Iscariot, one [of] his disciples, and the one who would betray him, said, ⁵"Why was this oil not sold for three hundred days' wages and given to the poor?" ⁶He said this not because he cared about the poor but because he was a thief and held the money bag and used to steal the contributions. ⁷So Jesus said, "Leave her alone. Let her keep this for the day of my burial. ⁸You always have the poor with you, but you do not always have me."

Common elements within this story in the accounts of Mark, Matthew, and John, in addition to its placement as part of the introduction to the passion narrative include the locale, Bethany; a complaint about the waste; Jesus' defense of the woman's action and his explanation of why it is appropriate. Jesus interprets the action in function of his burial. He comments that the poor "will always be with you."

There are also distinctive elements in these three accounts, although Matthew follows Mark more closely than John does. A brief table of comparison indicates some of these differences:

Mark 14:3-9	Matthew 26:6-13	John 12:1-8
Jesus at house of Simon the leper	Jesus at house of Simon the leper	Jesus where Lazarus was
woman is unnamed	woman is unnamed	woman is Mary, sister of Martha and Lazarus
disciples complain about the waste	Some asked themselves, "Why this waste?"	One of his disciples, Judas who would betray him, asked . . .
	Jesus said, "Let her alone . . .	Jesus said, "Let her alone . . .
Why do you trouble her?	Why do you trouble her?	
She has done a beautiful thing for me,	She has done a beautiful thing for me,	

The poor are always with you	The poor are always with you	The poor are always with you
but you do not always have me	but you do not always have me	but you do not always have me
She anointed me for my burial	She anointed me for my burial	let her keep it for the day of my burial
and wherever the gospel is preached	and wherever the gospel is preached	
what she has done will be told in memory of her.	what she has done will be told in memory of her.	

THE ANOINTING IN MARK AND MATTHEW[47]

Mark begins the passion narrative with a brief notice that the "Passover and the Feast of the Unleavened Bread" were to take place in two days' time (Mark 14:1). The religious leaders were seeking to put Jesus to death before the festival. After saying this, Mark inserts the story of the woman's anointing of Jesus. Immediately following this story, Mark recounts that Judas Iscariot, one of the Twelve, went off to conspire with Jesus' enemies to "hand him over" (14:10-12) for money.[48] This is the story that launches the reader into the fast-paced action of the passion of Jesus.

The open, courageous action of the woman is clearly contrasted with the secret plot of the leaders. Bethany is located just beyond the Mount of Olives, a short distance from Jerusalem. Jesus is eating at the house of Simon the leper. According to Mark, Jesus had healed a leper in Galilee at the beginning of his ministry (see Mark 1:42-44), but we cannot conclude that this is the same man. Yet we can probably assume that this Simon

---

[47] For our purposes, we need not comment on differences between Mark and Matthew; their accounts of this story are similar.

[48] The conspiracy against Jesus is alluded to before and after the anointing story, another example of inclusion. By thus enveloping the anointing episode, John puts the actions of the woman in stark relief against the machination of Jesus' enemies, including Judas, whom John further identifies as one of Jesus' own disciples.

was considered cured of the disease that was known to be highly contagious. The moniker "leper" is consistent with the tradition known to all the Gospel writers that Jesus associated with outcasts.[49]

In the Old Testament people were anointed for a number of reasons. Prophets were anointed, a way of recognizing their authority as coming from God. Kings and priests were also anointed. Oil was used in the anointing ceremonies that ritualized the community's willingness to follow the guidance of such leaders. The term Messiah means "anointed one." The woman anoints Jesus' head, a clear symbol of messianic recognition. Her action signified her acceptance of Jesus' messiahship. This story is more about her action than her identity; Mark and Matthew do not qualify or name her.

Some witnesses complain among themselves, Mark tells us, without further indicating who they were. Mark does add that their contention is that the expensive ointment might have been put to better use by selling it and giving the money to the poor. This prompts Jesus to defend the woman's action as well as to comment on the poor.

Jesus says that although the poor will always be with them, he himself will not always be. Mark could be thinking of the question of fasting Jesus had addressed in 2:19-20. When questioned about why his disciples did not fast, Jesus answered, "Can the wedding guests mourn while the bridegroom is with them? . . . The days will come when the bridegroom is taken away from them, and then they will fast" (see also Matt 9:15; Luke 5:32).[50] The time is near when Jesus will be "handed over" and taken away, just as he had warned his disciples repeatedly on his way to Jerusalem. The "muttering" of the disciples recalls the complaints of the Israelites in the desert, who "murmured" and complained every step of

---

[49] Note that this is in contrast to Luke's story, which identifies Jesus' host as Simon the Pharisee; Luke shows a preference for contrasting the individuals of his story, in this case a religious expert as opposed to the "woman known as a sinner" who anoints Jesus.

[50] That there was a Christian tradition that identifies Jesus as the "Bridegroom" is also clear in Matthew 25:1, 5, 6, 10; John 3:29; Rev. 18:23.

the way. In contrast, the unnamed woman does a "good thing" on Jesus' behalf.

The time now is to watch, to observe, as Jesus warned in the last words of the eschatological discourse (see Mark 13:33-37). The woman does this. Mark's Gospel began with a notice that "now" the kingdom of God is at hand; this is the *kairos*, the opportune time. Meanwhile, Judas and his enemies search for the "opportune time." It is the woman who names and seizes it. Jesus predicts his death, interpreting her action as a burial anointing. The feast day and the Sabbath will prevent Jesus from receiving a proper burial. The woman, who symbolizes the attentiveness Jesus called for all along the route to Jerusalem, anticipates a necessary service.

Jesus makes a pronouncement that is both breathtaking and ironic as Mark tells it. Jesus says that what the woman has done will be told in memory of her. Although her action is recorded, the woman herself is not even named, much less remembered. She has no name, no face; we do not hear further of her. Ironically, Jesus' traitor is named, but the woman who anointed him is not.

Yet Jesus' words are somehow true, as if the story of his passion and death could not be told had she not done her part. There's a similarity with the way Mark tells the resurrection story. He ends by saying that the women told no one (see Mark 16:8), but then, we wonder, how did the word get around? In fact, we do know the Gospel because of the memory of this and the other women who made it possible. We cannot otherwise explain the persistence of the collective remembrance of these women. The male writers would not have been apt to invent or preserve their stories, unless the telling of the Gospel would have been impossible without them.

This woman is the type of the faithful, authentic disciple. She distinguishes herself among his followers for her courage, her insight, her singlemindedness, and her generosity. She incorporates many of the elements Mark has used to describe a true disciple. In contrast to the many failures of the male disciples, including Peter as well as Judas Iscariot, the action of this woman is praised and commended by Jesus, not to be forgotten.

THE ANOINTING IN JOHN

To more fully appreciate what John is doing here, consider this incident of anointing in the light of the wider context of John 13. There John has substituted Jesus' washing of the feet of his disciples for the account of the "Last Supper" of the Synoptics.[51] Since there is no other meal associated with this washing of feet, the final or "Last Supper" in John is this one, when Martha serves and Mary washes Jesus' feet and anoints them. John's has been called the "Community of the Beloved Disciple";[52] in chapter 11 John says that Jesus loved Lazarus and Martha and their sister Mary. John features Jesus saying in his last discourse to his "friends": "This is my commandment: love one another as I love you" (John 15:12).

John identifies Judas as the one who objects to Mary's action on the grounds that the money ought to have been given to the poor (John 12:45). Jesus quickly and sharply silences him with the abbreviated "Leave her alone." John adds that Judas was a thief and held the money bag for the group (John 12:6); in the next chapter Jesus dismisses Judas into the night, saying, "What you are going to do, do quickly" (John 13:27). John adds to this another allusion to the money and the poor, explaining that "some thought that since Judas kept the money bag, Jesus had told him, 'Buy what we need for the feast,' or to give something to the poor" (John 13:29).

John definitely is describing events linking the anointing by Mary to the last meal Jesus shared with his disciples. As with the transposition of the meaning of the memorial sharing to chapter 6, John could have had several reasons for doing this. Perhaps he wanted to "demystify" the Eucharist, to stress

---

[51] Note that John transposes to the multiplication of loaves and the "Bread of Life" discourse in chapter 6, the eucharistic interpretation of Jesus' action of self-giving. Thus there is no meal described in John 13; rather, "after supper" (13:4) Jesus washed the feet of his disciples and then commented on the meaning of his action.

[52] This the title of a important book written by Raymond E. Brown, one of the foremost Johannine scholars: *The Community of the Beloved Disciple: The Life, Loves and Hates of an Individual Church in New Testament Times* (New York/Mahwah: Paulist Press, 1979).

its meaning rather than to exaggerate it as a ritual. So, for example, by assigning eucharistic overtones to the multiplication of loaves, John is emphasizing the meaning of the Eucharist as Jesus' gift of himself, his flesh and blood, for the salvation of the world. Also, by making the washing of the feet more significant than a meal the night before he died, Jesus is underscoring the meaning of both and the importance of this memory when the disciples gathered as a community.

These reflections shine a whole new light on John's presentation of the anointing. They also suggest another dimension to Jesus' prophecy that "wherever the gospel is preached, what [the woman] has done will be told in memory of her." The words and deeds of Jesus were not preserved because they have historical significance; in fact, that may be the least significant of their possible meanings. They are part of the sharing tradition because they were used by the community to instruct, to correct, to give direction as the Church was growing and spreading and for its future development.

From this story we can see that women were not only witnesses but participants in all levels of ministry: they heard the word, they believed, they bore witnesses, they made converts, they had authority. When "some" (men and women) objected, Jesus sided, at least in this instance, with the woman. If Luke can be accused of using the Mary-Martha tradition against a more active role for women and to preserve traditional roles more acceptable to the Roman world he lived in, John does just the opposite. The words of Jesus are evoked by John to defend the role of Mary against the objection that she serve in a more traditional way, that is, by giving alms.

6. More Women and Discipleship

"His mother said to the servers, 'Do whatever he tells you'"
(John 2:5).

THE MOTHER OF JESUS

Suggested Reading: John 2:1-12; 19:24-30

Following the Prologue, the Baptist's testimony about Jesus, and the call of the first male disciples, John begins his Gospel with the "Book of Signs" (chapters 2–12). The first "sign" (the Johannine term for miracles) is Jesus' transformation of water into wine at his mother's implied request. The interaction and conversation between Jesus and his mother is almost as important as the sign itself.

Twice John gives us a cameo of Mary, whom he calls the "mother of Jesus." At the beginning she appears urging her son to inaugurate his mission at the wedding feast of Cana (2:1-11); this is followed by John's note that she went with him, his brothers, and disciples to Capernaum and "remained" with him (2:12). At the end, at the cross, Mary is there too. Both times Jesus himself addresses her as "Woman." In both scenes she is portrayed in terms of a disciple, in the language of faith, as the mother of those who follow him. Here is how John tells the story of Jesus' mother at Cana.

> ¹On the third day there was a wedding in Cana in Galilee, and the mother of Jesus was there. ²Jesus and his disciples were also invited to the wedding. ³When the wine ran short,

the mother of Jesus said to him, "They have no wine." [4][And]
Jesus said to her, "Woman, how does your concern affect me?
My hour has not yet come." [5]His mother said to the servers,
"Do whatever he tells you." [6]Now there were six stone water
jars there for Jewish ceremonial washings, each holding
twenty to thirty gallons. [7]Jesus told them, "Fill the jars with
water." So they filled them to the brim. [8]Then he told them,
"Draw some out now and take it to the headwaiter." So they
took it. [9]And when the headwaiter tasted the water that had
become wine, without knowing where it came from (although the servers who had drawn the water knew), the
headwaiter called the bridegroom [10]and said to him, "Everyone serves good wine first, and then when people have drunk
freely, an inferior one; but you have kept the good wine until
now." [11]Jesus did this as the beginning of his signs in Cana in
Galilee and so revealed his glory, and his disciples began to
believe in him.
[12]After this, he and his mother, [his] brothers, and his disciples went down to Capernaum and stayed there only a few
days (John 2:1-12).

There is a wedding at Cana in Galilee, and the mother of
Jesus and her son are invited. John begins his Gospel account of
Jesus' ministry. While at the feast, Jesus' mother appears to pull
him away from the general activity to report, "They have no
wine." The son takes the implication to mean that she expects
him to do something, and he appears to refuse her. He says,
"Woman, how does your concern affect me?"[1] The conversation
between Jesus and his mother is not easy to interpret. There almost seems to be some tension between the two. But this impression may be due more to John's style than to actual events.
John's style takes a little getting used to. It is full of symbolism.

For instance, it is surprising that Jesus would address his
mother as "Woman." While this may have been a polite enough
manner for a man to speak to a woman, it seems like an odd
way for a son to address his mother. John never uses her name;
in the only two times she appears in this Gospel (here and in

---

[1] It sounds a lot like the question of the demon to Jesus in Mark 5:7,
which makes the tone of this all the more surprising. This may be a Hebrew phrase that means something like "That is your business; it is none
of my business."

19:26 at the cross), she is addressed as "Woman." Jesus adds a reason for his apparent refusal: "My hour has not yet come." Elsewhere, "hour" means the time of passion and death (e.g., 7:30; 8:20). When this hour does come, this "woman" appears again. Then she is given to the Beloved Disciple as the mother (that is, model) of the perfect believer. Jesus rejects a purely human sphere of action for this woman in order to indicate for her a more important role—that of mother and witness in leading to deeper faith all who follow him.

The term "Woman" that Jesus uses in addressing his mother is more powerful when we see it against the background of the creation account in Genesis.[2] John has suggested that we keep that text in mind, since the first words of his Gospel are "In the beginning . . ." This wedding feast occurs on the seventh day, the end of the first week of the new creation described in the Prologue, when Jesus is restoring the cosmos back to God. John is not so much interested in twenty-four-hour periods when he delineates the first "days" in 1:29, 35, 43 and 2:1. Rather, John is using symbolism, preparing the stage on which the reconciliation of the world with God will take place.

On this seventh day the "woman," the new Eve (the name Eve means "mother of all the living," Genesis 3:20 tells us) appears and prompts Jesus to begin his work of redemption. Eve and Adam collaborated to bring sin into the world. His mother and Jesus will collaborate to give the world access to God. This woman leads the new Adam to manifest through signs the wisdom and the power of God. With the sin of Eve and Adam there came a promise (Gen 3:15): there would be enmity between the seed of the serpent (evil) and the seed of the woman (humankind). Jesus is the fulfillment of that promise and more. He has destroyed evil, including the last enemy, death, and restored friendship with God.

Jesus refers to his "hour" as that of his passion and death, which is actually the time when Jesus manifests his "glory" for John. But this miracle is not going to get Jesus into trouble, as

---

[2] This idea is really well said by Raymond Brown in *The Gospel and Epistles of John*, 28–29.

many of the miracles do according to the Synoptics. In this instance Jesus therefore does not see a connection between his mother's concern about the wedding wine and his own time of fulfillment of the Father's plan of salvation. But here John gives the first of many examples of dialogue between Jesus and someone, where they seem to be confusing each other more than communicating.[3] John uses *misunderstanding* as a literary device to help us progress through stages of ever deeper faith and real understanding.

In this instance it is Jesus who appears somewhat confused. He is only beginning his ministry, and the "hour" of his death is in the future; it is his mother who appears to reveal something to her son this time. In the bigger picture, the "hour" is when the world and its Creator are reunited. Wine at a wedding may not be part of the plan in Jesus' mind, but when he follows his mother's lead here, Jesus seems to be showing his disciples a glimpse of his "glory" and his mission. As John concludes in 2:11, "Jesus did this as the beginning of his signs in Cana in Galilee and so revealed his glory, and his disciples began to believe in him."

Jesus will have no argument from his mother. She turns to the servants and says, "Do whatever he tells you." There is a double vagueness in this response. Rather than answer her son, the woman speaks to the servants, using almost a conditional phrase: "If he tells you anything, do it." Jesus then gives them instructions. It would seem that Jesus' mother is somewhat impertinent. But the fact that she brings about the beginning of signs means that, for John, she and this interchange have a positive meaning. We can contrast her with Nathaniel in the immediately preceding scene. He was reluctant and incredulous until he witnessed the minor miracle of Jesus' saying that he had seen Nathaniel sitting under the fig tree, an image that means Nathaniel was studying the Law. Suddenly Nathaniel is impressed. And Jesus says something like, "You haven't seen anything yet."

---

[3] Other examples are Jesus' conversation with Nicodemus in chapter 3; with the Samaritan woman in chapter 4; with his disciples when he multiplies loaves of bread in chapter 6; with the blind man in chapter 9; with his disciples and Martha in chapter 11 about the raising of Lazarus.

Unlike Nathaniel, Jesus' mother requires no miracles but believes beforehand. The substance of her belief is in accord with what is laid out in the Prologue: she acknowledges Jesus as the link between God and creation. She turns to him, and even when it seems as if she is rebuffed, she does not turn elsewhere. She knows already what Peter will only discover much later: there is nowhere else to go (see John 6:68).

John presents Mary as the last in a series of witnesses to Jesus at the start of his mission. She believes before any sign that will manifest who he is (although many will be baffled). First there was John the Baptist, then two of his disciples. Then Andrew, one of the two, brought his brother Simon, who was called Peter. And Peter brought Philip, who brought Nathaniel. His mother is and has been there all along. She is the model of right believing from the start, in contrast to the shallow inadequacy of most conversions, as John will say at the end of this chapter: "Many began to believe in his name when they saw the signs he was doing. But Jesus would not trust himself to them because he knew them all" (see John 2:23-24). His mother is not corrected or rebuffed. In fact, it seems that Jesus cannot resist faith such as hers. The sign he does at Cana will show witnesses something of the meaning of his mission. So some will begin to believe in him (see 2:21).

There is a festive tone to this story. A wedding is a time of joy. John conveys the element of surprise in the unexpectedness of the transformed water—not only that it is wine, but the best of wine. And in such abundance. It is a messianic symbol. The bridal banquet is an image of Jesus' own ministry (see John 3:29-31). The Baptist testifies that he is the "best man" and Jesus is the bridegroom. Appropriately, then, the Baptist says, "He must increase, I must decrease." And so it is. John the Baptist does not appear again in John.

Those who knew the prophets might have thought of the abundance of wine they promised in messianic days (Amos 9:13-14; Isa 25). According to Proverbs (9:4-5), wine is a symbol of wisdom and teaching; for John, Jesus is the Wisdom and the Word of God. John shows here and throughout his Gospel how Jesus replaces Jewish rites and feasts with something better. The surprise of the steward symbolizes the amazing abundance and quality of God's generous grace.

Galilee is the first place to witness Jesus' glory, in John as in the Synoptics. It will also be the last. In chapter 21 Nathaniel and Cana are mentioned again. John uses *inclusion* here, reminding his readers at the end to remember what was said and done at the beginning. John is straightforward in informing us of his reasons for telling the story of Jesus the way he does. He is not only giving us information but is interpreting what he says, often using symbolism. John says: "Now Jesus did many other signs in the presence of his disciples that are not written in this book. But these are written that you may come to believe that Jesus is the Messiah, the Son of God, and that through this belief you may have life in his name" (John 20:30-31).

His mother's faith is not dependent on signs. But John does suggest that it is normal for signs to play a role in faith as a connection with conversion and also as a confirmation of faith. A sign is a miracle and more than a miracle. A sign points to a reality beyond itself. A sign reveals who Jesus is; those who really "see" a sign come to accept its meaning and attach themselves to Jesus. John's is the Gospel of symbols. Jesus revealed his "glory" through the sign. Many believed because of the signs Jesus did. The first sign brought about by Mary's intervention is the faith of the disciples.

John concluded this story by saying, "He and his mother, [his] brothers, and his disciples went down to Capernaum and stayed there only a few days" (John 2:12). The rest of Jesus' family and his disciples rallied to him, but their faith is inadequate, as will soon be made clear. It is based on "signs," often the first stage of faith. In fact, John tells us, his disciples will only understand many things after the resurrection (2:21). That is the lens by which they become enabled to see the whole ministry of Jesus.

Then John tells us that the Passover was near (2:13); Jesus went to Jerusalem and cleansed the Temple. In Jerusalem, Jesus was challenged by the authorities: "What sign can you show us for doing this?" (2:18). Many refuse to understand what Jesus does as "signs." He replaces old religion with the new reality of God's presence in God's Son. Jesus rids the Temple of all traffic between heaven and earth that impedes rather than fosters access to God. Jesus is the only true way to God, according to John. We should accent less the exclusiveness of this claim than the reality that Jesus provides direct access, making all other means to God obsolete.

The words of Mary to the servants come back at the cross. She represents the first of Jesus' obedient and trusting disciples. In John, her presence at the cross implies her presence all along. And this is reinforced by the other evangelists, who confirm that the women who followed Jesus were at the cross and at the tomb. Luke has Jesus' mother in the Upper Room, awaiting the Spirit (Acts 1:14). She is present throughout Jesus' ministry, to the end and beyond.

John puts this sign of the changing of water into wine just before Passover. The symbolic combination of water and blood is noted explicitly again at the cross. There John says that when the soldiers pierced the side of Jesus, water and blood came out. Thus this woman and the sign she advocated link the beginning and the end of Jesus' mission. Let us turn now to the other scene in which Jesus' mother is present. Here's what John says in 19:24-30.

> [24]So they said to one another, "Let's not tear it, but cast lots for it to see whose it will be," in order that the passage of scripture might be fulfilled [that says]: / "They divided my garments among them, / and for my vesture they cast lots." / This is what the soldiers did. [25]Standing by the cross of Jesus were his mother and his mother's sister, Mary the wife of Clopas, and Mary of Magdala. [26]When Jesus saw his mother and the disciple there whom he loved, he said to his mother, "Woman, behold, your son." [27]Then he said to the disciple, "Behold, your mother." And from that hour the disciple took her into his home.
>
> [28]After this, aware that everything was now finished, in order that the scripture might be fulfilled, Jesus said, "I thirst." [29]There was a vessel filled with common wine. So they put a sponge soaked in wine on a sprig of hyssop and put it up to his mouth. [30]When Jesus had taken the wine, he said, "It is finished." And bowing his head, he handed over the spirit (John 19:24-30).

Only John has Jesus' disciples standing so near the cross that Jesus could speak to them.[4] And so he does. His last words

---

[4] An idea linked by Gail O'Day to the intimacy theme so evident in this scene: see "John," in *Woman's Biblical Commentary*, 300.

are a gift: "Woman, behold, your son." And to the disciple(s) whom he loved, "Behold, your mother." The designation "the disciple he loved" is introduced late in John's narrative (first in 13:23-26; also see 18:15-16, "the other disciple;" these designations are linked in 19:2). But John accepts as fact that Jesus' mother, the woman who was there at the beginning, is there at the end. Jesus' mother represents continuity with Jesus' earthly ministry, and the Beloved Disciple represents the believing community of the present and future. "At the heart of Jesus' ministry is the creation of a new family of God."[5]

Both Jesus' mother and the "Beloved Disciple" are symbolic figures. The symmetry of the parallelism in Jesus' words reinforces that fact. Neither of them is named. Both are empowered to persevere because they recognize themselves as loved. John comments that there are five (possibly four) people at the cross.[6] In entrusting his mother to the "disciple whom he loved" and vice versa, Jesus would not have been excluding anyone. Each and all of them could have identified with Jesus' mother and with the Beloved Disciple.

The language of intimacy in John can hardly be overestimated. Once we move beyond the limits of literalism, of our own expectations or imaginations, we can see how John's symbolism gives new challenges and new dimensions to our interpersonal relationships with God and Jesus and within the Christian community. Jesus' interaction with his mother is far from cold or off-putting. Rather, it is based on a deeper appreciation of their relationship as part of the revelation of God

---

[5] Ibid.

[6] The gender of the Beloved Disciple here is not so clear. There are at least three women referred to. The "mother of Jesus" heads the list of disciples in John (cf. John 2:12, she is the first one mentioned of those who, after Cana, went with him to Capernaum). Next is his mother's unnamed sister (recall that Mark named the second woman, Salome; and if she could be the same as Matthew's third woman, the "mother of the sons of Zebedee," this would make Zebedee's sons Jesus' cousins). Mary, the wife of Clopas could be a third woman or she could be in apposition with "his mother's sister," although it is rare to call two sisters with the same name. The third or fourth woman is Mary Magdalene.

and the basis of Jesus' mission to reveal God. In John, the disciples are commanded to "Love one another" (e.g., John 13:34-35). After he had washed the disciples' feet, Jesus said, "I no longer call you slaves . . . . I have called you friends" (15:14-17). The quality of this friendship is an expression of Jesus' relationship with God and is modeled on family relationships: Father and Son, mother and son, brothers and sisters. John suggests ample room for reflection on how to make family relationships more a revelation of God's love and how to make relationships in the faith-community more a revelation of belonging to the family of God. Jesus' mother shows the way.

Besides Jesus' direct statement to his "disciples," John's portrait at the foot of the cross has a number of other references to the community of faith. Just before mentioning those who stayed with Jesus to the end, John referred to the game the soldiers played for Jesus' "seamless" garment. John says, "But the tunic was seamless, woven in one piece from the top down. So they said to one another, 'Let's not tear it, but cast lots for it to see whose it will be,' in order that the passage of Scripture might be fulfilled [that says]: / 'They divided my garments among them, / and for my vesture they cast lots'" (John 19:23-24). John has few Scripture citations. When he does quote the Scriptures, it can be expected that they are adapted to his purposes. If John used the Synoptics (as many interpreters believe he did), he would have read in Mark and/or Matthew their use of Psalm 22 to express Jesus' sentiments on the cross: "My God, my God, why have you abandoned me?" (Ps 22:1).

Rather than convey Jesus' feelings of abandonment, John uses the same psalm to "explain" the soldier's game. But again, John's imagination is highly symbolic. He quotes Psalm 22:19 which says, "They divide my garments among them, / for my clothing they cast lots." In John this becomes a reference to the baptismal mystery as suggested by two points.[7] First, the principal earlier reference to "clothes" in John was at the foot washing (which clearly had baptismal significance in addition to its eucharistic symbolism), where John says that Jesus took his

---

[7] Countryman, *The Mystical Way*, 129.

clothes off to perform this service (13:4); second, Jesus' tunic is described here as "woven in one piece from the top down," using the same Greek word *(anothen)* used by Jesus in speaking to Nicodemus about baptism (see John 3:3, 7, 31; the term can mean "from above" or "again"). This term is rare enough to catch the eye of John's reader. We ought to remember that a person was "baptized" naked by immersion in the Johannine community. Afterward the new disciple put on the robe of baptism. She now has a new identity.

Raymond Brown says that "With this commission to his mother, Jesus has finished the work he came to do."[8] This work started and ended with his mother. Her remaining by his cross is an expression of her enduring faithfulness. For John, as for Luke, perseverance is a mark of a disciple. Initial faith may depend on miracles and signs. But in the end, faith involves "staying with," remaining with Jesus.

Jesus' death is portrayed by John as a free, gratuitous act of love. Jesus is in charge; he is victorious over death and over separation in the end. His death is not an isolated event that only affects him. The interchange among Jesus, his mother, and the Beloved Disciple confirms that Jesus' death creates the Church, "the discipleship of equals."[9] Jesus' gift of love is to be replicated in relationships between disciples. The woman moved from being only *his* mother to *the* mother; in a comparable way, the disciples proceed from identification as "his" to belonging to a new family in Church. John's baptismal imagery yields to eucharistic imagery. Jesus finally accepts the wine and declares, "It is finished" (John 19:29-30). And "blood and water," symbols of the sacraments, symbols of the Church, came out of his pierced side (19:34).

---

[8] Brown, *The Gospel and Epistles of John*, 94.

[9] This phrase, first used by Elisabeth Schüssler Fiorenza, has almost become her trademark; like so many other ground-breaking insights she has, it has been appropriated by authors who cannot overestimate her leadership in feminist interpretation and especially historical reconstruction, so that we can finally say we are beginning to see what women meant to the early Christian communities represented in the New Testament.

"It will come to pass in the last days,"
God says, / "that I will pour out a portion of my spirit upon all
flesh. / Your sons and your daughters shall prophesy. . . . /
Indeed . . . my servants and my handmaids . . . / shall prophesy"
(Acts 2:17-18).

WOMEN OF THE UPPER ROOM:
TABITHA, MARY, AND RHODA

Suggested Reading: Acts 1:13-15; 9:36-43; 20:8; see 12:12; 13:13

The first chapter of Acts gives us a tantalizing glimpse into the early days of the Church. There Luke links the earthly ministry of Jesus with the early Church before the descent of the Spirit. There are a number of ways Luke makes these connections. He reiterates stories about Jesus' appearances to the "eleven and those with them" (Luke 24:33-46; Acts 1:6-13), the ascension of Jesus, and the command for Jesus' followers to wait in Jerusalem until the Spirit comes (Luke 24:47-53; Acts 1:6-26). Then in Acts, Luke prepares the scene for Pentecost, recounting the election of Mathias to fill the place vacated by Judas. Acts 2 will begin a brand new phase, when the Spirit empowers the frightened disciples, whom Luke estimates to be about one hundred and twenty persons, to go out from the Upper Room and bear witness to Jesus to the "ends of the earth" (Luke 24:47-48; Acts 1:8).

Interpreters have noted that in his two-volume work known as Luke-Acts, Luke traces three phases of salvation history: the age of the prophets, which was completed with the death of John the Baptist; the age of Jesus and his disciples, including the Twelve who represented the twelve tribes of Israel; and finally, the age of the Church, which is empowered by the Spirit to reach all the world. While the Gospel focused on the first two stages (the end of the prophets and the ministry of Jesus), Acts tells the story of the beginning of the new age.

There is both continuity and discontinuity in the progression of these stages. For example, Luke stresses the fulfillment of the Old Testament in John's ministry, in the election of the Twelve, who fulfill the promises made to the patriarchs, and in the prominence of Jerusalem, the goal of Jesus' ministry and the initial setting for the last stage, the age of the Church. In particular, chapter 1 of Acts has some significant points of continuity with the Gospel. For example, the city of Jerusalem, which was the goal of Jesus' journey in the Gospel, is the starting point of the Church, which spreads out from there. Likewise, the replacement of someone to fill the vacancy left by Judas and fill up the component "Twelve" is still part of the old age. After the coming of the Spirit, the role of the "Twelve" as transition team is over. Now is the dawning of the new age. So, for example, when James, the son of Zebedee, is killed (see 12:1-3) by Herod, there is no need to elect someone to take his place. The Twelve belong with the time of Jesus' earthly ministry, which is now past.

Of course, Luke cannot name all the original disciples and fill in the events they experienced until their deaths. Luke will only focus on two disciples: Peter, who represents for Luke the connection with Judaism, and Paul, who is called to be the Apostle to the Gentiles. Even Peter, then, represents a transition. He had a significant role in the Gospel. But in Acts his mission is eclipsed by Paul, who takes the Gospel to the Gentiles, even to Rome.

Others who have significant roles in Luke's Gospel are also linked with the beginning of the Church, including women. So Luke notes that gathered together waiting for the Spirit were the Eleven, some women, and Mary, the mother of Jesus. Here's what Luke says:

> When they entered the city [Jerusalem] they went to the upper room where they were staying, Peter and John and James and Andrew, Philip and Thomas, Bartholomew and Matthew, James son of Alphaeus, Simon the Zealot, and Judas son of James. All these devoted themselves with one accord to prayer, together with some women, and Mary the mother of Jesus and his brothers.
>
> During those days Peter stood up in the midst of the brothers (there was a group of about one hundred and twenty persons in the one place) (Acts 1:13-15).

The women form the link with the cross, burial, and resurrection message of Luke's Gospel account. Mary reminds the reader of a return to Galilee, where she was first introduced as someone who heard the word and kept it. Consistent with his treatment of Mary all along, Luke places her with Jesus' disciples. Her "blessedness" and greatness are as a believer and faithful disciple. Luke takes for granted that women were present from the beginning and continued to be present all along the way. Therefore, although he only occasionally mentions the women or names some of them, Luke assumes their presence as the Gospel spread and the Church grew. One of the specified places where women's presence was felt was in the "Upper Room," which, along with the "house of Mary," is the designated home "base" of the Church in Jerusalem. Although Luke does not identify these places as one and the same, many have suggested that a woman named "Mary" is the host of the Jerusalem Church and that her house is the location of the Upper Room.

With the outpouring of the Spirit, the Church will move out beyond Jerusalem and even beyond its roots in Judaism. The gifts of the Spirit are universal. "All flesh shall see the salvation of God," as Luke quotes Isaiah (see Isa 40:3-5; Luke 3:6). The Gospel interprets Jesus as the Messiah who brings the "last days," when all the Old Testament prophesies will be fulfilled. In Christ there is a unity, a new creation, in which "there is neither Jew nor Greek, there is neither slave nor free person, there is not male or female; for you are all are one in Christ Jesus" (Gal 3:28). The usual lines of distinction between people are erased. The "last days" (which Luke relates to the coming of the Spirit, the age of the Church) is when the prophecy of Joel finds fulfillment. As Luke writes,

> "It will come to pass in the last days," God says, / "that I will pour out a portion of my spirit upon all flesh. / Your sons and your daughters shall prophesy, / your young men shall see visions, / your old men shall dream dreams. / Indeed, upon my servants and my handmaids / I will pour out a portion of my spirit in those days, / and they shall prophesy. / And I will work wonders in the heavens above / and signs on the earth below / . . . and it shall be that everyone shall be saved who calls on / the name of the Lord" (Acts 2:17-21, quoting Joel 3:1-5; see Isa 2:2; 44:3).

The universal scope of the Gospel is one of the signs of the dawning of the "last days." What needs to come to pass is that the lines of separation and distinction between peoples are eliminated. When people witness "daughters" as well as "sons" prophesying, this is a sign of the last days. When "handmaids and servants alike" are filled with the life of the Spirit, the Church has begun to bear the "fruit" of the word.

These quotations are part of Peter's initial, rousing speech in Jerusalem from which the Church sets out. The rest of Acts might be considered an illustration of the truth and fulfillment of Peter's prophecy. No limits or chains can stop its growth. Women and men are, as Jesus promised, dragged before synagogues and governors and kings. Luke takes this prophecy of Jesus as a kind of programmatic description of the route of the Church to follow Jesus' command to go to the ends of the earth. The "Way" has an ever-widening following until the Gospel has been preached throughout the world. And the Church takes quite seriously the mandate that women and men both bring about the fullness of the Spirit's prophecy. With baptism comes the fullness of life Jesus promised. Although the Church Luke describes will only accept Gentiles with some hesitation, they never questioned the full and complete participation by women in baptism and therefore in the salvation it represents.

Acts 1:13 is not the only reference to an upper room; there is also mention of a Jerusalem Upper Room in Mark (14:14-15), followed by Luke (22:11-12). These Gospels tell us that Jesus sent disciples ahead of him to Jerusalem to begin preparations for his last meal. This place would become important not only for the celebration that year of the Passover but for the Church's later celebration of the "Lord's Supper" (as it is called in 1 Cor 11:20). A commemoration of this meal would mark the birth of the Church and the occasion the Church's gathering as it was dispersed and spread throughout Judea, Galilee, and to all the Gentiles. Although we cannot know whether the "Upper Room" used by Jesus and his followers and then by the "one hundred and twenty" disciples, was one certain room or several, the spiritual meaning of the interior space of a home came to have special significance for the early Christians.

Besides Jesus' mother, another woman named Mary is associated with a gathering place in Jerusalem. That woman is Mary, mother of John, also called Mark (see Acts 12:12, 25; 13:13; 15:37). Her home will be the locus of much Church activity. For example, Peter knows to come there when he is miraculously released from prison (12:12-17). It appears that missionaries went out from there, after being fortified by the love and prayers of the community. Since the home and its interior space is the domain of women and since Luke takes for granted their presence and their ministry in the early Church, we can safely and fairly assume that there were a lot more women active in the Jerusalem Church in a variety of capacities. As Clarice Martin puts it,

> Women in Acts are seen as recipients of the Holy Spirit, active agents, missionaries and witnesses in spreading the Christian faith, hosts of churches in their homes, teachers, exemplars of good works, prophets, beneficiaries of God's healing and liberating power, and as hailing from diverse economic groups, including the very wealthy and the economically disenfranchised.[10]

Women acted alone and in concert with others. They are widows and partners, people of influence, and people enslaved. They are itinerant preachers, and they are resident faithful who hosted the gatherings, providing for the needs of the Church, preparing food for the assemblies, including bread and wine for the celebrations, testifying to the presence of the Spirit in their lives. In fact, Luke links the support and the spread of the Church, indeed its very survival, to the activity of the women.

THE RAISING OF TABITHA (ACTS 9:36-43)

The Upper Room may have quickly become a symbol for the Christians, if we can read between the lines of Acts. In two other localities, an upper room is the locus for a resuscitation story: the first is in the town of Joppa, not far from Jerusalem, where Peter raises Tabitha from the dead. The last is in Troas, where Paul spends a final evening before returning to Jerusalem with the collection, a trip that will end with his arrest and ultimately his voyage to Rome in chains. It is there in an upper

---

[10] Clarice J. Martin, "The Acts of the Apostles," in Elisabeth Schüssler Fiorenza, ed. *Searching the Scriptures* (New York: Crossroad, 1993) 2:762–799, at 771.

room that Paul raises a young man from the dead (20:7-12). Then the community "breaks bread" as if in celebration of the resurrection they witness. The last sentence of that story is, "And they took the boy away alive and were immeasurably comforted." Thus Luke links the upper room, the resurrection, and the breaking of the bread. But it is the story of Peter's raising of Tabitha (9:36-43) that interests us here.

> [36]Now in Joppa there was a disciple named Tabitha (which translated means Dorcas). She was completely occupied with good deeds and almsgiving. [37]Now during those days she fell sick and died, so after washing her, they laid [her] out in a room upstairs. [38]Since Lydda was near Joppa, the disciples, hearing that Peter was there, sent two men to him with the request, "Please come to us without delay." [39]So Peter got up and went with them. When he arrived, they took him to the room upstairs where all the widows came to him weeping and showing him the tunics and cloaks that Dorcas had made while she was with them. [40]Peter sent them all out and knelt down and prayed. Then he turned to her body and said, "Tabitha, rise up." She opened her eyes, saw Peter, and sat up. [41]He gave her his hand and raised her up, and when he had called the holy ones and the widows, he presented her alive. [42]This became known all over Joppa, and many came to believe in the Lord. [43]And he stayed a long time in Joppa with Simon, a tanner (Acts 9:36-43).

Luke twice (9:37, 39) mentions that this miracle of the resuscitation of Tabitha takes place in an "upper room" in Joppa. Luke includes the raising of Tabitha as complementary to the healing of Aeneas (9:32-35), in keeping with his tendency to "pair" stories of men and women. These stories appear within the transitional chapters 9–15, where Luke concludes Peter's ministry and introduces Paul's mission. Paul himself enters the picture in chapter 9 but then remains off-stage, as if in reserve, for a while. Meantime Luke completes his Peter cycle of stories, focusing on Peter in the rest of chapters 9 and 10. There Peter inaugurates the mission to the Gentiles that will be the fertile arena of Paul's missionary endeavors.

In chapters 11 and 12 Peter will gradually recede into the background. He testifies to the validity of the Gentile mission in Antioch, one of the cities, along with Jerusalem, where the

Church is centered. In chapter 12 we learn of Peter's imprisonment for a time and his escape to an "unknown" place. He surfaces again in chapter 15 in Jerusalem, where he defends the Gentile mission before all the apostles and presbyters. After his testimony there, Peter exits the picture, and Luke says nothing further about him. After chapter 15 Luke concentrates on the mission of Paul.

The miracles in Lydda (the healing of Aeneas) and in nearby Joppa (Tabitha) introduce Peter to the milieu outside Jerusalem that is receptive to the Gospel. At the time Acts was written, Jerusalem was a city of great unrest and of persecution of the Church. In the Gospel Jesus lamented the lack of hospitality of the city and warned the "daughters of Jerusalem" to "weep for themselves and for their children." Luke continues in Acts the sad commentary of Jerusalem as the place of the Church's beginnings. But it is also a symbol of the persecution that will force Christians to extend their boundaries, eventually to include the whole world. Although Peter will not venture out as far as Paul does, his foray into the "countryside" of Lydda and Joppa represents a movement away from the Church's adherence to the limits of its Jewish origins.

Aeneas is a paralytic who is "raised up" from his bed and enabled to walk (Acts 9:32-35). Tabitha is a woman even more wondrously "raised up" from the dead. The cure of Aeneas prompts delegates from Joppa to come to Peter to ask him to reach out even further. These events also hark back to the Gospel where the cure of a paralytic man was among Jesus' first miracles (Mark 2:1-12; Luke 5:17-26). Later, Luke tells us, Jesus raised up two people from the dead: the only son of a widow (Luke 7:11-17) and the only daughter of Jairus (8:40-42, 49-56). A number of elements link these three resuscitation miracles found in Luke. There is extreme sadness and mourning of the families or communities associated with these people. And the restoration of life is described in two dimensions: a resuscitation and the return of the raised persons to their own people.

In the Gospel Jesus sends out his disciple-learners with instruction to do the work he did—preaching and working miracles. The Twelve (a number representing Israel) go out in Luke's chapter 9, and then seventy-two (a number representing the Gentile nations) are sent out, according to chapter 10.

Only Luke has this double-mission discourse with both groups being given the same mandate. Luke is a Gentile, writing for Gentile Christians. He is emphasizing the idea that the mission to the Gentiles had been part of God's plan for universal salvation from the beginning. But Luke is also saying that the Gentiles were included only after everything promised to Israel had been fulfilled. The Church began with Judaism. Salvation, as John says, is "from the Jews" (John 4:22).

The story of Tabitha exemplifies a number of Lukan characteristics. We see here an instance of "step parallelism" when we compare what happened to Tabitha with what happened to Aeneas.[11] She experiences the greater power. Aeneas is not referred to as a disciple, but Tabitha is when the feminine form of the noun *mathetria* is used of her. She is the only woman thus designated in the New Testament. The term "disciple" often appears in the Gospels and in Acts, beginning with 6:1; it designates the followers of Jesus, who is presented by Luke as a teacher-prophet. Two names are used of this woman: the Aramaic Tabitha and the Greek Dorcas. This may reflect the practice of many Jews living in the Diaspora having two names, one Jewish and one Greek or Latin, used more commonly in that milieu.[12] Luke only gives hints such as this of his own relatively cosmopolitan background. He inserts this local story into the larger Gentile framework.

Also Lukan is the description of Tabitha as a model of a pious Christian woman. She has distinguished herself with a life full of good deeds and almsgiving (Acts 9:36). She appears to have been especially active in providing clothing and goods for the "widows." But her work was not limited to feminine circles. Note that it was two men from her community who were delegates to Peter, asking him to come to Joppa.

Peter has witnessed the raising of Jairus's daughter, according to Luke (8:51). Like Jesus, Peter banishes the crowd of mourners from the room. Luke had often portrayed Jesus at

---

[11] See Luke's use of this step-parallelism in the Infancy Narrative's comparison of John the Baptist and Jesus; above, Chapter 1, pp. 6–7.

[12] This is probably the explanation for the two names Saul and Paul attributed to the Apostle to the Gentiles. Up until Acts 13, when his Jewish credentials are discussed, Luke refers to him as Saul. In 13:9 both names appear; after that, only the Greek name Paul is used.

prayer in the midst of his active ministry. Peter knelt down and prayed, drawing on the same source of power that Jesus had. Peter then said to her, "Tabitha, rise up!" The reader necessarily makes a connection with the very similar Aramaic words of Jesus recorded by Mark: "'*Talitha koum*,' which means, 'Little girl . . . arise!'" (see Mark 5:41). Typically for Luke, the crowds of people form a chorus of praise and thanks for the wondrous deeds they witness. That is what happens here too. The story spread "all over," and "many people began to believe in the Lord" as a result of what was done for Tabitha.

The title "Lord" *(Kyrios)* for Jesus is one of Luke's favorites. It can mean simply a title of respect or honor, such as "Sir" might connote. But it also was a title given to a benefactor or ruler, one who is revered by the people because of privileges they enjoy. Thus those who recognize Jesus as "Lord" are also implying their own indebtedness. Paul identifies the community of believers as "those who call upon the name of the Lord" (Rom 10:9) and those who bend the knee at the "name" of Jesus (Phil 2:9). Paul calls himself the "slave" of Jesus the Lord. In Luke's world, "Lord" represents a universal Ruler, one who has authority, power, and renown. By his raising of Tabitha, Peter exemplifies the attitude of the model disciple. He prays and gives credit to God. The benefits of this miracle go far beyond Tabitha and the community of widows who so mourned her death. The Church spreads and grows because of this miracle. The crowd echoes what Peter had said to Aeneas: "Jesus Christ heals you!" (9:34). These miracles inspire faith.

A final note is that this resurrection occurs in a "house," more specifically in a "room upstairs," as Luke twice notes (Acts 9:37, 39). The Church is on the move away from Jerusalem and out of the synagogues, into homes, including the homes of women. The "upper room" may be an intentional signal to reflect on the healing, restorative, life-giving benefits of the community of believers, especially as gathered for their weekly memorials of the Lord's Supper, signified in the "breaking of the bread."[13] The community of believers is a community of

[13] Note that the last reference to an "upper room" in Acts 20:8 is also the scene of a resuscitation story, this time of Paul's raising the young man who had fallen out of the window to the ground below and died. It is

new life. As the Church moves away from and beyond Judaism, it establishes itself in households that "believe in the Lord." And so it grew and spread.

This story will be followed by Peter's going to Caesarea Maritima, to the house of Cornelius, a Roman centurion and his family. Peter eats with them, stays with them, and preaches to them, finally baptizing them. Cornelius had sent messengers to Peter to ask him to come, and he inquires about Jesus as a result of a vision. Peter follows the messenger to Caesarea also because of his own vision. This is how he will explain the validity of the Gentile mission to those in Antioch (chap. 11) and later in Jerusalem (chap. 15): "they, like us, are saved by grace."

RHODA (ACTS 12:11-17)

The story of Rhoda, while not particularly flattering to women, implies their very active role is nurturing and maintaining the environment in which the Church grew, despite persecution. A major dynamic of the progression and development of the story of the early Church is Luke's effective use of "bad news, good news" synergy. On the one hand, Luke describes in vivid terms a fledgling Church secreted in the corners of private homes, pursued and persecuted by powerful people such as Saul with his letters of authorization from high-ranking Jews, and Herod with his Rome-appointed authority by which he abused his own subjects. But God is working another plan that no human power, however strong, can withstand.

> [11]Then Peter recovered his senses and said, "Now I know for certain that [the] Lord sent his angel and rescued me from the hand of Herod and from all that the Jewish people had been expecting." [12]When he realized this, he went to the house of Mary, the mother of John who is called Mark, where there were many people gathered in prayer. [13]When he

---

significant that Luke explicitly links this upper room with the "breaking of bread" which is shared by believers in response to this miracle. The resurrection provides the context in which the Christians reinterpreted the Last Supper as the Lord's Supper, a commemoration of Jesus' death and a vigilant memorial "until he comes again" (see 1 Cor 10:16).

knocked on the gateway door, a maid named Rhoda came to answer it. ¹⁴She was so overjoyed when she recognized Peter's voice that, instead of opening the gate, she ran in and announced that Peter was standing at the gate. ¹⁵They told her, "You are out of your mind," but she insisted that it was so. But they kept saying, "It is his angel." ¹⁶But Peter continued to knock, and when they opened it, they saw him and were astounded. ¹⁷He motioned to them with his hand to be quiet and explained [to them] how the Lord had led him out of the prison, and said, "Report this to James and the brothers." Then he left and went to another place (Acts 12:11-17).

This chapter 12 begins with the senseless persecution of the Church by Herod, who has James, the son of Zebedee, killed, and when he finds that that pleases some people, he arrests Peter (Acts 12:1-4). The reader of Acts might just have been able to imagine how the Church could finally begin to grow through Peter's courageous move to the Gentiles. Now the Church is threatened by the imprisonment of Peter and the possibility of his execution. It is not by accident that Peter went to Caesarea to preach to Cornelius and stay with him. Nor is it accidental that Herod goes to Caesarea (12:19), where the Church was growing, despite Herod's attempts to destroy it. But it will be Herod who will be killed in Caesarea, not the Church.

Nothing, however, can prepare for the possibilities of God's power manifest this time in breaking the hold of torture and death, freeing Peter through a miraculous earthquake and an angel's guidance. Before he knows what happened, Peter is on the outside of the tomb of his imprisonment. He heads straight for "the house of Mary," where he knows he will find shelter and safety. Even in his stupor, Peter instinctively knows where he will be received and taken care of. In the meantime, the cowered Church is praying ceaselessly for his release. In this humorous way, Luke tells of the answer to their prayers, although they don't know it.

Rhoda is a maid in the house of Mary. She hears a knock at the gateway to the courtyard and goes to answer it. As Luke tells it, Rhoda recognized Peter's voice but forgot to open the gate. Instead, she flees back to the sanctuary of the house, exclaiming that she heard Peter and that he must have been miraculously released. It may be poetic justice that Luke uses next, when he reports that the insiders thought her out of her mind (Acts 12:15). Wasn't that Peter's own reaction to the women's report of Jesus' resurrection from the tomb? They stand there arguing: Rhoda that she had truly heard Peter, and the others that it must be Peter's angel. Indeed it had been an angel, a messenger from God who had freed Peter. Meanwhile he is outside, still knocking at the gate.

Finally they all come to their senses. They let Peter in. He had to motion for silence so that he could speak. After he told them what had happened, he instructed them to "report this to James and the brothers"; then he disappeared from their midst. Luke simply tells us that he went to another place. He will emerge again, one last time, in Jerusalem, to validate the Gentile mission. Then, like Jesus had at the beginning of Acts, Peter will disappear and not surface again for Luke and Acts. Peter's mission and his role have now been completed. The Gentile mission is launched. The rest is up to the Spirit working through Paul.

One of the delights of this story is that over against the impressive power of Herod out to wreak havoc on the Church is the household of a woman (Mary) and her young, vulnerable, somewhat disorganized servant Rhoda. But God is on the side of the defenseless, that is, Peter and the women. The Church is of such as they. Herod's plans to try Peter after the Passover are foiled. When Herod finds out that Peter has slipped out of his grasp, he has the soldiers killed instead. It does not take too much imagination to think back to the guards Pilate and the Jews planted at the tomb to make sure that Jesus did not "escape" or that his disciples did not take him away (see Matt 27:62-66). And when Jesus rose anyway, despite their best efforts to keep him imprisoned in the tomb, they conspired to tell a story that the disciples did, in fact, steal him (Matt 28:11-15).

This story of Peter's narrow escape is meant to stress God's power working to protect the Church against all the forces of evil. As a kind of anticlimactic ending to this story, Luke recounts the death of Herod himself, in terms that agree in essence with Josephus's reports of Herod's demise. He is punished for taking to himself the honor and allegiance due to God.

Herod made himself like a god in abusing and taking life. And when the people acclaimed him, he did not give God due recognition. No Herod ever had. Not Herod the Great, who tried to have Jesus killed as a baby but was foiled. Not Herod Antipas, who thought that John the Baptist and even Jesus were there for his entertainment and amusement. Nor this Herod, Agrippa, who murdered James and sought to do the same with Peter. He is struck down, "eaten by worms." Here Luke speaks of Herod's horrible death, using an image well known in Greek literature. The impression is that God has totally annihilated the enemy, a fitting end for those who do not honor God.

SUMMARY CONCLUSION

The "upper room" of a house is designated more than once in Luke as the place where believers form community, "break bread," and experience the resurrection. It is not possible nor necessary to identify the upper room with the house of Mary. The space became symbolic and paradigmatic of the place where the Church would gather for many years. The growing Church is presented by Luke as sponsored, nurtured, stretched, and challenged in a domain typically considered "women's space." No other space would be found to be so compatible with the community's goals. As the Church began to see itself as a discipleship of equals, it would experience this equality in a comfortable and safe setting. It created a new society based on the family.

The liturgy often provided the locus for the development of all aspects of the Church's teaching and missionary activity. As they celebrated meals within homes, where women have a major role, they reached back into the life of Jesus for guidance about Church teaching and morality. They shared memories with one another, which they could use to instruct new converts, to encourage people who were suffering and fearful and confused. The house, and specifically the upper room, has enormous symbolic significance for the Church.

LYDIA AND THE WOMEN OF PHILIPPI

Suggested Reading: Acts 16:11-18, 40; Philippians 4:2-3

After the so-called Council of Jerusalem around 50 C.E., Paul set out to visit again some communities he had established on his missionary journey with Barnabas. But then Paul had a vision in which he saw someone urging him to "come over to Macedonia and help us!" (Acts 16:9). So Paul set sail for Neapolis, and then traveled inland to Philippi, "a leading city . . . of Macedonia," as Luke describes it. A modern-day city named Kavalla is built over the ruins of Philippi. But the church of Philippi lives on in the minds of Christians, thanks in no small part to the Christian women we know from there. It is encouraging that their stories come down to us through Acts and Paul's letter to the Philippians, so that we can appreciate to some extent their significant contribution to that community. Here's how Luke tells the story.

> [11]We set sail from Troas, making a straight run for Samothrace, and on the next day to Neapolis, [12]and from there to Philippi, a leading city in that district of Macedonia and a Roman colony. We spent some time in that city. [13]On the sabbath we went outside the city gate along the river where we thought there would be a place of prayer. We sat and spoke with the women who had gathered there. [14]One of them, a woman named Lydia, a dealer in purple cloth, from the city of Thyatira, a worshiper of God, listened, and the Lord opened her heart to pay attention to what Paul was saying. [15]After she and her household had been baptized, she offered us an invitation, "If you consider me a believer in the Lord, come and stay at my home," and she prevailed on us.
> [16]As we were going to the place of prayer, we met a slave girl with an oracular spirit, who used to bring a large profit to her owners through her fortune-telling. [17]She began to follow Paul and us, shouting, "These people are slaves of the Most High God, who proclaim to you a way of salvation." [18]She did this for many days. Paul became annoyed, turned, and said to the spirit, "I command you in the name of Jesus Christ to come out of her." Then it came out at that moment. . . .
> [40]When they had come out of the prison, they went to Lydia's house where they saw and encouraged the brothers, and then they left (Acts 16:11-18, 40).

Luke presents us with a wonderful, complex narrative in several parts. First he describes the inauspicious beginning of this important community with the story of the encounter between Paul and Lydia, in the company of some other women, just outside the city, on the banks of a river. The church is established at her house. This encounter is followed by a double miracle story of the exorcism of a slave girl and an earthquake that both "saves" Paul from imprisonment and also "saves" the jailer and his household through faith. Finally Luke pictures the city fathers escorting Paul out of town after he had "consoled" the church at Lydia's house. Paul and his missionary band are sent on the next leg of their journey, which will further establish and promote the Church in Europe.

Paul's letter to the Philippians is well loved for its beauty and for the lasting image of the strong communal ties Paul shared with these model Christians. Paul holds up to others their example of faith. And he also sets before the eyes of the Philippians models to encourage their own faith and perseverance. Paul refers to the examples of Jesus, of Timothy, and of himself. He also challenges resident members of the community, among them the messenger, Epaphroditus, and two women, named Euodia and Syntyche. Luke's description in Acts and Paul's letter have one thing in common: the importance of the leadership of women in this exemplary community. To fully appreciate the implications of this, we need to do a little background on the city itself and then on the women who keep it alive in our Christian imagination.

Citizens of Philippi had mixed religious backgrounds. Philippi was a Roman colony, which means it was inhabited by former troops as a way of ensuring the loyalty of the population. The official religion was Roman, but there are indications that religion in Philippi was syncretistic, combining a variety of pagan divinities and cults. It was an honor to be named a Roman colony. Philippi copied Roman ways, using the Latin language a great deal, imitating the dress of the Romans, trading in Roman currency.

When Paul visited Philippi, Claudius had already expelled Jews from Rome (49–52). Anti-Jewish sentiments could well have affected life in Philippi. There was not a significant Jewish presence in Philippi, and apparently there was no synagogue. The practice of Judaism, although allowed by the Romans, was sometimes forbidden by magistrates of certain towns. This may have been the situation in Philippi. Acts tells us that the first charge brought against Paul and Silas when they were brought before the city's magistrates by the slave woman's owners was, "These people are Jews and are disturbing our city and are advocating customs that are not lawful for us Romans to adopt or practice" (Acts 16:20-21).

This implied animosity against Jews could explain why, on their first Sabbath there, Paul and his companions had to leave the city through its gates (Acts 16:13) to look for a suitable place to pray. Oftentimes a *proseuche*, which means "prayer" or a place to pray, was associated with water. So Paul and his companions headed for water, finding on the banks of the river a "group of women" who normally gathered each Sabbath, possibly for prayer. These women were Gentiles; among them was a woman known as Lydia, an immigrant from the region of Thyatira.[14] The city of Thyatira was located in a district known as Lydia, a name it had from Persian times.

The region of Lydia was also known for its prominent trade guilds, among them those that dyed cloth. Luke describes the woman Lydia as a resident of Philippi and a dealer in purple goods. That would imply that this woman would have been a business woman, perhaps a freedwoman known as an immigrant (that is, referred to as "the Lydian woman")[15] and also suggesting that Lydia was a former slave, since slaves were often named for their native region.

We also know from inscriptions that dyeing was a trade practiced by slaves, and selling purple goods was an occupation of former slaves. It seems that the eastern provinces of Rome traded in luxury goods such as purple dyes and perfumes. Wealthy people, most often wives who did the shopping, bought purple. Therefore, Lydia might have been a source of good contacts for Paul's message. As a head of a household herself, she was probably single, with a number of clients and maybe even workers associated with her. In any case, her household became the location for this most influential city of Christianity. She herself is representative of a type

[14] Thyatira will also be memorialized by the author of the Revelation as one of the seven churches addressed in the first vision (Rev 2:18-19).
[15] See Florence Gillman, *Women Who Knew Paul*, 31.

of this new Christian community, based among Gentiles who were relatively free of Jewish influence.

There is a river, the Gangites, about two kilometers outside of the city, which may have been the site of Paul's encounter with the band of women who went there to pray. But this is rather far away. An alternative to the Gangites is the springs located at the very edge of the city. A gate there was called the Krenides, which means "springs"; this site is still known locally today as "Lydia's river." Another suggestion is that the gate of the city that Luke mentions refers to the Neapolis Gate toward the south, leading to a small stream. Interestingly, an excavated Christian basilica on this site and claimed to be from the fourth century lacks a baptistry.[16] Some have conjectured that even after the basilica was built, baptism was performed in the nearby stream where Paul and Lydia met and where Luke implies that Lydia and her household were baptized (Acts 16:15).

Luke portrays Lydia as a model convert from the start. In only two verses she goes from being one of many pious woman who prayed by the river to a patron of the house church in Philippi. She is a "worshiper of God" who "listened" to Paul. By the banks of the river "the Lord opened [Lydia's] heart to pay attention to what Paul was saying." She understood the Gospel as something she wanted to accept; so she was immediately baptized along with her whole household. Then she challenged Paul, saying, "If you consider me a believer in the Lord, come and stay at my home." And so he did.

Lydia shared her resources with the missionaries who depended upon local patrons such as herself. She opened her home to the church at Philippi, just as Mary of Jerusalem had. Paul would experience a miraculous escape from jail (as Peter had), saved by an earthquake (just as Peter was: see Acts 12:2-19). Then Paul returned to the household of Lydia to "encourage" the brothers and sisters there, and no doubt also to be encouraged by their faith and more (Rom 1:11). Readers think of Peter going to Mary's house to gather his wits and belongings, to be comforted, and to regroup. And they then send him

---

[16] Ibid., p. 33.

off to "another place" (12:17). Surely Paul was also buoyed up as he continued his journey more deeply into Europe, by the good foundation of the Church symbolized by Lydia's enthusiastic and receptive household.

Luke inserts within the Lydia material a story of another woman who is quadruply marginalized according to the patriarchal and androcentric societal norms of the times:[17] she was undervalued because of her gender, her slave status, possession by a spirit, and economic exploitation by her owners. Luke tells us that this woman followed Paul everywhere. She was a fortuneteller. But she spoke the truth about him, testifying, "These people are slaves of the Most High God, who proclaim to you a way of salvation" (Acts 16:17). Her outbursts remind the reader of the initial exorcism Mark tells us about, when the demon of the possessed man kept shouting, "What have you to do with us, Jesus of Nazareth? Have you come to destroy us? I know who you are—the Holy One of God!" (Mark 1:24).

Paul became annoyed, not with the woman, but with the spirit that tormented her. So he ordered the spirit to leave her. "Then it came out at that moment" (16:18). A miracle becomes an opportunity for faith; or it can go the other way, and people can refuse to see the good that is done. Unfortunately Luke says nothing more about the woman who was healed. She is forgotten in the overall picture Luke creates by showing how adversity only serves to further the Gospel. The woman's owners seize Paul and charge him with disorderly conduct. The beating he receives becomes the means for Paul to challenge the magistrates the following day. Imprisonment works for the Gospel; it becomes a way for Paul to convert the jailer.

When the magistrates try to eject Paul from the town, he informs them that he is a Roman citizen who was beaten and jailed without due process. In their anxiety to right things, they escort him to the city gates, but only after he has gone and visited again with Lydia and the church at her house. Thus adversity means progress for the Gospel. The church is well established and taken care of by locals under the patronage of this amazing woman. Meanwhile, Paul and his missionary troop

[17] The phrase comes from Clarice Martin, "Acts of the Apostles," 784.

go off to another place, this time to Thessalonica, to start the church there.

It is true that Luke gives short shrift to the women in Philippi and more attention to the men.[18] But a perceptive reader can still read between the lines. The church was well founded and in good hands, thanks to the two women of Philippi, Lydia and the slave woman. Paul was called to move on to form other communities among the Gentiles that would always have this Philippian model.

Consider, for example, the difference in the way the jailer is described compared with Lydia (Acts 16:25-34). He represented the forces that were trying to silence and destroy Paul and his missionary band. Then, faced with the earthquake, he considered suicide. And it was only after Paul reassured him that the missionaries wouldn't run for it that he settled down to ask, "What must I do to be saved?" He meant save his skin, but Paul took it the best possible way and replied, "Believe in the Lord Jesus and you and your household will be saved" (16:31). And then, when it was clear that Paul would take care of the magistrates and the plaintiffs, the jailer and his household agreed to become Christians.

In contrast, Lydia was pious and eager to learn the truth from the start. She had nothing to gain from her conversion. She generously and freely offered all that she was and all that she had to the service of the Church. Her firm faithfulness must have made it much easier for Paul to leave and go on to spread the Gospel.

EUODIA AND SYNTYCHE (MORE WOMEN OF PHILIPPI)

Suggested Reading: Philippians 4:2-3

In his letter to the Philippians, Paul says, "I urge Euodia and I urge Syntyche to come to a mutual understanding *(phronein)* in the Lord. Yes, and I ask you also, my true yokemate, to help them for they have struggled at my side in promoting the gospel, along with Clement and my other co-workers, whose names are

---

[18] As noted, for example, by Clarice Martin, op. cit., 784–785.

in the book of life" (Phil 4:2-3). For emphasis, Paul repeats the verb "I urge," as if speaking to each of these women directly. Paul describes them as "fellow workers" *(synergoi)* who have struggled together *(synathlein)* with him.[19]

The concern Paul expresses about their disagreement suggests that they held positions of prominence in the community and that the whole community knew of and was affected by their dispute. This entire letter is an exhortation to greater unity, to taking on the same mind *(phronein)*.[20] Their disunity appears to have fueled other problems in the church. It would appear from Paul's naming them that these women were well known to the Philippians, as were the basis and reasons for their disagreement. They were leaders, perhaps deacons or heads of house churches.[21]

Paul uses the verb *phronein*, "to think, judge, set one's mind on," or as in this case involving two persons, an abbreviated way of conveying the idea of "agree on," in the sense of "have a meeting of the minds." The "place" where their minds are to meet is "in Christ." Paul is doing something more than advocating that they think of Christ's sacrifice or that they be inspired by his example. They are empowered to be in union with one another because of the self-emptying of Christ, who won for both of them their salvation and their peace. In Philippians, this is a particularly significant term to describe the unity they ought to strive for. In Philippians 2:2 and 2:5, for example, Paul enjoins the Philippians to have the same mindset among themselves as they have in union with Christ, who emptied himself of his equality with God for the sake of hu-

---

[19] *Synergoi,* meaning "fellow workers" or some derivative occurs eleven times in Paul; *synathlein,* meaning to "strive together," appears only here and in Philippians 1:27 in the New Testament. There are an unusual number of compound words with the *"syn-"* prefix (meaning "together," "with") in Philippians, another indication that the theme of this letter is unity.

[20] This term occurs eight times in this short letter: see Phil 1:7; 2:2 (twice), 5; 3:15, 19; 4:2, 10; see also 2 Cor 13:11.

[21] See Carolyn Osiek, "Philippians," in *Searching the Scriptures,* ed. Elisabeth Schüssler Fiorenza (New York: Crossroad, 1994) 237–249, at 238. Also Gillman, *Women Who Knew Paul,* 46.

mankind. In the light of this use of *phronein* for Christ's saving action, and Paul's mention of these women by name, it seems that their disagreement had to do with leadership and how it was to be exercised. It is probably not accidental that the names of three women are associated with this community, since there is good evidence that in Macedonia women had long had a much more significant role in public life than in many other regions of the Greco-Roman world.[22]

The people Paul names in this letter have Greek and Latin names, supporting the Gentile makeup of the community. A man named Clement appears to be already working to help Euodia and Syntyche to be reconciled. But we do not know anything more about him. Epaphroditus is the fourth person Paul names in this letter as a member of this community (2:25-30). He is the bearer of the Philippian community's gifts to Paul and probably the bearer of this letter back to them. In the two verses referring to the quarrel of these women (Phil 4:2-3), Paul addresses someone he calls a "yokemate," whom some have suggested could have been Paul's former jailer turned believer. That is conjecture. Another interesting suggestion is that although the form is masculine, it could be used of one's wife, who shared the "yoke" of marriage.[23] Although taken literally this is unlikely, since Paul denies he is married (see 1 Cor 7:7-8, 9:5), the possibility exists that he is addressing a woman of the community to which they are both "yoked." We do not know anything more about this person for sure.

It seems odd that Paul would not mention Lydia, whom Luke thirty years later identifies as the founding patron of the Philippian church. But there could be reasonable explanations for this. One is that Paul often brings up people and issues because there is a problem concerning them. Maybe there was no problem relating to Lydia. Maybe, as in the above suggestion, Lydia is the "yokemate" Paul exhorts to help the partners, Euodia and Syntyche, resolve their differences. Also, the letter suggests a fair amount of communication between Paul and the Philippians. His failure to mention

---

[22] See Osiek, "Philippians," in *Searching the Scriptures*, 238.
[23] Ibid., 247.

her in one letter does not indicate that she ceased to have a significant role in this community. Paul (and Luke) leave us longing to know more.

PHOEBE AND THE WOMEN OF ROME

Suggested Reading: Romans 16

Romans 16 offers some really interesting avenues of exploration to those interested in women in the New Testament. We are introduced to a world of possibilities for women in the early Church, women whom we would not know about were it not for this chapter. In Romans 16 we hear of women who were leaders in local churches, as well as independent traveling missionaries, deacons, and patrons, like Phoebe. Prisca, the well-traveled, scholarly missionary who was a patron to the church in Corinth and Ephesus and who partnered with her husband in business as well as religion, is mentioned again here. Junia, together with Andronicus (perhaps her husband?), is called an apostle. Women named Mary, Tryphaena, Tryphosa, and Persis formed commendable partnerships in fruitful missionary endeavors. Since Tryphaena and Tryphosa are paired in Paul's greetings, they possibly lived together in mutual support as well. In fact, ten of the twenty-four people we know from this chapter are women, many having a name in their own right, with or without reference to a man who is husband, father, or son. The collage Paul constructs in this list of greetings only hints at the significance of each woman mentioned. We wish we knew more, but at least we know this much from what Paul says:

> [1]I commend to you *Phoebe* our sister, who is [also] a minister *[diakonos]* of the church at Cenchreae, [2]that you may receive her in the Lord in a manner worthy of the holy ones, and help her in whatever she may need from you, for she has been a benefactor *[protastis]* to many and to me as well.
> [3]Greet *Prisca* and Aquila, my co-workers in Christ Jesus, [4]who risked their necks for my life, to whom not only I am grateful but also all the churches of the Gentiles; [5]greet also the

church at their house. . . . ⁶Greet *Mary,* who has worked hard for you. ⁷Greet Andronicus and *Junia,* my relatives and my fellow prisoners; they are prominent among the apostles and they were in Christ before me. . . . ¹²Greet those workers in the Lord, *Tryphaena and Tryphosa.* Greet the beloved *Persis,* who has worked hard in the Lord. ¹³Greet Rufus . . . and *his mother and mine.* . . . ¹⁵Greet . . . *Julia,* Nereus and *his sister* . . . and all the holy ones who are with them. ¹⁶Greet one another with a holy kiss. All the churches of Christ greet you (Rom 16:1-7, 12-13, 15-16).

The relationship of this chapter 16 to the rest of the letter to the Romans is debated, because the material in this chapter appears to be so different from the impersonal tone of the rest of the letter. In chapter 1 and again in chapter 15, Paul makes it clear that he has not yet visited the Christians in Rome. Although he had long since desired to go to Rome, he says, he has been hindered so far from doing so. But he anticipates the opportunity to visit there soon after he completes a final mission; that is, he must take the collection gathered from the Gentile churches to the "saints" (that is, the Jewish Christians) in Jerusalem, who were suffering a famine. Then he sets his sights on finally traveling to Rome. The letter to the Romans is a kind of "introduction" to himself and to his preaching, as if to prepare the Romans for a future visit from Paul and to set the record straight in case they had heard things about him. (On the basis of his history even with communities he knew well, such as the Corinthians, he was often misunderstood, it appears.)

But suddenly, in chapter 16, Paul changes his tone and greets by name a number of people he seems to know very well. He recommends Phoebe, insinuating as he does that she is the bearer of this letter. This change in tone and content is noticeable on many levels beyond merely going from impersonal to personal. Paul moves from theology to history, from the universal to the particular, from speculation to experience; and all this has given interpreters pause. They have asked whether chapter 16 is really an original part of a letter intended for the community at Rome. Or, is it possible, as some suggest, that chapter 16 is a kind of "cover letter" written after the completion of the other fifteen chapters? It might have been attached to chapters 1–15 and sent to another community, perhaps

Ephesus, making it a kind of "circular letter," since it explained Paul's thinking so clearly and so well. Phoebe, from nearby Cenchreae, could have taken the letter there. Prisca and Aquila, we learn from Acts, had lived in Ephesus for a while and had a house there where they hosted the church. They had stayed in Ephesus after they had been in Corinth, where they had gone after being expelled from Rome.

There is one more good reason for the theory that chapter 16 represents a kind of "attachment" to the rest of Romans: in some ancient manuscripts, the doxology of 16:25-27, which concludes the letter, is found at various places in chapter 15, as if to indicate that the letter had appeared minus the sixteenth chapter in some manuscripts and perhaps in some communities.

But there are better reasons to consider chapter 16 as part of the original letter that went to Rome along with Paul's defense of the Gospel he preached. Romans is at the head of the letters of Paul, not only because it appears first but because of its importance. The very significant, if still sketchy, glimpse into the rich life of the early Church, including the leadership of women seen there, ought not to be relegated to a peripheral subchapter just because such roles cannot be imagined by some interpreters.

This chapter serves as a letter of recommendation of Phoebe, who was probably also its bearer. In other places Paul refers to the practice, apparently popular among the belabored early Christians, of soliciting and using letters of recommendation from well-known and trusted leaders of the churches. So, for example, Paul challenges the Corinthians in a hurt tone, "Do we need . . . letters of recommendation to you or from you? You are our letter . . ." (see 2 Cor 3:1-2). Paul disparages the glowing letters of recommendation it appears others presented on their own behalf. But now he is writing one, and he must have thought about the woman whom he recommends as well as the others whom he implicitly recommends by his elaborate greetings to them.

Early on the Church experienced problems with false teachers. The Pastoral Letters suggest the difficulties with discerning the difference between true and heretical teachers. An apostle (a term that means "sent") represented the authority of the sender. Paul's letters themselves were a kind of substitute for his presence. They had to be entrusted to people who themselves were trustworthy.

All this gives greater weight to Romans 16 because it can be seen not only as Phoebe's credentials but as a recommendation of the others named there, including so many women. Further, even though we do not know much more about all these people beyond the words Paul says of them, they lived in the Roman community and, it is supposed, the Romans knew them or would come to know them. Paul is recommending them, too, along with Phoebe. And in doing so, he is assuring the community that since he trusts them, they should too. Now Paul needed this community. His hope was that they would help him get to Spain, the "ends of the earth." The first fifteen chapters are Paul's attempts to show that they and he share the same faith, the same Gospel. He would not and could not afford to jeopardize his relationship with the Romans. So he would be careful to include in his greetings people who would be acceptable to the Romans and helpful to Paul's long-term goal of gathering support for his mission to Spain. Paul is "putting his best foot forward" in Romans. When he greets all these people living there, he is also subtly endorsing their example and reinforcing their influence with that community.

Now let us consider what we can know about some of the women Paul mentions in Romans 16.

PHOEBE (ROMANS 16:1-2)

In Phoebe we have evidence that women were traveling missionaries, deacons, and leaders, whose authority and importance were recognized by Paul as well as by Christian communities in the fifties. We may be surprised at the terms Paul uses in reference to this woman, but apparently the Romans would not have been. Paul does not qualify or justify his language describing Phoebe, the way some interpreters and even translators have since Paul first recommended her. She is a "deacon" *(diakonos)*, which is grammatically masculine and is used in the New Revised Standard Version. Translations that feminize the term as "deaconess" also insinuate that she served in some subordinate capacity, not like the men named as deacons in Acts.[24] The New American Bible avoids using "deacon" for Phoebe and uses instead "minister," a more generic term that can more easily suggest a subordinate function considered proper for a woman. These sleights of pen illustrate that a translation is an interpretation and that an androcentric bias has been at work in the reading of the biblical texts for a long time.

In a comparable context, Paul described Timothy in similar terms (see 1 Thess 3:2), as "our brother and *diakonos* for God."[25] Interpreters do not seem to have a problem imagining a man's being called a deacon, but they balk when the terms are used for a woman, as here. As a delegate from Paul and emissary to the church he addressed, Phoebe seems to have performed the same functions as Timothy and Titus did to the communities at Thessalonica, Philippi, and Corinth. That she exercised these functions with regard to Rome could possibly have made her authority all the greater, since that church was so significant. That she is recommended to the church at Rome using the terms "deacon" and "benefactor-patron" without apology implies that such roles for women were acceptable in the churches. It was very important to Paul to be accepted by this Roman community. He needed them. He would not have been apt to experiment with their acceptance of Phoebe the person or with her role as his apostolic delegate.

The term *prostatis*, also used of Phoebe, means leader, chief, president, patron, guardian and protector. Paul says that she has fulfilled this role with regard to many, including himself. Unfortunately he does not specify further. But again, he makes no apology for his use of such a term of authority and leader-

---

[24] Romans was written around 58; Acts around 85. We ought to bear in mind that they represent two documents from very different times, aimed at very different audiences, with very different purposes, and reflecting very different world views, as well as situations of the Christian communities addressed. These differences affect how they ought to be compared and contrasted. In this instance Acts should not be seen as a standard for judging whether women in Rome could be recognized as deacons a generation earlier.

[25] Some manuscripts have *diakonos;* others substitute *synergos* ("coworker") in reference to Timothy in 1 Thessalonians 3:2.

ship with regard to a woman. Elizabeth Castelli shows how an androcentric bias has caused some interpreters to assert, without evidence or support, that we should not understand this term as ascribing the authority of its usual connotation to a woman.[26] According to Ernst Käsemann, for instance, citing the much later Book of Revelation, only in heretical circles do prophetesses have powers of leadership.[27] Käsemann says that with regard to Phoebe, *prostatis* means only that she took care of Paul personally. He claims this without helping us understand on what grounds he denies her the usual authoritative meaning of the term. Fortunately there are not many contemporary examples of this type of male bias in interpreting this verse.

Phoebe is further called "our sister," a designation used generally by Christians from earliest times. This familial term suggests the wide-ranging effect of modeling the community on the household, the family of God. Phoebe's status as a partner in the Gospel already gives her full mature identity in the new society of believers.

In later verses (see Rom 16:7, 11), Paul refers to some people as "kinsmen" or "relatives"; apparently he means it there in a more literal sense, because Christians in general are referred to as family members, brothers and sisters. If he meant it in this sense, why would he only call Andronicus and Junia and Herodion his relatives? There is a tradition that Luke refers to, namely, that some of Paul's relatives might also have been Christian. So Acts 23:16 says that his nephew, his sister's son, aided Paul when he was in Jerusalem. Yet there it is not clear whether his sister and/or nephew became believers. And still none of this is certain. In another instance Paul refers to Rufus's mother as "mine" (Rom 16:13), and there he probably means that she was one of his patrons, that she offered him hospitality.[28] But he does not seem to be saying that she is his own biological mother.

---

[26] Elizabeth Castelli, "Romans," in *Searching the Scriptures*, 272–300, at 278.

[27] Ernst Käsemann, *Commentary on Romans*, trans. Geoffrey W. Bromiley (Grand Rapids: Eerdmans, 1980) 411; quoted by Castelli, "Romans," 278.

[28] See Meeks, *The First Urban Christians*, 60.

The Apostle, Junia (Rom 16:7)

Junia is partnered with Andronicus, who probably was her husband. They are Paul's relatives, apparently by marriage or by blood. They were believing Christians before Paul. They were imprisoned with him, Paul says; we do not know which imprisonment he refers to. Now they are in Rome and Paul in Corinth. Together this pair are called "prominent apostles." Here we have an example of the lengths to which some will go to preclude the possibility that a woman was called an "apostle," a prominent one at that! Interpreters and translators since Jerome in the fifth century have masculinized her name, reading it Junias, struggling to work around the eventuality of naming a woman an apostle. Castelli calls it a case of "sex change by translation."[29] But in fact here is a good example of the lack of bias in Paul against the participation by women in all levels of leadership, work, and recognition.

For Paul, the credential of apostleship is an experience of the risen Christ. This is a divine call, verified by having "seen the Lord" (1 Cor 9:1; 15:3-8). When Paul recounts the foundational appearances, starting with Peter and ending with himself in 1 Corinthians 15, he says that Christ appeared to "five hundred brothers." He is certainly not excluding the appearances to women recorded in the Gospels altogether. The "brothers" generally means "brothers and sisters." There is no reason to deny the title of apostle to Junia.

Mary (Romans 16:6), Tryphaena and Tryphosa, Persis (Romans 16:12)

Along with Prisca and Aquila, Paul refers to these women as *synergoi*, the same term used of Paul's trusted associates Timothy (see Rom 16:21; 1 Thess 3:2), Apollos (1 Cor 3:9), Mark, Aristarchus, Demas and Luke (Phlm 24), Euodia and Syntyche (Phil 4:2-3). Paul includes women in all levels of missionary endeavors, and as local leaders. Romans 16 is testimony to that fact.

---

[29] Castelli, "Romans," 279.

Epilogue

> The Spirit said to Philip, "Go and join up with that chariot."
> Philip ran up and heard him reading Isaiah the prophet and
> said, "Do you understand what you are reading?" He replied,
> "How can I unless someone instructs me?" . . . As they
> traveled along the road they came to some water, and the
> eunuch said, "Look, there is water. What is to prevent my
> being baptized?" (Acts 8:29-31, 36).

We are like the servant of the queen of Ethiopia portrayed
in this story, needing teachers and models to instruct us, not
only so that we can "understand," but so we can be baptized
(that is, immersed) in the Scriptures. Fortunately we find teachers in the Scriptures themselves, people of faith, courageous
and generous in showing us the way.

We learn by imitation and example. It is almost sad to realize that in the third millennium of Christianity we are still surprised at how positive, consistent, and strong is the example of
New Testament women. We are surprised by the variety of
their experiences and intrigued by the possibilities of knowing
them for themselves. We owe them a "spiritual debt" for the
power we can take from their example. Women stand out among
the disciples, faithful to Jesus throughout his journey to the
cross and beyond. They are the first witnesses to the resurrection, and they distinguish themselves as worthy leaders in the
early Christian communities. They represent plurality at a
time when we expected uniformity. They are heads of households and servants, single women and wives and mothers. We
are surprised that the male writers of the Christian Scriptures

portrayed them so positively, and we are surprised that it took us so long to notice.

We are also delighted and intrigued, attracted to the hope the women of the New Testament inspire in us. Today more than ever we hear of the need for role models, for people we can identify with, whose lives testify to truth, beauty, goodness, love. We are not able to really "understand" unless someone shows us. The New Testament women of faith, courage, and integrity, like Mary, Elizabeth, Joanna, Lydia, Phoebe, and others, have shown us. Let their example empower us to be people of the Scriptures. Without our appreciation, understanding, and imitation, the stories of these New Testament women are frozen in time, an anticlimactic conclusion to the Gospel. And we become like those other Christians who thought their word nonsense and did not believe or act on it. But if we do believe that their lives are promise to us, we will enliven and continue their stories in our own. Then we will realize the promise of the words addressed to the community of Philippi we can envision gathered at Lydia's house:

> Keep on doing what you have learned and received and heard and seen in me. Then the God of peace will be with you (Phil 4:9).

Suggested Reading

Biale, Rachel. *Women and Jewish Law: An Exploration of Women's Issues in Halakhic Sources*. New York: Schoken, 1984.

Corley, Kathleen E. *Private Women, Public Meals: Social Conflict in the Synoptic Tradition*. Peabody: Hendrickson, 1993.

Gillman, Florence. *Women Who Knew Paul*. Collegeville: The Liturgical Press, 1992.

Newsom, Carol A., and Sharon H. Ringe. *The Women's Bible Commentary*. Louisville: Westminster/John Knox Press, 1992.

Nowell, Irene. *Women in the Old Testament*. Collegeville: The Liturgical Press, 1997.

Osiek, Carolyn, and David L. Balch. *Families in the New Testament World: Households and House Churches*. Louisville: Westminster/John Knox Press, 1997.

Perkins, Pheme. *Ministering in the Pauline Churches*. New York/Ramsey: Paulist Press, 1982.

Portefaix, Lilian. *Sisters Rejoice: Paul's Letter to the Philippians and Luke-Acts as Received by First Century Philippian Women*. Coniectanea Biblica New Testament Series 20. Uppsala: Almqvist and Wiksell International, 1988.

Reid, Barbara E. *Choosing the Better Part? Women in the Gospel of Luke*. Collegeville: The Liturgical Press, 1996.

Schneiders, Sandra M. *Written that You May Believe: Encountering Jesus in the Fourth Gospel*. New York: Crossroad, 1999.

Schottroff, Luise. *Lydia's Impatient Sisters: A Feminist Social History of Early Christianity*. Trans. Barbara and Martin Rumscheidt. Louisville: Westminster/John Knox Press, 1995.

Schüssler Fiorenza, Elisabeth. *In Memory of Her: A Feminist Reconstruction of Christian Origins*. New York: Crossroad, 1983.

_____, ed. *Searching the Scriptures*. Vol. 1: *A Feminist Introduction*. New York: Crossroad, 1993.

_____. *Searching the Scriptures*. Vol. 2: *A Feminist Commentary*. New York: Crossroad, 1994.

Streete, Gail Corrington. *The Strange Woman: Power and Sex in the Bible*. Louisville: Westminster/John Knox Press, 1997.

Tetlow, Elisabeth. *Women and Ministry in the New Testament*. New York/Ramsey: Paulist Press, 1980.

Thurston, Bonnie. *Women in the New Testament: Questions and Commentary*. New York: Crossroad, 1998.

Appendix

THE RAISING OF JAIRUS'S DAUGHTER

Mark 5:21-24, 35-43

²¹When Jesus had crossed again [in the boat] to the other side, a large crowd gathered around him, and he stayed close to the sea. ²²One of the synagogue officials, named Jairus, came forward. Seeing him he fell at his feet ²³and pleaded earnestly with him, saying, "My daughter is at the point of death. Please, come lay your hands on her that she may get well and live." ²⁴He went off with him, and a large crowd followed him and pressed upon him. . . .

³⁵While he was still speaking, people from the synagogue official's house arrived and said, "Your daughter has died; why trouble the teacher any longer?" ³⁶Disregarding the message that was reported, Jesus said to the synagogue official, "Do not be afraid; just have faith." ³⁷He did not allow

Matthew 9:18-19, 23-26

¹⁸While he was saying these things to them, an official came forward, knelt down before him, and said, "My daughter has just died. But come, lay your hand on her, and she will live." ¹⁹Jesus rose and followed him, and so did his disciples. . . .

²³When Jesus arrived at the official's house and saw the flute players and the crowd who were making a commotion, ²⁴he said, "Go away! The girl is not dead but sleeping." And they ridiculed him. ²⁵When the crowd was put out, he came and took her by the hand, and the little girl arose. ²⁶And news of this spread throughout all that land.

Luke 8:40-42, 49-56

⁴⁰When Jesus returned, the crowd welcomed him, for they were all waiting for him. ⁴¹And a man named Jairus, an official of the synagogue, came forward. He fell at the feet of Jesus and begged him to come to his house, ⁴²because he had an only daughter, about twelve years old, and she was dying. As he went, the crowds almost crushed him. . . .

⁴⁹While he was still speaking, someone from the synagogue official's house arrived and said, "Your daughter is dead; do not trouble the teacher any longer." ⁵⁰On hearing this, Jesus answered him, "Do not be afraid; just have faith and she will be saved." ⁵¹When he arrived at the house he allowed no one to enter with him except Peter and John and James, and the child's father and mother. ⁵²All were weeping and

mourning for her, when he said, "Do not weep any longer, for she is not dead, but sleeping." 53And they ridiculed him, because they knew that she was dead. 54But he took her by the hand and called to her, "Child, arise!" 55Her breath returned and she immediately arose. He then directed that she should be given something to eat. 56Her parents were astounded, and he instructed them to tell no one what had happened.

anyone to accompany him inside except Peter, James, and John, the brother of James. 38When they arrived at the house of the synagogue official, he caught sight of a commotion, people weeping and wailing loudly. 39So he went in and said to them, "Why this commotion and weeping? The child is not dead but asleep." 40And they ridiculed him. Then he put them all out. He took along the child's father and mother and those who were with him and entered the room where the child was. 41He took the child by the hand and said to her, "*Talitha koum*," which means, "Little girl, I say to you, arise!" 42The girl, a child of twelve, arose immediately and walked around. [At that] they were utterly astounded. 43He gave strict orders that no one should know this and said that she should be given something to eat.

THE MOTHER OF ZEBEDEE'S SONS (See Matthew 20:20-28; 27:55-56.)

Mark 10:35-45

[35]Then James and John, the sons of Zebedee, came to him and said to him, "Teacher, we want you to do for us whatever we ask of you." [36]He replied, "What do you wish [me] to do for you?" [37]They answered him, "Grant that in your glory we may sit one at your right and the other at your left." [38]Jesus said to them, "You do not know what you are asking. Can you drink the cup that I drink or be baptized with the baptism with which I am baptized?" [39]They said to him, "We can." Jesus said to them, "The cup that I drink, you will drink, and with the baptism with which I am baptized, you will be baptized; [40]but to sit at my right or at my left is not mine to give but is for those for whom it has been prepared." [41]When the ten heard this, they became indignant at James and John. [42]Jesus summoned them and said to them, "You know that those who are recognized as rulers over

Luke 12:50; 22:24-27

[50]There is a baptism with which I must be baptized, and how great is my anguish until it is accomplished! . . .

[24]Then an argument broke out among them about which of them should be regarded as the greatest. [25]He said to them, "The kings of the Gentiles lord it over them and those in authority over them are addressed as 'Benefactors'; [26]but among you it shall not be so. Rather, let the greatest among you be as the youngest, and the leader as the servant. [27]For who is greater: the one seated at table or the one who serves? Is it not the one seated at table? I am among you as the one who serves."

John 13:4-5, 12-17

[4]He rose from supper and took off his outer garments. He took a towel and tied it around his waist. [5]Then he poured water into a basin and began to wash the disciples' feet and dry them with the towel around his waist. . . .

[12]So when he had washed their feet [and] put his garments back on and reclined at table again, he said to them, "Do you realize what I have done for you? [13]You call me 'teacher' and 'master,' and rightly so, for indeed I am. [14]If I, therefore, the master and teacher, have washed your feet, you ought to wash one another's feet. [15]I have given you a model to follow, so that as I have done for you, you should also do. [16]Amen, amen, I say to you, no slave is greater than his master nor any messenger greater than the one who sent him. [17]If you understand this, blessed are you if you do it."

the Gentiles lord it over them, and their great ones make their authority over them felt. ⁴³But it shall not be so among you. Rather, whoever wishes to be great among you will be your servant; ⁴⁴whoever wishes to be first among you will be the slave of all. ⁴⁵For the Son of Man did not come to be served but to serve and to give his life as a ransom for many."

THE WOMEN AT THE CROSS (See Matthew 27:55-56.)

Mark 15:40-41

⁴⁰There were also women looking on from a distance. Among them were Mary Magdalene, Mary the mother of the younger James and of Joses, and Salome. ⁴¹These women had followed him when he was in Galilee and ministered to him. There were also many other women who had come up with him to Jerusalem.

Luke 23:49

⁴⁹but all his acquaintances stood at a distance, including the women who had followed him from Galilee and saw these events.

John 19:25-27

²⁵Standing by the cross of Jesus were his mother and his mother's sister, Mary the wife of Clopas, and Mary of Magdala. ²⁶When Jesus saw his mother and the disciple there whom he loved, he said to his mother, "Woman, behold, your son." ²⁷Then he said to the disciple, "Behold, your mother." And from that hour the disciple took her into his home.

Index of Authors